RIDING AND TRAINING

KING CHRISTIAN

Owned and ridden by Mr. Oscar G. Smith, Carolanne Farms, Norfolk, Virginia, winner of over fifty championships in amateur classes and stakes. And no wonder, for Carolanne Farms is managed by Eli Long, who is past master of perfectly broke show horses.

RIDING AND TRAINING

BY

EARL R. FARSHLER

ARCO
NEW YORK

EDITED BY EUGENE V. CONNETT

Second ARCO Printing, 1975

Library of Congress Catalog Card No. 72–2579
ISBN 0–668–02603–0

Printed in the United States of America

To horse lovers everywhere
I cordially dedicate this book.

PREFACE

When I wrote *The American Saddle Horse,* I started out merely to gather together some material for my own use, which I had been collecting over a period of years. I found that I had more material than I had supposed, and when I discussed it with a friend, he suggested that I put it in book form and publish it along with some suggestions for breaking gaited horses. I did this, adding the training suggestions quite hurriedly, as I did not at that time realize the interest that would be shown in that portion of the book.

As the book was sold, I began to perceive that it was those very suggestions that people were actually interested in and for which they were buying the books. I began to get quite a large volume of mail asking questions of all sorts and requesting that I publish a complete book on the riding and training of saddle horses.

Thus, this book was born; but as I have been continuously employed, it has been a part-time job, more or less, and has, therefore, taken me over ten years to complete. During this time I have made notes and have tried to be guided by the wishes of my readers, attempting to clear up especially those questions which were asked most frequently and trying to bring out the essential points in correct riding posture, as well as the generally accepted methods of training horses.

Riding and Training is therefore my answer to those hundreds of friends who have so kindly written me suggestions and questions. I hope it meets with your approval and thank you, each and every one.

PREFACE TO SECOND EDITION

Books about horses, their care, riding and training are quite abundant, but most of them deal exclusively with hunters and jumpers. It is almost impossible to find any literature about the five-gaited horse, the true Saddle Horse, the only horse in the world bred especially for beauty and ease of gaits, one of the few breeds of horses which originated in the United States of America, and the only breed which can be taught to correctly execute five perfect and distinct gaits.

As this field has been almost completely overlooked, this book deals primarily with The American Saddle Horse, but as I personally feel that any well rounded horseman should be able to do a creditable job on any type of horse, suggestions on training and riding other types, stock horses, hunters, and pleasure horses are also included.

My deepest appreciation goes to those who have helped me in the preparation of the book.

CONTENTS

ILLUSTRATIONS

Chapter I

ELEMENTARY EQUITATION

The arts of training and of riding are inseparable. In order for one to be able to ride really well, to get the most pleasure out of his ride, and to get his mount to obey him gracefully and easily, it becomes necessary that the rider know at least the fundamental principles of training and something of the course of training his horse has already gone through. It must also be remembered that the animal continues its learning each and every time it is ridden or is associated with human beings. It therefore becomes self-evident that unless the rider fully understands the principles involved in the training of horses, he may easily teach his mount bad habits without intending to do so, and without even being aware of what he is doing. How and why these bad habits are taught and how to prevent teaching them is nearly as important as how to teach correct habits. It should go without saying that before one attempts to actually train a horse he should be a superb rider; otherwise, no matter how much he may know about how and when the aids should be applied, he will find it impossible for him to use his knowledge to the best advantage. There are times when even the expert rider finds himself unable to use a specific aid at such time and place as will do the most good. The inexperienced are too concerned with merely staying on to be able to think of the results the untimely use of the aids may bring.

Riding, as well as training, is an art that has long been known to call forth the highest talent and skill. The beginner should recognize this, and while he enjoys himself on his daily ride he should constantly seek to improve himself. To become proficient he must apply himself just as studiously as if he were studying to be a painter or a musician, and he must realize that the very best of trainers are constantly learning and striving to learn more day by day. The trainer, of course, has a distinct advantage in being able to work with and ride a far larger number of horses than the average rider can. This continual striving to learn more and improve oneself is even more important for riders than for other artists, because the rider is not dealing with an inanimate thing, but with a living organism composed of brain, muscle, bones, and nerves very much like ourselves; and each individual not only presents a problem different from any other but even differing from its former self. In other words, even if one rides just one horse, he will find that each day new problems arise and new situations are to be met, as the animal shows itself to be versatile and capable of showing an ever-changing and new side to its rider.

For many centuries horses and trainers have been a necessity in every civilized country in the world. Until recently trainers were employed almost wholly by kings and nobles, and the training itself was designed to improve the horse for military purposes, the chase, or racing. Later on, horses began to be used for agricultural work and as a general means of transportation. Before the advent of roads, transportation was mainly by horseback, but, as fast as roads became built and improved, horses were hitched to vehicles and drew both people and luggage from place to place. It has been only in recent years, especially since the advent of the automobile, that the horse has come to be generally used for pleasure. The hunter was perhaps the first pleasure horse, and in some countries, is still the only one used for pleasure riding. In this country, as saddle horses became no longer necessary as a means of transportation, they came into use as a means of delightful recreation. Those persons who desire more strenuous competitive games turn to the hunter or polo pony. Nearly all of us seem to have an almost instinctive love for a horse, for the companionship and healthful exercise it affords. There is no other animal except the dog for which man forms that strong unbreakable allegiance.

Horseback riding is perhaps the most healthful exercise there is, as well as one of the most pleasant. It takes one out of doors and at the same time easily brings into play every muscle in the body to a greater or lesser extent, and is especially good for those inner abdominal muscles which are not called upon in so many forms of exercises. It is recommended by many prominent physicians and is endorsed by riders the world over, many of whom give it sole credit for long healthy useful lives. Riding gives a mental rest and gentle stimulation to children and grownups alike. There is an old saying, "The outside of a horse is good for the inside of a man."

The mounted man enjoys a certain prestige not otherwise obtainable. The mere physical fact that the pedestrian must look up to the mounted man, coupled with the sense of admiration at seeing a well trained horse respond to the stimuli of its master, and the realization of the vigorous training both must have gone through to achieve this perfection, all unite to cause admiration of the accomplished horseman. Throughout the ages the great men were commemorated in paintings or statues astride a horse, a compliment to both horse and rider. To be able to ride well is a special grace as well as a delightful recreation, and the nobility of all countries are thoroughly schooled in the arts of equitation as a matter of course.

Horse trainers have always held a peculiar niche or station, solely their own, in society. As a general rule they were not wealthy or titled, yet in most cases they worked for nobility and were held in the highest esteem. In many countries today, in order to become a horse trainer one must go through a very thorough course of training or school, lasting several years and including

ILLUSTRATION I

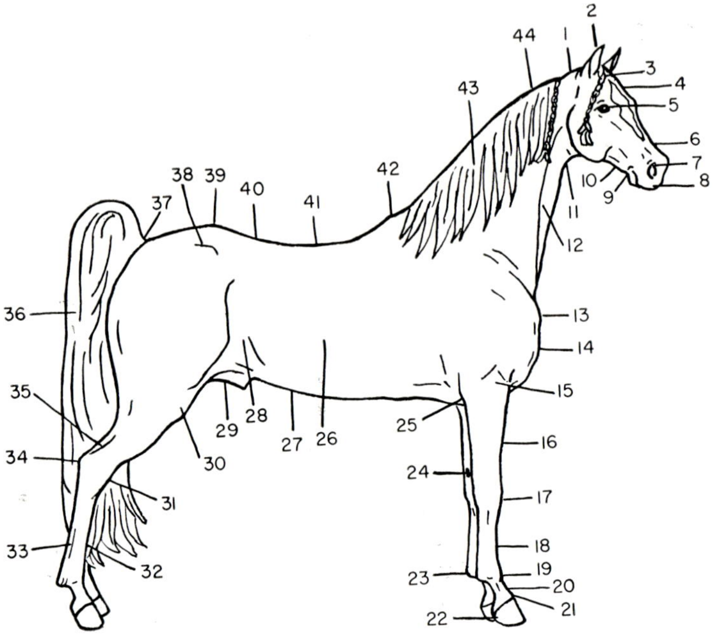

PARTS OF A HORSE

1. Poll
2. Ear
3. Forelock
4. Forehead
5. Eye
6. Nose
7. Nostril
8. Muzzle
9. Chin Groove
10. Jaw
11. Throat
12. Neck
13. Point of Shoulder
14. Breast
15. Arm
16. Forearm
17. Knee
18. Shank
19. Fetlock Joint
20. Pastern Joint
21. Coronet
22. Hoof
23. Point of Fetlock
24. Chestnut
25. Elbow
26. Ribs
27. Belly
28. Flank
29. Sheath
30. Stifle
31. Hock Joint
32. Cannon Bone
33. Tendon
34. Point of Hock
35. Ham String
36. Tail
37. Dock
38. Point of Hip
39. Croup
40. Loins
41. Back
42. Withers
43. Mane
44. Crest

fundamentals of saddle making, horseshoeing, and veterinary work. Trainers in this country are nearly all expected to have at least a workable knowledge of horseshoeing and minor veterinary work, as well as to be able to give advice on the purchase of tack and horses, if not doing the actual purchasing themselves.

When the beginner first feels the urge to learn to ride he will find it profitable if he can go to a good riding school and secure the services of a good riding master for at least a few lessons—the more the better. In doing this, he should be careful to select a capable riding master even if the cost per lesson is greater. A thoroughly competent riding master can teach more and teach it right in a few lessons than a less experienced man can do in several, and there is always the danger than an incompetent instructor may get one started wrong and the beginner may establish habits that are hard to break. It does not logically follow that any man who can ride a horse well, or look well on a horse, is qualified to teach riding. If the finances are limited I would surely advise one to take fewer lessons and if necessary pay more for them, but to be very sure that the instructor is thoroughly experienced and competent. One should also ride different horses to become familiar with all types, so that he will be able to select the type which will suit him best when he eventually decides to buy his own. This, I believe is the ultimate desire of nearly all horse lovers. Nearly all beginners want to ride a beautiful and spirited mount, but these are always the hardest to ride and control, which is the reason all riding academies have animals that are slightly dull witted and lazy. This is the type of horse on which one should begin. After one becomes more competent and confident he may gradually graduate to better class animals. It may be well to state here that owning a nice saddle horse is not nearly so expensive as some people think. In a later chapter more advice will be found on selecting and buying a horse for a hack or for a special purpose, with approximate prices which might have to be paid. In the chapter on stable management one will find hints on the actual cost of keeping one or two horses along with the work to be done, as well as more complete instructions for the larger stable.

When one first takes up riding he should learn the names of the different parts of the full bridle and saddle. He should also learn how and where to place the saddle and how to fit the bridle. If the reader will look at *Illustration II,* he can easily familiarize himself with the various parts of the saddle and bridle and be able to recognize them instantly. He should, if possible, practice taking apart and putting together a full bridle.

On first approaching a horse one must always speak to it. The horse, when standing idle, often relaxes its muscles and dozes and if startled it may kick; therefore, one must approach all horses quietly, speak to arouse them, then pat or caress them. These movements should all be firm and gentle with a view of inspiring the horse with confidence in the rider.

In placing the saddle on the animal's back it should not be thrown on, but rather lifted and placed gently on the back, a trifle ahead of the correct position, then slid back into place in order to smooth down the hair under it. It should not be set up on the animal's withers, as is so often the case, and cinched there. This is the cause of many sore backs, withers, and shoulders. The pommel rubs the animal's withers, and the tree and skirts rest upon the shoulders, rubbing and causing stiffness or galling. Referring to the United States Army drill regulations in the cavalry drill manual, we find it stated that the saddle should be placed far enough back so that four fingers may be placed between the shoulder blade and the front of the saddle tree. This is approximately the correct position, varying slightly with different animals and for different uses. The skirts on the stock saddle may confuse some, but we must remember that the wooden tree is the factor

ILLUSTRATION II

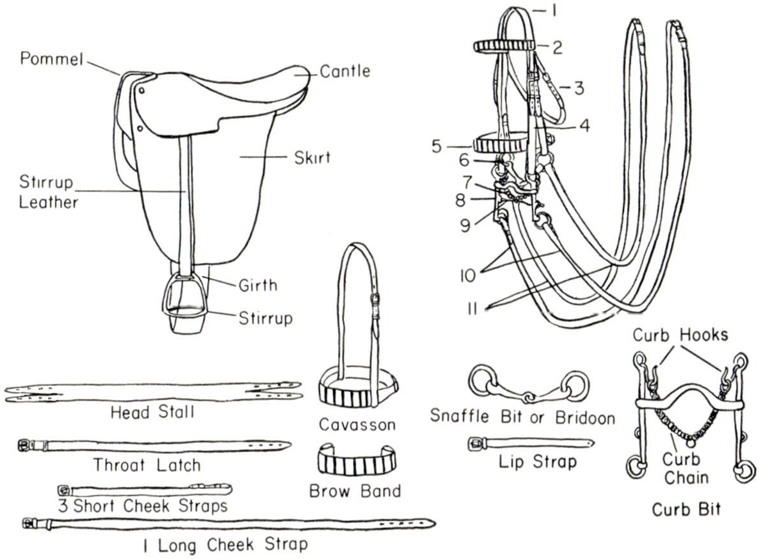

PARTS OF THE FULL BRIDLE

1. Head Stall
2. Brow Band
3. Throat Latch
4. Cheek Strap
5. Cavasson
6. Snaffle Bit or Bridoon
7. Curb Chain
8. Curb Bit
9. Lip Strap
10. Curb Reins
11. Snaffle Reins

that governs the position. In no case should the saddle tree rest upon the shoulders or withers.

On an English saddle the stirrups should have been drawn up before the saddle was removed from the previous horse and should be left that way until the saddle is in position and cinched up. If they have not been drawn up before, they must be now. This is done by lifting the stirrup strap with the left hand and grasping the stirrup with the right, then slipping it up the under strap. The whole stirrup leather is then brought down through the stirrup. When desiring to lower the stirrup again it is only necessary to grasp it and pull sharply. The girth is attached to the right side of the saddle and thrown over it. The saddle is then lifted (with the left hand grasping the pommel and the right hand grasping the cantle) to the horse's back. It is placed a little ahead of the proper position and gently slipped back where it belongs, which makes sure that the hair is laid properly and not curled backwards. The girth is then fitted under the belly about four inches back of the animal's elbows, then tightened from either side. Notice that the girth is not fitted too far forward or close to the animal's legs, as this will often cause sores. The stirrups may now be pulled down.

The stock saddle, being much heavier, may be thrown on if the horse will permit. This is done by grasping the pommel in the right hand and swinging it up. In this case, the saddle blanket has already been placed in position and slipped back a trifle to lay the hair down. The saddle then need not be placed ahead of the proper position nor must it be placed too far back, making it necessary to slide it forward and undo the good already accomplished with the blanket. If the stock saddle is to be lifted into position like the English saddle, the girth and off stirrup should first be laid across it.

To put on the bridle, the bit should be laid across the left hand between the thumb and index finger, and the headstall grasped with the right hand. (*See Illustration III*). The horse is approached from the near side and the animal's chin is taken in the left hand, gently pressing the thumb into the mouth forcing it to open to receive the bit. The horse cannot bite, for in this part of the mouth between the nippers and grinders there are no teeth. There is a variation of opinion as to whether or not the reins should be placed over the animal's neck before putting on the bridle. It is a little easier to do it this way, as the reins are disposed of immediately and one may control the horse a little better. However, unless the animal is tied it may run away, taking the bridle with it and tearing it up. The safest way is to slip the halter back over the neck and buckle it there, the animal thus being tied until the bridling is done. After the bits are inserted into the mouth between the nippers and grinders, the headstall is gently slipped over the ears, which are very sensitive and must be handled with care.

The throat latch is fastened loosely. It should never be fastened tightly, because when the animal's head is low and relaxed, the neck at this part is thinner than it

ILLUSTRATION III

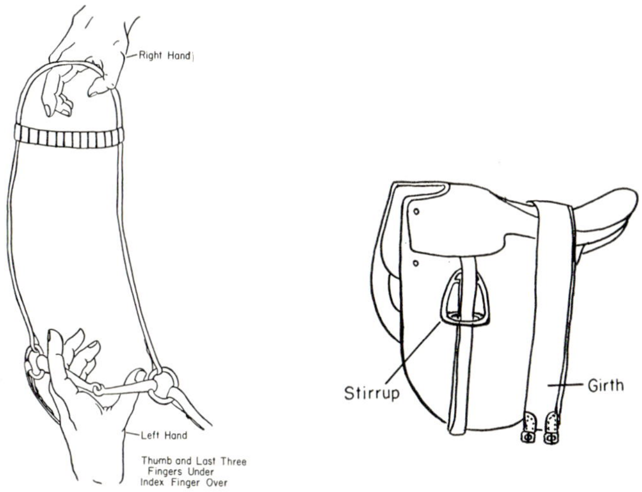

HOW TO PUT ON BRIDLE AND SADDLE

will be later on when the head is lifted and set. A loose throat latch will give the horse the appearance of having a finer neck. The bridoon on a single bridle is fitted snugly against the lips without causing them to wrinkle or draw up. On a double bridle the snaffle bit may be taken up one hole tighter to allow room for the curb, which is fitted just below the snaffle but not so low that it touches the horse's tusks. It is fitted to that part of the mouth where there are no teeth and rests against the bars or gums of the animal's mouth.

The curb chain is then fastened so that it lies flat in the groove, commonly spoken of as the chin groove, into which it naturally falls. Its only effect should be to stabilize the top of the curb bit or fulcrum, and it should therefore never be twisted. To do so defeats the primary purpose of the curb bit, which is to tuck the animal's head. A twisted curb chain will often cause the horse to toss its head. As there should be a little play before the bit takes hold, the curb chain should not be adjusted too tightly, but, if adjusted too loosely, it will have practically no effect. The exact adjustment will depend largely upon the particular horse in question. The animal now being saddled and bridled we are ready for our first ride.

Before mounting, the pupil should grasp the reins, as well as the mane or withers, with the left hand and should stand facing the rear, at about the horse's shoulder; then hold the stirrup with the right hand while inserting the left toe. Next he should grasp the pommel (or front) of the saddle with the right hand and spring up. (*See Illustration IV.*) The beginner should remember not to pull himself up, as will no doubt be his inclination. Instead, he should spring up from his right foot, throwing his leg well over the rump so that his foot does not come in contact with the rump, and then gently slide into the saddle.

It will be noticed that two things are particularly emphasized. First, the grasping of the pommel instead of the cantle with the right hand as one often sees done. This is very important for several reasons; namely, it is easier to mount this way when one once becomes accustomed to it, it does not pull the saddle to one side, which may cause sore backs, and most important of all, it is safer. If the horse is nervous or attempts to move off, this movement aids the rider in mounting and there is no necessity of letting go or changing grips until the rider is firmly seated in the saddle, thus avoiding many spills and runaways. The second thing which was emphasized was to gently slide, not drop, into the saddle. When the rider constantly drops down into the saddle with a thud it hurts the horse's back and loins, and will eventually cause even the mildest mannered animal to run away at the crucial moment.

The military method of mounting is very similar to the foregoing, except that the rider stands farther back and faces forward instead of to the rear before mounting. Then, as he mounts, he makes a distinct pause as he reaches the standing position and clicks his heels before throwing his leg over. This of course makes for greater uniformity and is therefore all right for military purposes, but serves no useful purpose to the individual rider. It also places the rider in a position where he may be easily kicked if the horse is so inclined.

The first thing that should be done after mounting is to adjust the stirrups to the right length and get the correct position in the saddle. Then the reins are properly gathered before starting off. Some of this may seem absurd to the beginner or even to the more experienced horsemen who do most of these things subconsciously, but they are really the result of many years, yes many centuries of study and practice in the art of riding by the best masters in the world, all of whom concur on the main essentials.

There is a definite reason for everything we do. In order to get the proper position one should slip forward in the saddle, reach around behind each thigh and pull out the breeches, then grasp the muscles along the inner side of the leg from the rear and pull back slightly. This will bring the flat side of the leg into closer contact with the horse. The legs are allowed to hang naturally with the toes down, and the stirrups should be adjusted so that the tread hangs about to the ankle bone. This length may be varied slightly to suit the individual's make-up. However, most beginners have a tendency to adjust the stirrups too short. This inclination must be overcome, for if the stirrups are adjusted too short, the knees are forced away from the saddle, and contact with the horse is lost. On the other hand, I have found that a number of riders want to lower the stirrups much too long, as soon as they begin to feel a little more confidence in themselves. I understand that this is done in imitation of some show riders who ride what is often referred to as Kentucky Style. Neither the beginner nor even the more experienced rider should do this. The trainer and showman have their special reasons for riding this way. They are not riding in order to spend a pleasurable half-hour, but to improve their mounts for a specific purpose and to show them off to the best advantage. Furthermore, this style of seat does not lend itself to everyone's conformation. Many show riders do not wear extremely long stirrups, but sit well back in the saddle and keep their knees bent and their lower legs well back, which often makes the stirrups appear longer than they actually are. We must also remember that most professionals are of necessity better riders than the average amateur and have had much more experience, often riding more hours in a few months than the average amateur does during his entire lifetime. He is therefore able to ascertain correctly the minor seat changes or stirrup lengths that are best suited to his particular needs and his build.

On the other hand, the average amateur generally rides for the pleasure he gets out of the ride. He should therefore adopt as comfortable and firm a seat as possible. Not until he becomes very good and experienced in riding the correct and comfortable way, should he learn show ring riding if he feels he wishes to do so. It can then be learned very easily and with only a few minor seat changes. Beginners and others who are trying to learn to ride correctly should resist the impulse to sit too far back in the

ILLUSTRATION IV

The Author demonstrating correct position in preparing to mount. Registered Arab Stallion, Jinon 2219, used.

saddle and to lengthen the stirrups too much. In the following chapter the reader will be taught how to sit and ride three- and five-gaited show horses. It is absolutely essential that one first learn to ride correctly, to manage his mount properly at all gaits, and to derive pleasure, comfort, and relaxation from riding.

After the rider has his seat secure and his stirrups adjusted to the proper length, he then inserts his toes into the stirrups until the ball of the foot rests squarely on the tread. The heel should drop lower than the toe. This will be the case if the rider is perfectly relaxed, but in most cases the beginner feels a slight fright, or at least feels himself in an alien environment and tenses his muscles, thus causing his heels to fly up higher than his toes. This will be more pronounced later on at the faster gaits. Therefore the beginner must at all times force his heels lower than his toes until this becomes a fixed habit. This will be the case when he is perfectly relaxed and confident in himself. The feet should be nearly parallel with the horse's body with the toes pointing slightly out. Never should they point in. The exact angle will depend upon the build of the rider. As long as the knees are always in close contact with the horse, and the rider is not consciously trying to turn the toes either in or out and is perfectly relaxed, the position of the feet will be found correct for that particular individual. We must always remember that what may be correct for one individual may not always be correct for another of different height, weight, or build. I have always found that the fastest and easiest way for the beginner to learn to ride is for him to relax and enjoy his ride, and not to try to be too particular about maintaining correct position. Trying too hard generally defeats its own purpose, as it invariably causes one to stiffen his muscles and thus lose correct riding posture. When riding (and this applies to the more advanced student as well as to the beginner) if one feels himself becoming stiff, tense, or tired at any time, it is best to pull the horse down to a walk or, better still, stop, dismount, and relax. The rider will soon find that he can learn faster by taking things easy.

The knees should be slightly bent with the lower legs hanging loosely and naturally. The buttocks rest squarely in the saddle; the rider sits up straight, but not stiff, with his head up, chin in, shoulders squared, abdomen in, and his back slightly curved. The arms hang naturally to the elbows which of course are bent and the forearms are held at such an angle that the reins and forearms form an unbroken line from the elbow to the bit.

I prefer to have the beginner start with the single bridle having either snaffle bit or bridoon. In this case there is only one pair of reins for him to handle, one of which is carried in each hand, coming in under the little finger, passing through the hand, and coming out over the index finger and held down with the thumb. (*See Illustration VIII, figure G—next Chapter.*) The hands are held nearly vertical, as in this position one will have perfect flexibility of the wrists, whereas if they are held horizontally, flexibility of the wrists is greatly reduced. If the full bridle must be used, the snaffle reins are held in the same position stated above and the curb reins are also carried one in each hand, coming into the hand between the ring and middle finger, passing through the hand under the snaffle and coming out over the index finger exactly like the snaffle and directly under it. (*See Illustration VIII, figure B, in next Chapter.*) I am aware that most riding masters say that the curb rein should pass between the little and ring fingers and that this is the military method (*Illustration VIII, figure A*), but I have always found that one has more control of reins and can more easily use them individually or simultaneously as the occasion demands if they are carried in the way I described. I know I have helped a lot of riders get more perfect control of their mounts by merely suggesting this small change in the position of the curb rein.

It should go without saying that the off reins are carried in the right hand and the near reins in the left. One will find it much easier to learn to ride and control his mount with the reins held in both hands this way than if he attempts to hold them all in only one hand. An experienced rider always uses both hands when schooling or showing a horse, using one hand only when he is relaxing. When this is the case the reins may be held as in *Illustration VIII, figure F,* with the near snaffle rein coming into the hand under the little finger, the near curb between the little and ring fingers, the off curb between the ring and middle fingers, and the off snaffle between the middle and index fingers, all lying flat and coming through the hand together and out over the index finger. This is the position generally taught for holding four reins in one hand, because it is the easiest position in which the rider can get the full effect of either the snaffle or the curb reins, or both. There are other positions for carrying the reins in one hand and many others than those which I have described for carrying the reins in two hands, some of which may be used for special effects, and some because they seem to adapt themselves to a particular rider. These will be explained later, and after the rider has become adept he may choose and use any position which may seem to best suit his purposes. The methods I have just described will be found to be the most convenient to the majority of people on the greatest number of horses and should be mastered thoroughly by the novice rider before he attempts any of the other positions. All the others are but modifications of those above.

The beginner, having his seat and hands properly and firmly settled, is now ready to gather his horse and move off. Always before a horse is started in to a walk or an increased gait, he should be gathered in order to let him know that something is to be asked of him. In other words, gathering is a preparatory command. It is done by squeezing with the legs and taking a little hold of the reins. As he is ready to be moved out, the pressure of the bit is somewhat relaxed and the pressure of the legs increased simultaneously. There should be no clucking or jerking.

The animal should move out at an even flat-footed walk, and the beginner will do well to ride only at a walk until he becomes perfectly accustomed to sitting this gait upright, yet relaxed and full of confidence. It is at this gait that one can most easily develop a good firm seat. I especially like to have students ride at a walk over rough terrain if possible, without holding onto the pommel of the saddle for support. One should learn to use both the leading and the bearing rein for turning and controlling his mount. With the leading rein, the animal's head is turned slightly in the direction in which it is to go, and the bearing rein is used with a slight pressure on the opposite side of the neck to encourage the horse to turn, yet keeping its head in a straight line with its body. Cow ponies, polo ponies, and some hacks, especially in the West, are taught to turn by the use of the bearing rein only, and when riding just for pleasure it is perfectly correct to guide a broke horse this way, although I personally believe that all students should first learn thoroughly the use of both leading and bearing reins.

Let me emphasize the fact that the embyro rider and even the more advanced student cannot get too much riding at a walk. Fillis contends that it takes twenty-five years to learn correctly and completely to ride the walk and proportionately more for the faster gaits, inferring that that is the only gait any of us can completely master. Most trainers ride from a dozen to a score of horses daily, yet I doubt if there are any who are not sometimes caught slightly off balance at a high fast trot or other increased gait.

When the pupil is ready to begin trotting his mount, it should be gathered, as explained formerly, after which the pressure of the legs is increased and the pressure of the bits decreased until the animal moves out to a slow trot. In my opinion, the beginner should not be in a hurry to move faster than a slow trot, nor should he be in a hurry to learn to post (that is, rise to the trot). He should first learn to sit the slow trot. To do this, he must relax completely and sit square in the middle of the saddle with his body leaning slightly in rear of the vertical. The horse must be allowed to trot very slowly, and the rider should learn to take up the slight jolt completely in the small of his back. The jolt will be lessened proportionately as the rider learns to relax his muscles completely. This was once explained to me by the following: "If a sack is filled full of pig iron and placed on a horse's back it will fall off at the first motion of the animal, and if held down it will bounce up and down; but if, on the other hand, a sack is partially filled with oats or other loose material and balanced across a horse's back it will ride almost indefinitely and with no apparent bouncing." Therefore, to sit the trot comfortably the rider must balance, loosen his muscles, and relax. He should always ride by a sense of balance rather than by gripping with his knees. Even the experienced rider will improve himself by riding a few minutes each day at a slow trot without the aid of stirrups. The beginner should not take the stirrups off the saddle but keep his feet hanging loosely in them just in case he begins to lose his balance. Riding a few minutes each day at a slow trot without the use of the stirrups will help give anyone a firm secure balanced seat which is an absolute necessity for a good rider.

The reins must not be used as anchors nor must they be used for the purpose of helping one to retain his balance. In the next chapter we shall discuss good hands, but at this stage the less use the rider makes of his reins, except for directing the movements of his mount, the better it will be. Pulling leather or holding onto the pommel of the saddle is bad form, bad horsemanship, and will destroy instead of increase the confidence of the rider.

Except as a last resort to keep from falling from his horse, the student should never take hold of the pommel of the saddle while riding.

After one has been riding the walk a great deal and the slow trot for a few days, and begins to feel confidence in himself and gets the rhythm of the animal's foot movements at the trot, he may begin to learn to post or rise to the trot. Generally speaking, I find that the more riding the student has had at the slow trot, the quicker and easier he will learn to post the trot. This is not always the case, however, as there are some people with a natural rhythm and grace who seem to catch the feel of the horse almost instinctively and immediately. I have had many such students begin posting the trot within ten minutes after they were first mounted. Nevertheless, even these people should not omit practice at the walk and slow trot, as one may be able to post quite well and still not have a firm seat in an emergency. Correct posting does not necessarily indicate a firm, secure seat, but merely indicates that one is in perfect time with the animal's movements.

It is desirable for the horse to move out at a faster rate of speed when the student begins to learn to post the trot, as it is only by doing so that its hind legs impart enough of a jolt to throw the beginner forward in the saddle. The expert may be able to post a slow trot by catching the slightest movement, but the novice should be helped by a harder, more definite movement. The mechanics of posting are quite simple. The primary thing is to be in perfect time with the animal. The rider inclines his body forward and allows himself to be thrown forward in the saddle by the impulsion of the horse's hind leg. He then balances himself in that position for an instant, while the opposite hind leg moves forward, then gently slides back into the saddle just in time to receive the next impulse from the same hind leg. Thus, posting is actually bouncing slightly on every other movement rather than on every one. Please note: it is not an up-

and-down movement, but more of a forward-and-backward movement with a slight rising and lowering of the body at the same time. The body must lean forward from the hips in order to receive the impulse correctly. The United States Cavalry School properly advises the beginner to place his hands on the animal's neck in order to be sure that he leans forward, as well as to increase his sense of equilibrium. This, of course, greatly exaggerates the position which the rider will take later on, but, while learning, it is just as well to exaggerate to a certain extent. It generally takes the student a little time to get the feel of the thing and to do it correctly, but once he catches it, it is his from then on even if he fails to ride a horse for a number of years.

The trot is a two-beat gait with the diagonal legs moving in unison. That is, the left front and right hind feet strike the ground at the same moment, and the right front and left hind feet do likewise. What actually happens when posting the trot on the right diagonal, is that when the left hind leg, beginning to move forward, throws the rider's weight slightly up and forward, he in turn sustains himself there an instant, then gently slips back into position in the saddle and is then ready to receive the next impulse from the left hind leg of his mount. It will be noticed that there is very little effort required from the rider. He must be ready to receive the impulse from the horse's hind leg at exactly the right instant. In other words, he must be in perfect unison with the horse and must sustain himself an instant at the height of the movement in order not to return to the saddle too soon. That is all the energy the rider should expend. He does not raise himself in his stirrups, for the movement is almost entirely from the knee up. The lower leg should move very little on an evenly trotting horse.

When the beginner fails in the first few attempts, there is always the tendency for him to try to lift himself up or to force the post. This, of course, spoils the whole movement and defeats its own purpose by causing him to get out of time with his mount, rather than in unison with it. A far better plan for the beginner is to start his animal at a smart trot and try to catch the beat a few times; then bring the animal down to a walk. The rider should then adjust his seat and relax a few minutes before he tries again. When he is learning to post he should never try too long at any one time, especially if he is getting tired or feels that he is working under a strain. The minute one begins to strain, all further attempts are futile. He must neither become impatient, nor expect to catch the idea quickly. Sooner or later the feeling will come to anyone, and once experienced correctly, it will never be lost. Some may take several days acquiring it and others may master it almost immediately. Above all, an instructor cannot help his pupil by grasping under his arm and attempting to force him to post. This only throws the student to one side causing him to lose his balance and making it harder for him to get in time with his mount. The instructor can give valuable advice and coaching. The pupil must remember to keep his legs back, his heels down and his body bent at the hips, but the back must not be rounded. With the foregoing instructions, I know that any normal person can learn to post the trot in a short while. *Do not try too hard.* This is a mistake nearly every beginner makes. The effort must come almost completely from the animal.

The next step for the beginner is to learn to ride the canter and to make the mount canter at will. The actual riding of the canter is quite simple, for there is no rising as in posting the trot. The canter is a series of jumps, as it were, and in order to ride it easily without bouncing, one must sit in the saddle loosely, leaning slightly in rear of the vertical, and allow one's buttocks to roll in the dish of the saddle with the movement of the horse. With a little practice this will come easily and the canter will be found to be one of the easiest of all gaits to ride. However, making the horse canter at will and on whichever lead is desired, is not always quite as easy.

The canter is a three-beat gait, with the animal leading out with one front leg, followed by the diagonal pair and lastly propelled by the other hind leg. In taking the canter with the left lead, the animal leads out with its left front leg, followed and propelled by the left hind and right front simultaneously, after which the lone right hind does the propelling. When traveling in a circle or taking a turn, it must always lead with the inside leg, which is the reason it must be taught to lead with either leg the rider sees fit. If one will watch a horse running loose in the pasture field, he will notice that it changes leads whenever necessary, and when cantering in a circle it will nearly always lead with its inside leg. However, when being ridden it cannot be depended upon to do this. It seems to depend upon the rider to give directions and the rider must know how to give the directions properly.

For this purpose, we assume that the pupil, or reader, is riding a well broken mount, which should always be the case for a student rider. One cannot expect a beginner to force a green horse to do its gaits, as that really comes under the head of training. For the student, the well broke horse should take any gait which is asked of it, and take it promptly and easily. It is always easier for a beginner to learn to ask for the proper lead in a ring or circle which is enclosed by a wall or fence. If the rider is now riding in the ring to the left (with his left hand toward the inside), he will wish to take the left lead. The animal is gathered, then the rider's weight is shifted a little to the rear and to the right (outside), and the animal's head is lifted with the snaffle bit a little to the outside. The left heel is then used just behind the girth and the right heel further to the rear. (*See Illustration V.*) It will be noticed that each of these movements is designed to relieve the animal's near or left shoulder of weight and to force its hindquarters slightly to the left. These move-

ILLUSTRATION V

ments should be performed simultaneously, and the animal will take the canter on the circle to the left leading out with its left leg. The rider relaxes and allows his body to lean back slightly and his buttocks to roll in the saddle, but does *not* allow his feet to fly forward. They must be kept in the same position as when trotting, i.e., legs back and heels lower than the toes. The arms must not flop like a pair of wings, but they should rather be held gently against the rider's sides.

When cantering to the right and using the right lead, the exact opposite aids from those just explained will of course be used. After the rider has learned to ask for and to obtain the inside lead of a canter on a circle, he should learn to ask for the canter on a straight line with either lead he may desire to use. He, of course, uses his aids the same as when asking for the canter in a circle. The animal must not be cantered all the time on the same lead. It should be cantered on one lead awhile, then halted, turned around and cantered on the opposite lead. Asking the horse to canter on a straight line is a trifle harder than on a circle, but if the rider will persist he will soon accomplish it. The two important things to remember is to lift the mount's head toward the outside of the ring, the opposite side that he wishes his mount to lead with, and to remember that the opposite heel from the lead being taken is the one used further back and most vigorously.

The canter should always be taken from a walk, never from a trot. There is a very good reason for this; the canter is the natural gait a horse takes when wishing to move faster than the trot, and if allowed to take the canter from a trot under the saddle, it will learn to break into a canter when the rider wishes to urge it into a fast trot. This it should never do. The animal should never be allowed to break from one gait into another, and if it is always taught to take all gaits from a walk and that practice is always followed when riding, it will never learn to mix its gaits.

On the other hand, the saddle horse is always brought back to a walk, from any fast gait, through a trot. That is, if one wishes to slow down or halt his mount from any fast gait, it is first slowed down to a trot for a few steps, then down to a walk, etc. This applies to a canter, a gallop, a rack, or an exceedingly fast show trot. The cow pony or polo pony must, of course, stop almost immediately from any gait. This, however, requires very good horsemanship, and, even so, it is done at the risk of the animal's hind legs, and is even worse on the fore legs, if the rider should allow the horse to stop on them instead of the hind legs. This risk is all a part of their work but not a part of a riding horse's work. In riding the canter the rider's arms should move with the animal's head. If there is any feel of the mouth it should be a light, steady feel with no jerks or bumps. The canter and gallop are the same gait except that the gallop is faster. Let me say here that the rider who wishes to really learn how to ride a horse should avoid fast speeds. Being able to sit on a horse as fast as it can go is not a test of horsemanship, but usually denotes a novice. If the reader will go to any of the bridle paths, he will soon find out for himself that the ones who race their horses are precisely the ones who do not know how to ride any other gait. They haven't learned to enjoy the slower gaits, so they kill off their horses by racing them all the time. A saddle horse is bred and trained to give one a pleasant comfortable ride, and not to be raced. I don't mean that a good rider never lets his horse gallop. Nearly everyone who owns a good hack likes to allow it to gallop occasionally, but the good rider does so only occasionally and always keeps his mount well within itself.

After learning to ride the forward gaits, the student should learn to back his horse properly in a straight line. The pupil should, of course, be mounted upon a well broke hack. He first gathers the horse to let it know that something is to be asked of it, then leans slightly to the rear and gives a light pull on the reins, keeping his legs in contact with the animal's sides and well back. The tension on the reins is very soon released and repeated, having a give and take effect. The animal should begin to back easily. The rider's legs should keep in contact with the animal's sides all the time, and the give and take effect in this case should be a little more take than give, never a steady backward pull. To stop the horse from backing, merely increase the pressure of the legs and release the rein pressure. A horse must never be allowed to back of its own accord. The rider must always keep the forward impulse even when backing. To help insure this the rider should always ask his mount to take at least one step forward after it has been backed, and at the beginning, he should back it no more than two or three steps. If the animal is allowed to back of its own accord, or is not moved forward a step or two after being backed, it will often teach the horse to get behind the bits, in which case the rider has lost all control.

In halting the animal it is first gathered, after which it is brought to a slower gait or to a halt, with a give and take effect of the reins. If the animal should happen to get out of control for the beginner, especially at the canter or gallop, he must not forget this give and take effect and use it as hard as necessary, and always against, rather than with, the stride.

To dismount, the student gathers his reins in the left hand and places them on the withers or crest of the neck. The other hand is placed on the pommel of the saddle. The rider then slips his right foot from the stirrup, and swings his leg over the animal's rump without touching the rump, and brings it down beside his left foot. He now leans against his mount with most of his weight supported by his hands which are still in the position described above. The left foot is then slipped free of the stirrup and the rider springs to the ground, at the same time pushing himself a little bit away from the horse. Mounting or dismounting is, of course, always done from the animal's "near" (or left) side.

While the beginner is learning the rudimentary principles of riding explained in this chapter he should not bother the animal with the reins, but should use them as little as possible; mainly to guide and halt the horse, otherwise he should have little feel of the animal's mouth. Later on, he can learn the exact use of the reins, but it is first necessary for him to learn to ride absolutely independent of the reins, so that when he does begin to use them properly he may become very skillful with them and be able to use them with as much force, and only as much force, as is required, and only at such times as force may be required. To do this, he will need a perfectly secure, balanced seat in which there is positively no dependence upon the reins.

Chapter II

HIGHER EQUITATION

Part A—In the Ring or Riding Hall

While the foregoing riding may have been done either in the ring or on the trails, the work in this section can best be grasped in the ring or riding hall. It is here that one can acquire the fullest attention of his mount and therefore exercise more complete control over it. It is also true that in the ring the instructor has the distinct advantage of being better able to watch every move of his pupil and to offer concrete suggestions for improvement. While it is no doubt true that the riding hall is the best place for all phases of collected riding, it is also true that both horse and rider are apt to become bored by this type of riding alone. It is therefore suggested that one should ride in the ring, with advanced instruction if possible, every other day, and ride on the trails on off days, either alone or in a group.

To my mind, all training and riding, no matter how far it is carried, should be designed to help the rider secure instant and perfect control at all times, and to teach the animal that it must respond instantly to any of the aids. The prime purpose of the saddle horse, with the exception of those used entirely for the show ring, is for transportation or for going places. It may be either to carry the soldier to the place of battle; the hunter after his game; the cowboy to examine stock or fences or to catch a steer; the polo player after the ball; the horse lover over the trails or merely for a pleasant ride over the bridle paths, or in the ring for a short hour's enjoyment. The easier the animal does this and the quicker it responds to the aids of the rider, the easier and more enjoyable a ride the equestrian will have.

Before proceeding further with this chapter, we must not only assume that the reader is thoroughly familiar with all parts of the first chapter but also that he can actually put them into practice, and that he has a firm secure seat. All this requires much practice, and not merely reading about it. Therefore, it will be useless for the reader to go ahead with this chapter until he has had a great deal of experience in riding, can post the trot well, can get either lead of the canter at will, can properly make the horse stop or back, and, most important of all, that he has a good seat, absolutely independent of the use of the reins. He is then ready to go ahead and learn what good hands, often inappropriately called "light hands," actually are, as well as other phases of riding which are more advanced than in the former chapter. The student should still be riding a well broke mount for all phases of instruction.

GOOD HANDS, AND THE TECHNIQUE OF PRODUCING A FLEXION

Up to this point, the reader has been told to ride with little, if any, feel of the animal's mouth. Now, that statement must be modified. The reins have a very definite purpose and should not be allowed to hang loosely. This advice given previously was to insure the development of a firm seat, without any reliance upon the reins, so that when this phase of instruction came they could be used as directed, absolutely independent of the seat or of the gait the animal may be taking. The following is the final and highest requisite of good or light hands; that the reins may be used whenever necessary with as much force and only as much force as is required to exact obedience, no matter what the gait of the horse or the circumstances.

If force is absolutely necessary, it does not constitute poor hands to use force, as is so generally believed. This is why I believe the term "light hands" is a misnomer. I also think that, due to the general use of this term, the correct significance of it is so generally misunderstood. We can easily see how the term came into general usage and why authors as a rule continue its use. The reason is that these same authors advocate training the horse to such a degree that very little force is necessary to exact obedience. This, of course, is the ideal for which we all strive, but in a book on equitation it is necessary to take cognizance of the fact that many readers are not riding such well broke horses, of which there are indeed few. Those riders who must ride at public schools cannot hope to get a mount that obeys so readily. Because of the large number of inexperienced people who ride at public stables, no matter how good a mouth a horse may have when it first enters such stables, it will not stay that way long. Therefore, we will stick to the term "good hands" instead of "light hands," always remembering that in order to exact obedience, force is to be applied only when necessary, and only in the amount required for that particular animal.

We have taken little notice of the bits and their real use. On the Saddle Horse, the snaffle bit is used primarily to lift the head, and the curb bit to set the head and obtain a flexion. Of course, it is possible to flex the head with the snaffle bit by using it either with a running martingale or with the hands held low, so that it works on the bars of the mouth like a curb bit; however, with a double bridle the snaffle bit is used only to raise the head, with the pressure applied to the lips. The saddle horse is trained to lift its head when it feels the pressure of the snaffle and to set its head and flex at the feel of the curb bit or pressure on the bars of the mouth. This setting of the animal's head is done not only to improve its looks, which of course it does, but also to flex it and make it far easier to handle. We are now coming to the finer points of equitation; the production of a flexion of the animal's neck at the poll, which in turn relaxes the muscles of its whole body. The problem of teaching a colt to flex comes properly under the heading of training, but it is now necessary to learn to produce a flexion in a well-trained mount.

This flexion of which there is so much talk is, I am afraid, little understood. The pressure of the bit on the bars of the horse's mouth causes it to give to this pressure or relax its jaws, which in turn relaxes the muscles at the poll and makes the animal light-mouthed and easy to handle. A heavy-mouthed horse is simply one which has not learned to flex itself properly and the degree of light-mouthness of the animal, depends almost entirely on its willingness to flex itself correctly. This flexion really brings the center of propulsion closer to the center of gravity or center of weight. The closer together the two are brought, the easier the horse will be to handle, the quicker it will be able to obey signals such as to stop or turn, and the higher action it will have. This, then, is the real reason for setting the horse's head and obtaining a flexion or, in other words, collecting the mount.

It must not be thought, however, that just because one's mount has its head in the proper position that it is fully collected. If the animal is pulling on the bits or fighting them, it is not properly flexed no matter what position its head may be in. As we shall soon find out, the rider must at the same time use his legs to draw the animal's hind legs under it and increase propulsion in order to obtain complete collection. The horse must be brought under perfect and complete submission to the will of the rider.

To obtain this flexion, the rider lifts the head with the snaffle reins and takes in a little with the curb. As soon as the animal gives to the pressure of the bits on the bars of its mouth, the rider must give to the horse, or relax his hold a trifle. That is, for the time being, he does not "take" any more or keep pulling, for this in time will spoil even the best animal. However, he does not allow his reins to become entirely loose, for if he does this he will lose all he has gained. He merely holds what he has and attempts to take no more. This is what is generally called "give and take," a term which is also often misinterpreted. It is not a continual process of jerking and turning loose, but rather it is a light pull followed by a steady hold. The rider takes and the horse gives; then the rider takes no more for the time being. After a short while the rider again takes, asking his mount to give, until he finally has the horse's head in the position he wishes, after which he rides with a somewhat fixed hand, keeping only a slight feel of the animal's mouth with both snaffle and curb reins, thus keeping the animal well flexed.

I realize there will be a storm of disapproval at my expression "fixed hands." However, it is the most appropriate term I can think of. I certainly do not mean a rigid wrist, but merely a light, supple wrist with the hands maintaining continuous even contact with the animal's mouth. He is then riding at a collected gait, and at a collected trot, the animal's head will move only slightly. At a walk or at a canter the animal's head will move, and the rider's wrist must be supple enough to maintain the same light even contact with the animal's mouth. The rider's whole arm must move if it is necessary, in order to keep that even contact with the horse's mouth, without any semblance of jerking or bumping the mouth.

From several experiences I have had lately, it appears to me that collection is very little understood even by those who have been taught and should know the technique of collection. There are many students who, when asked to take a collected trot, merely pull their horses down to a slow trot without getting any degree of collection in the least. Perhaps this is partly the fault of instructors who, for some reason, are not able to impart the idea that collection implies propulsion and movement, the horse at the same time being well under control. I have talked with several instructors on this point and many agree that that is one of the hardest things to instill in the minds of their pupils. Personally, I have always been able to do quite well by demonstrating just exactly what collection is, rather than just talking about it. As it is impossible to do that in a book, I am giving it special emphasis in trying to define it in understandable language, and I will include several pictures demonstrating true collection in this book.

The animal may travel just as fast at a collected gait as when it is traveling free hand; the difference being that when it is traveling free hand, its head is loose and fairly relaxed and it is up to the horse to pick its own way and often its own speed. In trail riding, especially mountain climbing, etc., one rides free hand. On the other hand, when the animal is collected it is picked up. The rider takes a feel of the reins and uses his legs to draw the horse's hind legs well under it. The horse is not pulling or boring, but is up on the bit, ready to move forward. change gaits, stop, or do anything which it is asked to do, immediately. It is completely flexed and perfectly under control of the rider. When one collects his mount before changing gaits, it is a kind of preparatory command. In the Army, the soldiers are given this same preparatory command before each command of execution, so that each man may, at the same instant, prepare himself and be ready to follow the command of execution. When one rides at a collected gait he keeps his mount prepared for any instant change which he may ask of it. The experienced rider easily senses when his mount is collected. It feels perfectly alive and full of spirit, yet supple and anxious to go, and is perfectly submissive to the will of the rider. Even when trail riding or riding free hand, the horse should always be collected before being asked to start, stop, or change gaits. (*See Illustration VI.*)

So far, we have talked primarily about the use of the rein aids in collecting our mount. However, the leg aids must be used at the same time that the rein aids are used,

Illustration VI

JEAN CAMEO 16657

A Saddlebred Gelding by Cameo Kirby, bred by Revel English and owned by Ted C. Buck, Indio, Calif. Ridden by the Author. A very good example of a horse traveling at a high fast trot in complete collection. Note the all-around action, especially the position of the hock and hind leg. Also note the position of the head and how the horse is well up on the bit without pulling. Notice the position of the rider's legs and the close contact with the horse's body.

ILLUSTRATION VII

A PARADE HORSE

A good example of a modern day parade horse and the trappings which are now a part of all parade horse classes. This horse owned and ridden by Mr. Don Groom of Oakland, California, who has owned and ridden some of the top winning parade horses on the West Coast.

in order to secure perfect collection. The legs, heels, or spurs impart the idea of impulsion and gather the horse's hind legs under it, and the rein aids set the head and translate part of the impulsion into action and spirit. When all this is done together true collection is obtained. Without the use of the legs in connection with the reins, the animal will learn to get behind the bit. This is about the worst possible fault a horse can acquire, and once learned it is generally a very hard vice to cure. On the bridle paths, the animal will seldom be asked to go in a collected walk, but will often be collected at other gaits. In the riding hall, the horse will be taken at a collected walk more often, but not all the time, as the walk will be used a great deal to rest and relax the mount, and the horse will be ridden in full collection at the faster gaits.

After thoroughly digesting the foregoing, the reader will readily see that the curb bit is not at any time a mere emergency brake to stop the horse when all other means fail, as is so often taught by a certain class of instructors and which is practiced by a great number of persons who consider themselves good riders. When asking the horse to stop, one should bring it into full collection by using the legs, as well as the reins, and by applying gentle, successive pulls on the bits. All saddle horses, with the exception of the polo pony or cow pony, should be brought to a halt from the faster gaits, through a trot, then a walk, and gradually a full halt. *Illustration VI* shows correct flexion obtained at the poll.

We should now familiarize ourselves a little more with the different aids and their uses. There are what are known as the three natural aids and the three artificial aids. The natural aids are the legs, voice, and the rider's weight. We have already seen how the weight may be used in asking for the canter. It is also used in slowing down or halting the horse by sitting down firmly in the saddle before signaling the halt, and is often used in teaching the colt to rack on and in starting some of the high-school gaits. The legs are used in collecting the mount and controlling the hind quarters, as well as inducing mobility and starting the animal into faster gaits. There are few authors, instructors, or riders who stress the value of the voice as an aid, or use it to its full advantage. It should not be used for a continual clucking to the mount, but it is a very effective instrument in obtaining the horse's attention, gaining its confidence, and quieting it when necessary.

The artificial aids are the bits, spurs, and whip. The bits are used for obtaining collection, control, and calling for the gaits; never for punishment. The following are the names and uses of some of the rein aids. The first and most common is called the leading rein. It is the rein that nearly all beginners, with the exception of those who ride cow ponies in the far West, are first taught to use. It is, of course, used in guiding the horse, by pulling its head around the way one wishes it to go. Next we have the bearing rein, which is either used to keep the animal's head in a straight line with its body when it is turning, or for guiding a horse which has been taught to neck rein. It is pressed on the opposite side of the neck from that which we are turning. That is, if we wish to turn to the right, we use the left bearing rein, and vice versa. We also have the rein of direct opposition which is used straight back with the give-and-take movement. It is used in order to produce a flexion, or to ask the horse to slow down, halt, or back up. The indirect rein of opposition, used both backward and against the animal's neck, is used when asking the mount for two-track work and to help hold the forequarters in place when turning on the forehand. These are the rein aids most commonly used. The spurs are an artificial aid and are used for increasing the force or efficiency of the leg aids, when the animal does not respond properly to the lower legs. In rare instances they may be used as a medium of punishment, but the horse should not be continually poked or prodded along with them. The whip, if used correctly, can be an important instrument in securing control and attention, as well as for direction and demanding obedience. It may also be used for punishment if necessary.

DIFFERENT METHODS OF HOLDING THE REINS

When one becomes quite a proficient rider he will often find times when he feels that the method of holding the reins explained in the preceding chapter is not sufficient for all his needs. By experimenting himself, he may find one or more other methods which may fill his needs and perhaps entirely replace the original position advised. When one knows how to ride well and knows what he is doing with each hand, we cannot say that any special method is wrong, unless he intends to ride in equitation or horsemanship classes, in which case one will always have a better chance if he uses a standard method. Other than this instance, as long as any one particular rein can be used separately and independently, when needed, and any combination can be used at will, and the rider is able to shorten his rein or reins at will, the position he has found for himself is correct for him. Nearly all professionals have their own pet way of holding the reins, and one method produces just about as good results as the other. Many use different methods of carrying the reins to get different effects or different gaits, or on different horses. In order to help our reader to find the particular method which may be best for him, we will explain some of the most common methods used. He will find these pictured in *Illustration VIII.*

The method already explained for holding four reins in one hand (*Figure F*) is no doubt the simplest and easiest, and nothing further need be said on that score, except that in rare instances it may be varied by placing the curb reins on the outside and the snaffle reins on the inside. I understand that this is the English custom. The main reason for using them in this manner is to obtain greater leverage on the curb bit when riding an animal which needs to be ridden more on the curb than on the snaffle. All other methods are for two hands.

The one most generally used and that which is no doubt the best for the average rider, and which is made compulsory by the United States Government for cavalrymen, etc., is the one explained in the first chapter. (*Figure A.*) The English method is just the reverse; that is, snaffle and curb reins are transposed. Many riders carry three reins in one hand and one in the other. This does not give the lopsided effect which at first glance may be supposed, for in this case the two curb reins are held on either side of the middle finger and are used primarily to obtain the flexion, while the snaffle rein comes into the hand under the little finger and through the hand directly over the curb reins and is thus used independently. The opposite snaffle may be carried in any way desired, although the usual way is to put it under the little finger, just as the snaffle is carried in the other hand. (*Figure C.*) When using this method, the three reins are generally carried in the left hand and the single one in the right, as most riders have learned to use their left hand with greater versatility than the right. Nevertheless, there can be no objection to carrying the three in the right hand, if one so desires. I find this method very useful in riding many gaited show horses. When I first saw it described quite a number of years ago, however, in my own mind I condemned the author and criticized this method for being unnatural and lopsided. Then one day I noticed that I was carrying my own reins in that position and perhaps had been doing it without realizing it; for how long, it is impossible to say. I then realized that it must be somewhat of a natural position and studied its possibilities further. This method may be changed by transposing the curb and snaffle reins.

If a whip is carried, it will of course be carried in the right hand, which makes it almost necessary to carry the three reins in the left hand. There are a few good riders who hold two reins in each hand, with the snaffle coming in under the little finger, passing through the

ILLUSTRATION VIII

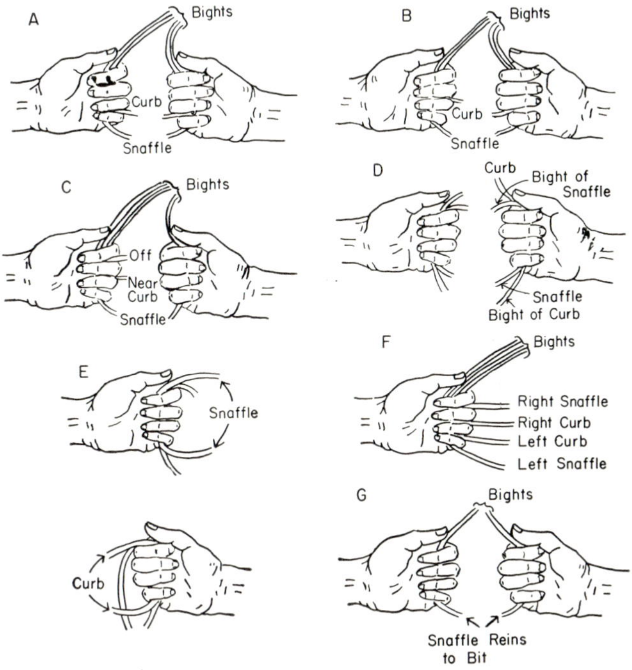

DIFFERENT METHODS OF HOLDING REINS

hand and out over the index finger and the curb coming in the hand over the index finger, passing through the hand and out directly below the snaffle rein. (*Figure D.*) Here again, the reins may be transposed if one wishes to do so. I do not especially advocate this position, as it seems to me that it destroys the mobility and suppleness of the wrists, which should be kept supple and flexible at all times, as the wrists and fingers, not the arms, should control the horse's mouth. There is also the problem of shortening one or more reins which seems to me to be much harder when one uses this position.

There is one other method that is used successfully by some people. This consists of holding the snaffle reins in one hand and the curb reins in the other. (*Figure E.*) Those who advocate this method have a very convincing argument for it, in that it is easier to raise the head with the snaffle and set it with the curb when the reins are held in this way. On the other hand, producing a flexion should be done on a well broke horse with only a slight bit of pressure, not with force. I find that this method makes it difficult to take in slack when necessary and destroys the suppleness of the wrists and makes turning difficult, unless the animal has been trained to neck rein, which is true of few show horses. The experienced rider may try any or all of these positions until he finds the one which seems to fulfill his needs the best.

ELEMENTARY DRESSAGE

There is another commonly used method of asking a horse to take a canter, beside that explained in the first chapter. In order to differentiate between the two, we shall call the method previously explained, the use of the diagonal aids. That method is the most logical, the most beautiful in transition, and is the method which should be taught to most saddle horses, many of which have not been taught by that method. However, polo ponies and stock horses no doubt respond better to the use of the lateral aids, especially when changing leads at the fast gallop, and are therefore taught to take the canter by this method. The use of the lateral aids is also learned easier in a circle. In contrast with the former method, the rider uses the outside bearing rein and throws his weight forward on the animal's inside front leg, at the same time using the heels just in rear of the cinch. These movements must all be done simultaneously and with only as much force as is necessary. They are more effective if given at the exact moment when the horse begins to make a sharp turn, as it is then forced to take the correct lead and avoid becoming overbalanced. One often finds it easier to start colts to canter in this way, rather than by the use of the diagonal aids. In this case, the trainer generally switches to the use of the diagonal aids as soon as the colt begins to get the idea of the canter. Horses broke to one method will generally refuse to take the canter if the other method is tried.

I believe the use of the diagonal aids is superior to the use of the lateral, because the former is a graceful movement, pretty even in transition, while the other is a sloppy, haphazard affair that has little to recommend it except that it works. In the use of the diagonal aids, the skilled rider asks for the lead of the canter from the rear, forcing the horse to lead out with the correct hind leg, in which case, a true united canter is always the result. When the lateral aids are used, however, the lead is asked or forced from the front and the horse often does what is called a disunited canter. This gives one a choppy, bumpy ride and looks very bad until the horse finally decides of his own free will to get straightened out and canter united. When he does this, he is very likely to change his lead in the front rather than in the rear, in which case one is riding on the wrong lead.

In horse terminology when speaking of gaited horses, we usually mean a five gaited horse instead of the three gaited one. The five gaited horse according to the rule book must do a flat footed walk, a square trot, a canter on either lead, a rack and a slow gait. The slow gait may be any one of these three, a running walk, a fox trot or a stepping pace; however, in actual practice today, all use the stepping pace as a slow gait. The words "gaited horse" are also much used in referring to the American Saddlebred Horse, both three and five gaited. It is one of those American figures of speech which may be interpreted two ways and must therefore be related to the whole thought in order for one to get the correct interpretation. Gaited Horse people use the word Saddle Horse in the same sense to distinguish that particular breed of horse from all other types of riding horses.

What are commonly known as schooled horses are those which have at least the rudiments of high-schooling. These horses are apt to be of the thoroughbred type, although a growing percentage of them are either part bred or pure bred American Saddle Horses. Of course true High-Schooling was originated and carried to the peak of perfection at the world famous riding schools of Versailles and Vienna, where the breed of Lippizaner horses was created for that express purpose. Only stallions were thought worthy or able to be high schooled or were even ridden there. Perhaps the leading trainer of schooled and high schooled horses in this country is Captain Hyer, now living in Sarasota, Florida. He came here from Holland in the mid-thirties to work for Ringling Brothers Circus.

His first experience with five gaited horses was with some which had been spoiled, and he couldn't understand them nor the idea of gaiting horses. We had many a friendly argument on the merits of five gaited horses in which his favorite expression was, "But, I can't understand, you work to get horses off-gait, while we work to get them on-gait." Recently I had an opportunity to visit with him again, and he has done a complete about face. He now works five gaited horses as well as high schooled horses, and prefers to use American Saddlebreds even for his exhibition high school horses. He claims they are more naturally supple and take to schooling easier than thoroughbreds.

In attempting to explain what a schooled horse is I am afraid we have digressed from the issue at hand. Yet it is necessary for one to know the distinction between a schooled horse and a gaited horse. The canter is one of the principal gaits of a schooled horse, while it is more or less secondary for the gaited horse. The gaited horse is never required to change leads while cantering, whereas the schooled horse is. He may be asked to change leads while cantering very slowly and should always be broke to the use of the diagonal aids, as it is only in this manner that the movement may be precise and beautiful. A well broke, schooled horse will change leads at any time it is asked and as often as it is asked to do so, even to the extent of every jump or every other jump, etc. To do this, the animal must be traveling in perfect collection and the change must be asked for on the silent beat, when all four feet are off the ground. It must also be asked for the change from behind, that is, its hind legs change before the forelegs, otherwise, if it is asked or is allowed to change on the forehand, it will result in a disunited canter. By asking for the change on the silent beat, the rider can easily obtain this change from the rear. I have previously stated that the canter is a three-beat gait and sounds about like this—tat tat tat —tat tat tat—tat tat tat. Now in order to change leads on this silent beat, the rider must have his mount perfectly collected and prepared for a change, and then give the signals for the change just at the sound or feel of the third beat, which gives the horse a fraction of a second to change during the silent beat.

Other elementary dressage movements which all good riders should learn are: Change hands, half turn, half turn in reverse, pivot on the haunches, pivot on the forehand, and some two-track work, at least at the walk. Two-track work at the faster gaits requires extreme skill, and is part of the high-school gaits. At the command "Change hands," all riders ride to the far end of the ring around the end, then diagonal across the hall to the other end and take the track on the opposite hand to which they had been previously riding. In this movement all riders follow one another unless part of them are on one side of the ring and part on the other when the command is given, in which case the first rider to reach the correct corner begins the movement, and as the riders cross the center they must all be careful of the approaching riders, and alternate in crossing. There often seems to be a little difficulty in teaching students the meaning of taking the track on the right (or left) hand. If, while entering the ring, one is asked to take the track to the left, he must first turn to the right to do so. This is probably the cause of the confusion. However, it will be easy to remember if one just thinks that taking the track on the left hand means with his left hand on the inside. The horse will then be cantered on the left lead. The opposite will, of course, apply if one is asked to take the track to the right. Just remember that track to the right means right hand inside, and track to the left means left hand inside.

The half turn is executed individually by each rider. At the command, each rider makes a semicircle toward the center of the ring at the same gait at which he has been riding, unless told by the instructor to take a different gait. At the completion of the semicircle, he then rides on a diagonal back to the track and is of course traveling in the opposite direction, or riding on the other hand. The size of the semicircle should be about four feet in diameter at a walk, about eight feet at the trot, and about twelve feet at the canter. At the command "Half turn in reverse," the rider first diagonals away from the track to the prescribed distance, then makes a semicircle, coming back to the track on the opposite hand. This movement is also executed individually, and the size of the semicircle should be the same as prescribed for the half turn.

The command "Reverse," given in the show ring where gaited horses are being shown, actually means half turn in reverse. However, many gaited-horse showmen make a half turn instead, and it is the generally accepted practice in this case to allow either half turn or half turn in reverse, as long as the riders turn and take the track in the opposite direction. If the command is "Reverse and canter," which is sometimes the case, the rider will find it much easier to get his horse to take the canter on the other lead, if he executes the half turn in reverse correctly and asks for the canter on the turn. It should be understood that it is a little harder to get the five-gaited horse to take the canter correctly on a straight line than it is to get the schooled horse to do so. I am sure it would make a more beautiful show if all riders would obey the command "Reverse" in the same way, instead of some doing it one way and some another.

Two-track work is often thought to be extremely difficult and to be one of the highest phases of dressage. However, any horse which is well broke and which has been properly trained to have its hindquarters controlled by the rider's legs, should be able to do two-track work quite easily at a walk. This is especially true if it has been trained to the use of the bearing reins; that is, if the horse neck reins. All that two track means, is that the hind feet do not follow in the same path or track that the front feet have made; therefore, two track. All these aforementioned movements may be done two-track and if taken at a walk, they are quite easy; yet they help develop the horse and teach it to respond to leg pressure and the bearing rein.

Along with this work, the rider should learn to turn his mount either on the forehand or on the haunches, as he wishes. I do not mean the circus trick of making the horse pivot on the forehand with its front legs wrapping around each other, but rather, making the hindquarters move around the forequarters, the former making a larger circle than the latter. This is done by using the leg, or spur, well in the rear of the side away from which we wish the horse to turn; the purpose being to force the rear quarters around. At the same time, the indirect bearing rein of opposition is used on the same side as the spur is used.

This rein is, of course, used to help keep the mount from moving forward and to make it move its front feet in a small circle, while at the same time the hind legs are making a larger circle. In doing any work of this type, the animal must be asked to go first in one direction, then in the other. Otherwise it will soon get the habit of going only in one direction and will respond only to one spur, which will be exactly the opposite effect from that which is wanted. All this sort of work is designed to help both horse and rider in using and obeying all the aids.

To turn on the haunches, both leading and bearing reins are used to cause the animal to turn the forehand, but the outside spur is used further back than the inside spur. This prevents the animal from making a circle with the hind legs following in the same path as the front. By using the outside spur in this way, the hind quarters are held in a smaller circle than the forequarters, which is the result wanted.

PART B—RIDING DIFFERENT TYPES OF HORSES

THE TRAIL HORSE

In this case, for the purpose of designation, we will define the trail horse as the western broke horse which is used over the mountain trails and ridden western style with a stock saddle. Correctly speaking, there are a number of types of trail horses; the hunter hacks could be placed in this classification, as well as Walking Horses, when so used, and gaited horses are often used for trail riding, especially through the states where that type of horse is very prevalent. I have ridden both walking and five-gaited horses through the mountains of Kentucky, Tennessee, and California. To me, horses of this type represent the ideal pleasure horse, and I have seen them take hard trips as well or better than their cold-blooded brothers. However, gaited horses and hunter hacks will be dealt with a little later on in this same chapter. Trail riding is essentially the same no matter where one happens to be riding or what type animal one's mount may be.

With the western horse one rides a stock saddle, which is ideally suited for mountain riding. The rider who has been used to riding flat saddles may find some types of stock saddles seem to fit too tight, and often the horn annoys such a rider. In all such cases one should secure one of the more modern types, especially those built on a roper tree with quite a long seat, low cantle, low pommel, and low horn. These are generally quite comfortable for a long ride.

A single bridle with some form of curb bit, spade bit, or a hackamore is used. The animal is ridden for the most part on a loose rein and is guided by neck reining. By a loose rein I do not mean that the head is turned entirely loose, but that the mount is not kept in a collected gait. A very light feel of the mouth should be maintained as an aid against stumbling, etc. The reins are held in one hand, generally the left, although on a long trip one will find it relaxing to change off from one to another now and then. They really should enter the hand from the bit from below, that is, under the little finger and out over the index finger. They may well be separated by one or two fingers, the little finger or the little and ring fingers. The hand will, of course, be held vertical in order to keep the wrist supple. The stirrup length must be adjusted for comfort; a long enough length that the knee is not cramped by too much bending, yet short enough so that one does not need to reach for his stirrups. Comfort for both horse and rider is a prime requisite, and one rides loose and relaxed, but certainly not in one side of the saddle, as this will soon cause sore backs. The animal's comfort is always taken into consideration before the rider's, as it is upon the horse that we depend for transportation.

If overnight trips are planned, plenty of grain must be carried for the horses, and a suitable camping spot with both forage and water should be sought. For overnight trips, it will generally be necessary to take along a pack horse for every three or four horses, in order to carry enough food, bedding, etc., unless the riders wish to more or less rough it. Taking along a pack horse can generally be managed quite easily, as nearly all such riding is done at a walk. If the pack horse is inclined to lag behind, one of the riders must stay behind it to help force it forward and relieve the strain from the rider doing the leading. Of course, it is only courtesy for the different riders to take turns leading the pack animal.

When on the trail, the riders should keep about one horse's length apart, and when climbing mountains, a halt must be called after every hard climb, to allow the animals to get their wind. Everyone in the group should be accomplished riders before any of this type of riding is attempted. The animals must never be allowed to take an increased gait down grade, and the group should keep well together at all times. An unusually good rider should lead and set the pace, and if there happens to be any in the group who are not quite as experienced as the rest, they should be placed well to the front and preferably between two exceptionally good riders. If it becomes necessary to cross a highway, the leader should always wait until there is a lull in traffic before crossing, and all horses must be walked across hard roads. If the whole group does not get across at one time, those who have already made the crossing should wait until the others cross before resuming the trip. If it is necessary to ride along a highway, all riders should stay on the same side of the road and as far off the pavement as possible. Riding along the highway must always be considered very dangerous, as many automobile drivers seem to take a special delight in driving as close to a saddle horse as possible and occasionally toot their horns, not realizing how serious an accident they may cause by so doing. A frightened horse will slip and fall very easily on a hard road, which can cause either horse or rider to break a bone.

Before starting on a trip with a group of riders, one excellent horseman who is mounted on a fast horse should always be delegated to take charge in case of a runaway. All other riders should be instructed that should such an event occur, they must stop, dismount, and not attempt to help or interfere in any way, as several running horses will become excited and it may lead to serious trouble for many of them. A good horseman can generally head off an animal that has bolted from fear or from other cause. It will not always be necessary for him to even put his mount into a gallop, for the easier he can accomplish the result, the better for all concerned, and the less danger of bad accidents. If all the riders are competent and the horses are ridden well in hand at all times, no such thing should ever occur. Nevertheless, this is a good precaution to take.

A horse may and should have water as often as possible on a trip, but one must be sure it is fresh and clean, and that the animal doesn't take too much at one time, especially if the weather is hot. Very little hay should be fed in the morning before starting a trip, but the horses should be given a good feed at night. Plenty of grain should be fed them in the morning and not too much at night; and if they are brought in warm they should be fed no grain for two or three hours. A little grain and forage, if possible, should be given during the noonday rest. All shoes should be examined before beginning a trip, as a loose shoe or one that may come loose, may be lost and the animal will soon become footsore and lame. If the trip is to be a long one, dismounting and leading the horse about five minutes out of every hour will rest both horse and rider, and will help a great deal in preventing the rider from becoming sore and stiff. Nearly all other things will be governed by common courtesy, and if each rider will stop and think a minute before rashly doing anything on the spur of the moment, the ride can be a pleasant experience for all.

THE STOCK HORSE AND POLO HORSE

These two types of riding horses may as well be handled together, as both are broke and ridden in much the same way. Most persons riding such horses are already accomplished riders, and it is not the intention of this book to try to correct any method of riding adopted by one who really knows how. All good riders eventually develop certain peculiarities of their own which they find are best adapted to themselves and their own makeup, both physical and mental. Some readers may think that I am entirely wrong in saying that these two types of horses are broke and ridden in much the same manner; as the polo horse is ridden with a flat saddle and generally a pelham bit, while the stock horse is ridden with a stock saddle and some form of spade or curb bit. On closer examination, it will be seen how nearly alike the two are. The stock horse is usually started off with a hackamore and gradually changed over to the use of the bit, while the polo horse is started off with the snaffle and gradually changed over to the use of the pelham, but the net result is about the same. Both types are taught to run fast for short distances, get away fast, turn quickly on a dead run, and to be fearless of anything swinging around its head or rump. In the case of one it is the rope, and in that of the other it is the polo mallet. The polo horse is trimmed, while the stock horse wears its mane on the near side, in order to keep it out of the way of the rope. Both must be extremely agile. The stock horse must be taught to hold a steer or calf that has been roped, which, of course, is a duty the polo horse never performs. With the exception of exhibitions, the stock horse is a work animal, while the polo horse is used purely for sport. Riding on either of these horses is purely secondary to getting the job done, whether it be roping a calf or hitting a ball. Therefore, such riding is merely a means to an end and not an end in itself.

THE JUMPER AND HUNTER HACK

This is the age of specialization. Nevertheless, to my way of thinking, we can carry this idea of specialization too far. It is of course true that for an animal to become a top-notch contender in its class, it must be a specialist and must be worked and trained for that particular type of work. It does not follow that just because a rider rides different types of horses that he should become poorer on one particular type of horse. I firmly believe that a man who calls himself a good rider and an accomplished horseman should be able to get on nearly any type of horse and turn in a creditable performance. I, myself, am a gaited horse rider and trainer, because I prefer that type of animal. Nevertheless, I feel that if I were asked to fill in in a game of polo, partake in a hunt, or take a mountain trip on horseback, I should be able to do so, and that experience would not detract from my ability to ride gaited horses. There are employers however who would not think of hiring a man to ride a jumper if they knew that man had always ridden a gaited horse or vice versa. Several years ago I was asked to show a jumper at a state fair horse show. I felt perfectly capable of doing so, as I was riding and breaking jumpers when I was twelve years old. Nevertheless, I refused, because at such a large show there might very well have been someone who at some time or another might consider hiring me, and I knew that the fact that I had been seen riding a jumper would be of no advantage, to say the least. For this reason I haven't been on a jumper in public for over fifteen years, yet there is a certain thrill to riding horses over jumps, and if I ever am so situated that I no longer need think of hunting for a job, I shall own a good hunter hack, and I believe every person who aspires to become an excellent horseman, should learn to ride jumpers and should ride them occasionally.

In riding the hunter or jumper, one rides what is commonly known as the forward seat. The stirrups are about one or two holes shorter than those used for bridle path riding. The rider should be well in the middle of the saddle with his body inclined slightly forward from the hips. One should first learn over low jumps on a thoroughly experienced and reliable jumper. In order to negotiate the jump, the rider raises himself in the stirrups and leans well forward over the animal's neck. Jumpers that are well schooled and especially those which are used in the hunting field, should be able to jump equally well from either lead, although many horses jump better off one lead than the other. When this is the case, the rider should see that his mount has the advantage of being on the lead it likes to jump from the best. The beginner leans well over the animal's neck, balancing himself on the neck or by means of a rope or strap around the neck for that purpose. The rider maintains this position, with his legs well back and his knees firmly gripping the saddle, until the horse has completely negotiated the jump and is on the ground and has taken a stride or two at the gallop. He then slips gently back into the saddle, in his former position, until about half a dozen strides before the next jump. The rider must never allow himself to be thrown back into the saddle while going over the jump, or at the conclusion of it. The reins are used only to direct the animal to the jump. In no case should they be used in an attempt to lift the horse over. This is as foolish as trying to lift oneself by one's own bootstraps.

It is generally better if the beginner will have no feel of the horse's mouth during the jump, but after one becomes experienced in jumping he should then maintain a light, even, contact with the animal's mouth at all times. The horse must have absolutely free use of its head at all phases of the jump, as it uses it to help balance itself when going over. It learns the proper time and place to take off during its schooling period and must be allowed to gauge this for itself.

In recapitulation, it will be noticed that the rider balances himself over the horse's neck at all phases of the jump, thus allowing the horse's hind legs which are the propelling power to work to the greatest advantage without being disturbed. He does not disturb the horse's head at any time during or immediately after the jump, allowing free movement of the animal's head and assuring no bumping of its mouth. The legs are kept well back and the rider does not slip back into the saddle until his mount has completely negotiated the jump and has regained its former stride. If the rider does not observe the latter rule, he will most surely develop the habit of dropping or being thrown back on the animal's loins, and at the same time jerking its mouth with the reins. This will discourage the horse from jumping, and even the best jumper will begin to refuse jumps if it finds out it gets hurt both on the loins and mouth every time it takes a jump. The horse must not be allowed to rush the jumps. If the reader will stop and think, he will recall that when a man jumps, he does not run as hard as he can towards the jump, but merely takes a smooth stride. The horse must do the same.

In making broad jumps on the horse, the same forward seat is used, but in this case, the animal must move along at quite a fast pace. Its very momentum will help it to jump farther. At no time should the rider allow his feet to fly forward, as this will disturb his equilibrium and interfere with the balance of his mount. It is a good idea for the beginner to learn over very low hurdles at the trot, until he has developed a sound technique. This is especially true if there are no mounts available except those which desire to rush the jumps. All in all, while jumping is quite spectacular, it is not nearly as hard to learn as many of the less spectacular feats of horsemanship, and any fairly good rider should soon become quite proficient.

THE FIVE-GAITED AND WALKING HORSE

The primary gait of the Walking Horse is what is called the plantation walk or running walk. This is a distinct gait, not merely a fast walk as many people seem to think. It is a kind of easy saddling gait about six miles an hour, somewhat similar to an old-fashioned very slow, singlefoot. Many people own and ride horses that do a plantation walk and never know just what it is that their horses are doing. The Plantation horse need not trot, but should do a good flat-footed walk and a canter on either lead as well as the running walk. Many of them are bred along similar lines to the American Saddle Horse, and some are registered as Saddle Horses, but were foaled natural gaited with no trot, or a very poor one and were then trained as Walking Horses. Due to this fact, many people consider the Walking Horse to be but a sub-breed of the American Saddle Horse, especially as the registry for the latter breed was started about forty years earlier than that for the Walking Horse. Such a view, however, cannot be considered correct, as it is partly to the Walking Horse that the gaited horse is indebted for its gaits in the first place, and such natural Walkers in the Saddle Horse registry must be considered as throwbacks to the original. The Walking Horse is distinct from the gaited horse in that the former is natural-gaited, while the latter is for the most part forced-gaited. The gaited horse, having been bred for style longer, is much more of a peacock and is generally quite a lot finer than the average Walking Horse.

The Walking Horse is perhaps one of the easiest of all horses to ride. The rider requires a stirrup length about one hole longer than that taught in the first chapter of this book. This will help one maintain his balance easier, which is all that is necessary on this type horse. Many of these horses, if allowed to go much faster than about six miles an hour, will swing into a pace, which is, of course, the most unpleasant of any gait to ride. For this reason, they should not be urged to a much faster speed than is their natural one, by anyone except an expert. A lot of these horses have been spoiled by such riding. While these horses are without a doubt the easiest of all

ILLUSTRATION IX

GLEAM OF GENIUS 28581

Showing the correctly executed rack with both form and reach which denotes speed.

Gleam of Genius is by King's Genius 9500, out of Donna Gleam 18544. She is a Champion Mare, winner of seven firsts in mare and stake classes in 1944. She is owned by Miss Sara Elizabeth Wilhite, daughter of Mr. and Mrs. Stacy D. Wilhite, Cookeville, Tenn. Earl Teater up.

for an amateur to ride, they are not to be recommended to the student, as he can learn but little from them, and if he rides them very much before he has acquired perfect mastery of the basic three gaits, he will generally develop many faulty habits which he will find hard to break.

We now come to the riding of the only true Saddle Horse, bred and raised for centuries for its easy riding qualities, as well as beauty, style, action, spirit, and docility. This horse that along with the walk, trot, and canter, which all horses do, does a slow gait (which may be a running walk, a stepping pace, or a fox trot) and a rack. Until one has had the pleasure of riding a good racking, five-gaited horse he does not know what real riding is. He who has never felt the thrill of a good racking horse beneath him, has missed the greatest ride that a horse can give and the ultimate experience to the lover of horseback riding. I know of a number of people who were finally persuaded to buy a gaited horse for pleasure riding and forever after they consistently refused to consider any other type for pleasure riding. I venture to state that I believe there are only a very few persons who ride for pleasure who would ever consider anything but a gaited saddler if they would once get a really good one and learn to ride it correctly.

One should be quite a good rider before he attempts to ride gaited horses, and I certainly do not recommend one for a beginner, because they are more nervous and more highly trained than the ordinary hack, and therefore are more easily spoiled. When one first begins to learn to ride a five-gaited horse, he should remember that it has five gaits, all of which are to be used at intervals each time the animal is taken out. Thus, the rider gets not only the supreme, thrilling sensation of riding the rack, but also the variety which will prevent any ride from becoming monotonous. Before changing from one gait to another the mount should be brought down to a walk and then asked for the new gait. This will prevent it from getting confused and from learning to mix its gaits. However, in changing from a stepping pace to a rack, he need not do this. This is the only time in riding that the horse should take a gait from anything except a walk.

In riding gaited horses it is generally desirable to have one's stirrups about one hole longer than the position described in the preceding chapter. The only time when the rider's legs need not be kept well back is when he is riding the rack. It is sometimes necessary on some racking horses to allow the lower legs to come slightly forward in order to help balance oneself.

According to the rule book the fox trot may be the slow gait of the five gait horse; however, it is no longer used as such. It is merely a slow saddling trot, about six miles an hour, which is easy to sit to instead of posting. It is ridden merely by relaxing in the saddle and rolling or giving to the very slight jar rather than by trying to post. It is an easy gait for both horse and rider, and the animal can continue it for long stretches. For this reason when much travel was by horseback, foxtrotters were very popular, and they are still sought after by present day cowboys. Today I doubt if any trainer attempts to use the fox trot as the slow gait for a five gaited horse, because that saddling trot will almost always be carried over into the fast trot, which is disastrous in a gaited horse.

The most generally used slow gait, and the one always used by show horses because of its flashiness, is the stepping pace. In my opinion this is a misnomer, for the lateral legs do not strike the ground at the same time as in the true pace, but the hind foot strikes the ground a little ahead of the front. The stepping pace is an extremely pleasant gait to ride, as the rider is not rolled from side to side as is the case when riding at the true pace. Speed is neither necessary nor desirable, but here again the animal should be well flexed, and hock action as well as knee action should be extreme. The horse is asked to take this gait by being sent ahead with the legs or spurs, the rider at the same time giving a light seesaw effect with the snaffle reins. This should not be a hard yank with first one rein and then the other, but rather, a light feel of the mouth, first on one side, then the other. As soon as the mount begins to step the pace, the motion of the reins should be discontinued and a light, even feel of the mouth be maintained with both bits, to help balance the horse in its stride. One should not keep the mount doing the stepping pace for long intervals at a time, as it may become leg weary and go to pacing. This is perhaps the greatest trouble that many amateur owners have with gaited horses. They spoil them by keeping them racking or by doing the stepping pace so long that the animal becomes leg weary and goes to pacing to relieve itself. Once the horse learns this, it will do it whenever it gets the slightest bit tired.

The rack is taken directly from a stepping pace, by moving the horse faster ahead and lightly shaking the reins. While racking, it is impossible to keep most horses as well in form, or as well flexed, as in the other gaits, but it should be kept collected as much as possible. The rack is a fairly fast gait, and in the show ring the faster a horse will rack and do it correctly and in form, the better. However, the amateur rider will generally get along much better and keep his mount doing its gaits true, if he does not push it to capacity. The gaited horse must do both the trot and the rack with considerable speed, but there must be no getting out of form in order to gain speed, and no semblance of a pace when racking. If at any time the horse attempts to break from a rack into a trot, it can easily be forced to hold the rack by giving a light see-saw motion with the reins; but if the animal has learned to reach for a pace from a rack, the only recourse is to slow down immediately.

It must be remembered that both the rack and the stepping pace are broken gaits; that is, each foot strikes the ground separately, instead of two at a time as in the trot or true pace. They are therefore very hard on the horse, while being easy to the rider. For this reason, the gaited horse should never be kept at either a rack or a stepping pace too long at any one time. The owner who has not been used to gaited horses is often so thrilled with the rack, that this is the only gait he will ask of his mount. Sooner or later, this will spoil almost any animal, either by teaching it to pace, or making it lose the trot entirely, or both. The trot remains the principal gait and should be the one that is used the most, especially where the going is likely to be a bit rough. The rack and slow gait should be used for variety, relaxation, and comfort; not for continuous riding. There is no reason to call upon the pleasure horse for excessive speed at either a rack or a trot, although a fair amount of speed in the rack is necessary to get proper stride action and gait.

Quarter boots should be worn on most gaited horses at all times, as at forced gaits the animal is very liable to hit its quarters, especially on turns, etc. The rack is ridden by sitting well in the saddle and using the stirrups merely as a slight aid to balance oneself. It is one of the easiest of all gaits to ride, as there is no rising as there is in the trot, nor any side movement as in the true pace, nor any up-and-down movement as in the canter. There is little movement felt except that of an exhilarating vibration.

A great many people who attend horse shows in various parts of the country comment on what is termed the Kentucky seat or show seat, adopted by most professionals when riding and showing gaited horses. Some of these comments are unfavorable and some are merely the result of astonishment at what is called "atrocious form." Let us tear it down and analyze it a little. In the first place, this seat is not so very different from the correct seat described in the first chapter of this book as is so often thought; and in the second place, it must be remembered, that professionals do not ride for pleasure, but as a business. Their jobs, and therefore their very lives, depend upon winning as many shows as possible, and by getting the greatest possible speed and action out of their charges. Riding well back in the saddle with fairly long reins, gives the mount the appearance of having a longer neck than otherwise, and its shoulder motion is better seen and its knee action enhanced. Many young riders attempt to imitate this show seat before they are thoroughly versed in the fundamentals of riding. They often imitate it very badly and present a ludicrous appearance, which brings further unfavorable criticism to the show seat and the show riders.

Before one attempts to ride a show seat on a gaited horse, he should be an excellent horseman and should know how to ride properly in correct form. When changing to a show seat, the change is not so radical as some people think. The stirrups may be lowered about one hole from the position explained in the preceding chapter, making them the same length on gaited horses as those used by the pleasure horse rider. The rider then slips well to the rear of the saddle and holds this position by gripping with the knees, which are kept bent with the lower legs back and heels down. The knees are pressed much more firmly against the side of the animal than when one is park riding. This gives the appearance of having longer stirrups than is actually the case, but many novice riders who try to imitate this style seat do so by merely pushing themselves back from the stirrups, which they have already lengthened several holes, and not paying any attention to the knees and lower legs. Doing this, of course, makes a very unbalanced and insecure position. In a correct show seat, posting is not so high as it is with the forward seat. The stirrup length stated above is really necessary for riding the rack; the position gradually became adopted by riders for both walk-trot and gaited show horses. Although there is only the change of position noted above, it requires considerable skill and practice to ride this style correctly, especially as one has to develop the muscles of the upper legs in order to keep the knee pressure necessary. The lower legs must be back and be free to move, to control the hindquarters of the horse. (*See Illustration VI.*) Note heels are well down and lower legs back.

Of course, a few professionals do use stirrups a little longer than stated above, but these men have found that such stirrups lend themselves to their physical make-up better than shorter ones do. Primarily, the position in the saddle makes the stirrups appear longer than they really are. Please glance through this book at the pictures of various professionals, on top-show performers and note the position of the knees and lower legs. The uninitiated often take a passing glance at professional show riders and conclude that all they need do is to lengthen their stirrups several holes and that they, too, can ride that style. They are the very ones who show bad form even to the point of standing in their stirrups, reaching for them with their toes, or pushing their feet far forward in an effort to ride "show style." Before attempting to imitate a professional rider, it must be remembered that the average professional rider often rides a dozen to a score of horses every day and may put in as many hours in a saddle in a week, as the average amateur does in a year. Their muscles are therefore hardened and adapted to a degree that few amateurs can ever attain, and if some of these professionals can use long stirrups to an advantage, it does not follow that many amateurs could do the same. We must all adapt our riding technique to our own capabilities, conformation, and amount of riding practice we may get.

In showing gaited or walk-trot horses, the fundamental aids are used as in riding pleasure horses, but a greater degree of collection is called for and kept. The three-gaited horse should be ridden in the show ring at a flat-footed walk, in partial form with its head up, on a nearly loose rein. At a trot it should be kept perfectly in form and completely collected at all times, but should not be ridden fast. Collection, brilliance, and extreme action is to be sought for, rather than speed. At a canter, the animal should also be kept well collected and cantered slowly and brilliantly. The rider may wear spurs if he wishes, or may carry a crop or light stick. In evening stake classes, the rider should be appropriately dressed, which in this case calls for a white bow tie, high silk hat, and narrow jodhpurs with no flare at the cuff, and a black stripe down the side of them.

The five-gaited show horse should also be ridden in partial form at a flat-footed walk and in a well-collected, balanced trot, somewhat faster than that of the three-gaited horse, until such time as speed is called for. Even then, form should not be sacrificed for speed, but the horse should be called upon for all the speed it can give and at the same time stay in form. At a slow-gait, collection and brilliance and extreme action are necessary, but speed is not, as all energy should be converted into action and brilliance. At the rack (*see Illustration IX*), the horse will lose some of its form, but it should retain as much of it as possible. When speed is called for, the horse should be pushed ahead as fast as possible, without losing all semblance of form. The gaited horse seldom has quite as high a degree of collection in the canter as the three-gaited animal, but it must be kept collected as much as possible and cantered slowly. In the case of both gaited and walk-trot horses, the animals will be called upon to take all gaits in both directions of the ring. The rider should, of course, be well acquainted with his mount before going into the ring. The rider should be dressed appropriately, which, in evening stake classes, will mean a dark suit, black tie, derby and jodhpurs with no stripes, but a flare at the cuff. He may carry a whip, or wear spurs if he wishes. A whip should be used for gaited classes and a crop for walk-trot classes.

The show rider should always obey promptly all the commands of the ringmaster, and when called upon to line up, he should do so immediately. He brings his mount to a halt and poses it until the judge has inspected it, after which he may, if his horse is warm, allow it to walk around in the center of the ring, until he is given other instructions by the ring steward. He should be prepared beforehand, in case the command, "strip saddles," is given.

In this case, of course, the groom should run into the ring and strip the horse, while the rider holds it, the latter trying meanwhile to keep it alert, with its ears up.

PART C—MOUNTED EXERCISES, DRILLS, GAMES

These mounted exercises and drills are designed to improve one's seat. The exercises may be done by the lone rider or in classes. If the latter is the case, the ringmaster must always give a preparatory command first, followed by the command of execution, both of which must be obeyed promptly with military precision, in order to make an effective showing. This is particularly the case with musical rides, which may be very beautiful if the horses are all under perfect control and the commands of the ringmaster are obeyed promptly. They may all be used in riding academies and clubs where a number are gathered to ride at the same time, and are done much easier in a riding hall. They make the ride more interesting and are invaluable in perfecting one's seat.

The advanced students should remove the stirrups for the exercises. Novice riders should be allowed to keep theirs, as a precaution against possible accidents, but they should use them as little as possible, perhaps even letting them dangle with the feet hanging out altogether, or if the rider or instructor feels it necessary, the novice may keep his feet in the stirrups. The rider takes a natural, easy seat in the center of the saddle and allows his legs to hang naturally with the toes lower than the heels. In a class, the animals must be kept evenly spaced, at approximately four feet from head to croup. While these instructions will be given at the slow trot, they may all be taken at a walk if the instructor feels that the students are not far enough advanced to do them at a slow trot.

The ringmaster commands, "Slow trot," whereupon each rider individually collects his mount until he gets the command of execution, which is "March." Then, each horse is asked to move off at a very slow trot, at about the rate of six miles an hour, still keeping the distance of four feet from head to croup. To keep one's seat at the slow trot, it is only necessary to keep perfectly balanced and relaxed. There must be no tension or exertion of any kind. One should not try to grip with the knees, but merely lean a trifle back and allow the legs to hang naturally. It is easy to see that these exercises in classes tend to induce the rider to keep perfect control of his mount and to obtain instant response from the aids.

While the animals are moving around the circle at a slow trot, and after each rider has become accustomed to his seat at this gait without stirrups, the ringmaster begins to give the exercises. If at any time a rider seems to be in danger of losing his seat, or slips from one side to the other, the instructor should give the command to "Walk," then "March." In this way, all horses are brought down to a walk at the same time and each rider can adjust his seat. In any case this should be done at intervals to allow all riders to relax and adjust their positions. The length of time between these rests will be governed by the experience of the riders in the class. If any rider begins to lose his balance and is not noticed by the ringmaster, he may immediately ride toward the center of the ring, out of the way of the other horses, then stop and adjust himself, and ride at a walk a few minutes in the center of the ring, before resuming his place on the rail. All students must learn not to anticipate commands. That is, when the command "Walk" is given the horse must *not* be brought down to a walk immediately but merely collected, in order that when the command "March" is given the response may be almost instantaneous. This is very necessary in any kind of class work, in order to avoid the confusion of having horses run up on each other.

The first of the exercises given is, "Flex the ankles." To do this, the toes are raised as far as possible, then lowered and turned round and round, all the time allowing the legs to hang naturally. Moving the ankles as much as possible helps make and keep the ankles supple, and they play a very important part in one's riding.

At the command, "Flex the knees," the lower leg is lifted as much as possible and then lowered. This should be done slowly and should not disturb the remainder of the seat. Only the knees are bent, and the feet should not come in contact with the animal's sides. The mount, of course, continues its slow trot keeping its distance from the horse in front of it. When flexing the knees, one should attempt to bring his heels to about the level of his knees. The next exercise given is, "Flex the hips." This should not be attempted by inexperienced riders, as there is a certain amount of danger of falling. The knees are raised and lowered as far as possible, but the rider's position should be disturbed only slightly. When first trying this exercise, it is perhaps better to raise only one knee at a time. This may make it easier for the beginner to keep his balance. When flexing the hips, the knees and feet should be kept away from the horse's body while they are being raised.

After the leg exercises, at the command, "Flex the neck," it is rolled from side to side and round and round. Each of these exercises should be done for only a short time, and there must be rest periods in between for the riders to relax. The reins are, of course, held in two hands at all times in the ring, unless otherwise directed.

The next exercise is, "Lean back." The whole body leans back, until the head touches the horse's rump, if possible, and is then raised to a sitting position. In this exercise, the legs should be disturbed as little as possible. The ringmaster should call attention to any rider allowing his feet to fly forward. One must be careful not to put any extra tension upon the reins. The body is both lowered and raised without the slightest aid from the reins. To do this, the hands must be allowed to slip back on the reins as far as necessary, to avoid pulling on them.

Now, at the command, the reins are all taken into one hand, namely, the outside one. If the track is being ridden on the left hand, then the reins will be grasped in the right. After everyone is settled and the slow trot has been resumed, the ringmaster will give the command, "Flex the arm vertically," at which time each rider raises his left hand above his head and describes a circle, above, back, down, and to the front, continuing this movement until told to cease. At the command, "Flex the arm horizontally," the arm is raised to the level of the shoulder and describes a semicircle from front to back, at the level of the shoulder. All the movements are continued until a different command is given by the instructor.

After a short while, the animals will all be brought to a walk, for a change of hands or reverse. Afterwards, each rider will, upon the command, change his reins into the other hand, which will again be the outside hand, and the command, "Slow trot," will again be given. The right arm will now be flexed both vertically and horizontally, the same as before. These are the principal exercises which are recommended by the United States Army for all mounted branches, and they are used in most of the better riding academies all over the country. Any rider who will spend ten or fifteen minutes a day doing them will find himself much more supple, and will be able to manage his mount more gracefully. He will also find that his seat is more secure after a few months than he would ever have thought possible. There are no perfect riders, but exercises such as the foregoing certainly lead a long way toward perfection.

Military drills generally follow a set routine such as, forming column of two's, column of four's, figure eight's, two single columns passing down opposite sides of the hall, where they may execute change of hands, passing each other alternately in the center, or where opposite columns meet at the end of the hall, forming column of two down the center of the hall, etc. These military drills are best adapted to groups of riders who are used to riding together, and may be varied as the director in charge sees fit. The beauty of these rides lies in having all riders keeping perfect formation, exact space, etc.

There are many other games for small shows, gymkhanas, class rides, etc., which lend themselves better to a diversified group. Mounted musical chair is played in exactly the same way as the game is played dismounted at parties and picnics. The riders take the track at the same gait, preferably the gallop, and a number of chairs are placed in the center of the ring, back to back, in a double row. The number must be one less than the number of riders, or for a large crowd, there may be two less for quicker elimination. There should be music, but if that is not possible the ringmaster may carry a whistle and use it, instead of stopping the music. When the signal is given, which in most cases will be stopping the music, all riders quickly dismount and try to get a chair. The ones who fail to do so are eliminated and must leave the ring. The music starts again and the riders again start riding around the ring as before, and then one or two chairs are taken from the ring. The whole process is repeated until all the riders, with the exception of one, are eliminated. This remaining one is declared the winner.

The potato race may be played in two different ways. One way is to have all riders start together from one end of the hall, at the other end of which is a pile of potatoes for each rider. Each rider races to the far end of the hall, picks up one potato at a time and returns it to his bucket and places it therein. He then returns to his pile of potatoes for another, and repeats the performance until all his potatoes are in his bucket at the starting point. He must of course take only one potato at a time. The first one to finish is declared the winner. Each rider must dismount to pick up each individual potato, but he may toss it into his bucket upon returning to the starting point. However, if he misses the bucket he must dismount and place it in the bucket before returning for another. Another way this game may be played is to have each rider equipped with a spear, and instead of dismounting to get his potato he merely spears one at a time, but he must carry it back to the bucket and place it therein without the aid of his hands. In other words, his hands must not touch the potatoes at any time, or he is disqualified.

The egg race is played by giving each rider a tablespoon with an egg in it. He must then race the others over a prescribed course without losing his egg, and he must not touch it with either hand, balancing it merely by the handle of the spoon. This race is particularly effective if it is over a course that requires the riders to stop and turn at one end of it. The course should not be too long, for if it is, it will be too hard for the judges to watch all contestants and we want at least one to finish with his egg. Touching the egg with either hand immediately disqualifies a rider.

The relay race, in which horses are changed, is always good for thrills, excitement, and entertainment for all concerned, particularly if riders must change saddles at each station. Horses should be kept bridled in order to prevent chances of runaways and an attendant should be on hand to hold the additional horse. Two horses are plenty for each rider, even if four to six changes are to be made, as the primary part is quick mounting, dismounting, and changing saddles and the distance between horses need not be great. Generally, the rules require that the same type saddle must be used by all contestants, and that all must start and finish with a standard fastening. However, during the race anything goes, and one may merely hold his cinch, or if he thinks he is able he may ride with the cinch absolutely loose.

In the apple-eating race, each rider has an apple tied to a string from above which hangs at about the height of his mouth. The point of the game is to see who can first eat his apple, while remaining mounted and without touching the apple with his hands.

The water-carrying race is also very interesting. Each rider is given an eight-ounce tumbler of water and told to race over a prescribed course, bringing back as much water as possible. In this case, certain points must be established beforehand, both for speed and for the amount of water to be brought back.

These games, music rides, and drills are used in various places in the country to promote interest in riding. Their success along this line is generally instantaneous, and as riders join the spirit of the games, they also learn to control their mounts better. Many small shows put on exhibitions of musical drills, which allow many people to exhibit themselves and their mounts, who could not otherwise do so. While an animal may lack the quality for a show horse, it may still be useful for these drills and games, and owners of these horses love them just as much as owners of higher class horses love theirs. Along with this idea, I should like to suggest to local horse show committees that they invite owners of horses which do a few tricks, to put on exhibitions at their local shows. Most horse owners will be delighted to do so, and they may be just the ones who have felt left out in the cold, because they do not own horses of high enough quality to compete in horse show classes. Trick horses, even those that are not letter perfect in their tricks, generally appeal to the audience, especially in the smaller shows where the majority of the audience is not always quite certain as to just what points are looked for in show classes, and they are therefore apt to become bored with nothing but three- and five-gaited classes on the program. The management can often break up and fill in the intervals between classes by utilizing these home talent trick horses. As a rule, show managers can learn some valuable lessons about keeping the interest of the audience at all times, by visiting some of the larger circuses.

Chapter III

COLT TRAINING

Breaking to Lead

We now enter upon the highest phase of equitation; namely, training the horse. We will start in with the young colt and follow through the different phases through which it goes, until the finished animal. The man who is training the hack may skip the parts referring to the jumper, the show horse, or even the gaited horse, if he intends his animal to be just three gaited. The same thing applies to the man who is training his mount for any particular work. He may skip any parts which do not apply to his needs. Further on in this chapter, the section devoted to breaking the colt to harness may well be applied to any colt for whatever purpose one might later intend to use it. Driving is good preliminary work for all types of saddle or riding horses, as they can be started younger, they can be made bridle-wise before breaking to saddle and their gaits can thus be strengthened. It also makes the process of breaking to saddle much easier and with less danger to both horse and rider.

If a man owns but one or two brood mares and has both the time and the inclination to start handling the colt at a very early age, it is nice to do so. The colt, at a week or so, is fairly easy to manage and by constant handling he will not get man shy, and later on, work with it will be facilitated. At this age, in order to begin teaching the colt to lead, one can take hold of its tail at the root with the right hand and the halter with the left and soon have it leading fairly well. A colt of this age will forget very easily and may even forget what it was taught the day before. In most cases, a colt of this age will forget everything it was ever taught in a week's layoff. Therefore, to be of any value, one must spend at least a few minutes nearly every day with the colt, up to the time when it is two, or even three months of age. It is about that time that they begin to remember a little longer.

One must not make the mistake of thinking that a very young colt is not dangerous. Those tiny hoofs can really cut, and even very small colts have a surprising amount of strength, as well as being quick as lightning. Consider the fact that the three-day-old colt can generally keep up with its mother, for short distances, in a gallop across the pasture. Therefore, don't underestimate the small charge. All work with colts or young horses requires a vast amount of patience, and very easy, gentle, unexcited handling. This is especially true when working with the very young colt, as about all one can really hope to accomplish at this tender age is to get it used to being handled, and not becoming man shy.

One principle to remember, when breaking in young colts, is that the pivot point is near the center of the body between the front and hind legs. By this, I mean that if it is touched anywhere from the front legs forward, it will back up and if touched in the rear it will move forward. By exercising a little common sense, the trainer can make use of this in teaching the colt to lead. If it is too large to lead by holding the tail with one hand and the halter with the other, the trainer can have an assistant walk behind, for the first few days, and gently tap the colt on the rump with his hand. After the colt is fairly gentle, the trainer may, if he finds it necessary, run a cotton rope through the halter and around the colt's hips in such a way that pressure can be exerted at the rear whenever necessary or desirable. If he does this, he should either use a short rope over the back to hold the other from falling around the colt's legs, or he may cross the rope over the back at about the withers, for the same purpose. One must not begin to use these ropes too soon, as they may frighten the colt and cause serious damage. To prevent burning the colt, one should use nothing but cotton ropes. As soon as possible, only the lead rope should be attached to the halter and the colt should be taught to lead by a pull on it. One can handle even quite a large colt, if he will not lose his wits and will take every advantage of the animal. For instance, if the colt of five or six months balks and refuses to lead, few men can pull it along in a straight line. However, if the trainer will move off to about a ninety degree angle and give a sharp pull, not a jerk, even a small man can overbalance the colt and start it moving off. If it stops again, repeat in the opposite direction.

When the colt is fairly well broke to lead, it should be tied up. It must be wearing a halter that is too strong for it to break and it is tied to a solid post at about the height of its nose, allowing just enough rope for its head to reach the ground if it throws itself, as it may do a few times. This is a good time to teach the colt to stand for being rubbed and handled. Rub and pat over all parts of the body, neck and head with the bare hand. I never use a brush until the colt is well gentled. I then teach it to stand for having its feet handled. I find that most young colts will throw themselves if the front feet are picked up first, but if the hind feet are picked up first, it will soon stand for having all four feet handled. With older colts, one must generally work with the front feet first.

In a great many cases, the colt will hardly be touched until weaning time, unless the mare is to be shipped away to be rebred, or if the colt needs treatment for scours or for injections of any kind which may be felt necessary. At weaning time, one has quite a different problem confronting him. The colt has increased in size and has gained considerable strength. In fact, at times one will be sure he is as strong as a matured animal. If the colt has been raised in a small lot and fed every day along with its mammy, it may be fairly gentle, and then again, it may not. On the other hand, the colt that has grown up in a large pasture along with other colts will very likely be man shy and may be quite capable of taking care of itself under most conditions. Many times one feels that he had just as well be in a cage with a wild animal as with a colt raised in this manner. A colt of this age, however, has developed a pretty good memory and will easily remember the lessons from the preceding day. Nevertheless, it is a good idea to handle such a colt at least once, or better still, twice a day for about two weeks until it thoroughly understands its elementary lessons.

Perhaps the best time to wean the colt is when it is five to six months old. I seldom let a colt nurse longer than six and I dislike to wean before five months. This will be more thoroughly discussed in the chapter on care of breeding stock. This is the time to break the colt to lead, if it has not been handled and taught to do so previously. In a few instances one may, by being very gentle, quietly approach the colt and caress it and finally slip the halter on very carefully. In most cases, however, one will have more trouble, and in some cases a great deal of trouble will be encountered in getting the colt haltered. When I find that no amount of coaxing will do any good, I herd the colt into an enclosure from twelve to twenty feet square, with no projections of any kind on which the colt may hurt itself. A sixteen foot box stall will do very well. I then proceed to whip-break the colt, but I do not carry the process so far that the colt will follow the whip, but only far enough so that it will stand to be petted or haltered. To do this, one must have a light training whip, and as he tries to approach the colt he will say, "Whoa, Baby" or any other name he prefers. He must always talk soothingly and gently. As the colt moves away, or turns its heels toward the trainer, he must crack it around the heels with the whip. On a hot-blooded or nervous colt, this may be little more than a tap, but it must be hard enough to sting. The trainer must be very careful that he does not get himself hurt, as many colts will retaliate by kicking viciously, or even striking or biting.

One should try not to rile up the colt any more than necessary, as this is no time to be breaking it of bad habits. It is merely trying to defend itself, and while it must not develop the habit of kicking, this is not the time for punishment of any kind, unless it is absolutely necessary. Instead, one should try not to aggravate the colt more than is absolutely necessary, and one should hit it around the heels only when it turns them toward him or when it kicks viciously directly at the trainer. This process must be continued as long as necessary, and the trainer must always try to approach the colt quietly as he continues to talk to it in soothing tones. Eventually, the colt will stand to be petted and finally haltered. This may take from ten minutes to two hours, but once the trainer goes in with the colt, he must be prepared to stay there until he gets the colt haltered. Above all, he must not lose patience, no matter how long it takes, and he must be generous in his caresses. He may have to repeat this process for two or three days each time he goes in to catch the colt and he should always be ready to do so. However, two to ten minutes will usually be sufficient after the first day.

The colt will now be brought into an enclosure to be led around. This enclosure should not be so large that the colt will attempt to escape. A riding hall or ring will be suitable; but it should, if possible, be away from sight of any other horses. One can always do far more with a colt if it has nothing in sight which may distract its attention from the trainer. The aisle of the stable may be used for this purpose, if nothing else is available, but one will have more trouble holding the colt's attention. It generally takes two men to teach a colt of this age to lead properly; one to lead the colt and the other to follow with a whip. At this time, the over-use of the whip can easily do more harm than good. For this reason, I like to have hold of the whip myself, to be sure that it is used properly in the right place, at the right time, and without any more force than is necessary. The proper gauging of these things takes time to learn and it can seldom be left to the discretion of an assistant. The whip should be used, when possible, to coax rather than to force the colt to follow the man who is leading.

The man who is attempting to lead the colt has his hands full at the moment also. It is his job to see that the colt is following him, and not leading or dragging him along. The colt should be brought to a halt several times and caressed, in order to try to take away its fear of man and to show it that it will not be hurt as long as it follows the man who is leading it; but that it must obey that man. The colt will progress much faster if it gets these lessons twice a day, for a few days at least. It need be led only about ten minutes or so each time. Very soon the leader will no longer need an assistant, and the colt may be taken anywhere.

The colt should then be taught to stand tied, by following the same directions as given earlier for younger colts. As soon as it learns to lead properly, with no thought of pulling back or running ahead, and will stand quietly when stopped or tied, it may as well be taught to pose. Some colts will learn this very readily and others seem to take an extra long time to get the idea through their heads. The trainer stands at the colt's head, carrying a light training whip that is long enough to reach the hind ankles if necessary. He waves the whip back and forth, holding it vertically to attract the colt's attention, and pulls on the halter strap at the same time, calling "Whoa." If the colt attempts to move forward with all four feet, the trainer tries to scare it into standing still.

At the same time he continues to pull the halter strap, first one way, then another, trying to get the colt to take only one step forward, with a front foot only. When he succeeds in this endeavor, he caresses the colt. Gradually, he will attempt to get the colt to step forward with both front feet, keeping its hind ones in place, and he should always reward it for the slightest correct attempt. He may have to tap it lightly on the front ankle, or even take one of its front feet and place it forward for a few times to try to get the idea across to it. The colt's attention must be held at all times and at all costs, and any slightest inclination to obey must be rewarded. One must not try to accomplish too much at any one time, nor must he strive for perfection from the start. As soon as the colt seems to be getting even a faint idea of what is expected, caress it and put it away immediately so it can rest on the idea. If practical, the colt should be worked two or three times a day, for just a few minutes at a time, until it is posing fairly well. Afterwards, once a day will be sufficient.

Let me say one word about correct posing. The colt or horse should not stand all stretched out when posed. That is absolutely incorrect, but is a fault seen very often. Rather, it should stand upright on all four feet, but not stretched out. To do so is bad form and causes most colts and many horses to appear low in the back, and may weaken the colt's back. Colts will often learn to overstretch of their own accord, and the cautious trainer will always be on the lookout for this tendency and not allow this to develop, as it is a habit that is almost impossible to break when it is once established. Many animals, in trying extra hard to please the trainer, will develop this habit if they are not carefully watched. It requires far more skill to teach a correct pose, than an exaggerated one.

This is the time to break the colt to cross ties. If it is in the stall it will make the job much easier, as the colt will not be as likely to back up or throw itself. It should be cross-tied a few minutes each day while it is being brushed and having its feet picked. If it must be tied in the aisle, this aisle should be narrow enough so that the colt will not be liable to turn in the ties. One should always have a whip handy in case it tries to pull back. In this case, it is far better to use the whip gently, if results can thus be obtained, because a hard crack may frighten the colt and cause it to leap forward, perhaps breaking the halter or ties, or throwing itself. It may injure itself badly if it does the latter on a hard floor. One will always find that the more gentle he can be with colts, the faster he will accomplish the desired results and the less chance there will be for accidents to occur. The older we get and the more experience we have, the more we all ccme to realize this truth.

If the colt is to be exercised in getting ready for a sale, it may be done by leading behind a cart, while jogging a broke horse, or by circling on a lunge rope. In the latter case, one will need the services of an assistant for a few days, until the colt gets the idea of going both ways around the circle. Ten to fifteen minutes a day, of this kind of work, will be sufficient. After the weanling has been taught to stand to be caught easily, to lead easily and well, to pose correctly, and to stand in the cross ties to be brushed and have its feet handled, it may as well be turned out until time to be broke to harness.

Before going on with the next step, this is perhaps as good a place as any to make a few observations that apply to all phases of training any type of horse for any purpose. Every animal must be treated as an individual; therefore, one must be instantly ready to change any method, or any rule, to suit the needs of any particular animal. The true skill of a trainer lies in his ability to note the temperament and individuality of each animal with which he works, and to change his methods to meet existing conditions. In other words, the good trainer must have had experience with a large number of horses, in order to get the different impressions of each type. He must know all the rules and, most important of all, he must know when, how, and why to break all known rules.

The following will illustrate more clearly just what I mean. I had a boy who worked for me for about three years and who was a pretty good horseman before he came to me. He had progressed to the point where he was halter breaking most of my colts, jogging many of them, and doing quite a little riding. He had gaited a few and, like most youngsters, thought he knew just about all there was to know. It so happened, that those he had gaited had gone along according to rule and he had done a very good job with them. Finally, he tried gaiting a little black mare that took the rack very easily, but she wanted to go too fast and consequently he couldn't hold her. He finally asked me to come out and watch him work this mare and see if I could help him, as he wasn't getting along as well as he thought he should. After watching him work a short while, I suggested that he try turning her away from the barn, whenever he tried racking her, and only allow her to walk when headed toward the barn. His reply was, "But you don't do that. You always say to start a colt by heading it toward the stable." I then proceeded to tell him that he was now learning what was perhaps his most valuable lesson in training horses. That was, to throw the rule book away when it doesn't work. I told him that any time he broke a rule of training and knew he was breaking it and why he was doing so, it would be perfectly all right.

So I say to the reader; know all the rules, but don't be bound by the book of rules. Use your own initiative and ingenuity. One other instance along this line may prove of some value to my readers. I had a very good boy working for me, who was getting along very well with the horses he had been working. I got hurt and was unable to ride for several weeks, but I managed to get around to watch what was going on. This boy was trying to start a gelding to slow gait and was not having much success. I would try to give the boy pointers to help him along. Then, I would go into the house and watch from the window, thinking that perhaps he would get along better if I weren't around and he didn't know I was watching; but he just couldn't seem to get the job done. The whole trouble was that he was holding onto the horse too much, and although it wanted to start slow gaiting, he would unconsciously pull it out. I told the boy to turn loose the reins, but he just didn't seem to be able to grasp the situation. Finally, I sent him to the barn and told him to put a halter on the gelding instead of a bridle, and to fasten the reins to that and then come and try again. Without liking the idea very much, he did it and soon had taught the horse to slow gait and finally to rack, before he put a bit in its mouth again.

What was more important, he had taught himself two things; one, not to hang onto a horse's mouth and, two, that sometimes by a change of method, results can be obtained that seem otherwise impossible. I have had dozens of these illustrations happen in all phases of training, all proving the point I am trying to make. While the reader may never run into a case calling for the same treatment, he may, and very likely will, run into many cases calling for his ingenuity rather than for the rule book. The reader should remember this, throughout all the following lessons on training.

Adjusting the Bitting Harness

To resume our present course in training the colt, the next step will be training to drive. Most riding horses and all gaited horses, should first be taught to drive. Whether the animal will later be used for jumping, trail riding, show work, or even work with stock, breaking it to drive first will be definite aid for later work, as it will become bridlewise and will have a good trot established before a saddle is ever put on its back. Furthermore, it can be broke much younger, and is therefore easier to handle, and it takes to training much more easily. Thus, the whole training course is facilitated. Of course, this is not an absolute necessity, and the man who does not want his animal broke to harness may skip this part and wait until the colt is about two and a half years old, before doing anything further with it. Perhaps the man with a cheap horse, that he intends to dispose of as soon as it is broke, may also skip this part to keep expense down; but the man who intends to keep his horse for pleasure, or for whatever riding purpose he will later use it, will do well to break it to drive. There are other practical reasons for this also. The owner may sometime be too busy to exercise his horse and if it is well broke to drive, the groom can easily exercise it on off days.

Driving is the way to make the trot of a gaited horse; in no other way can a true, well balanced, square trot be produced so easily and so thoroughly. The trot is the basis for all the gaits, but even aside from the training aspects a good driving horse can still be a pleasure to own. How many of you horse lovers have ever hitched a fine horse to a nice carriage in the evening for a short drive? When one tries it he'll usually find it more enjoyable than a spin in a high powered car, and I can think of nothing much more thrilling than to hitch a nice high stepping horse to a good cutter, equipped with chime bells, and to take a real sleigh ride on a cold snowy day. I'll personally guarantee one will receive more attention than the finest car will command.

I prefer to start colts off in the bitting harness before hitching them to a break cart. Perhaps about the best age to start colts to the bitting harness is about a year and a half, or during the late fall after they have become yearlings. They can then be well started in both bitting rig and cart and harness before cold weather sets in, after which they may as well be turned out for the winter, to be taken up in the spring to resume work as two-year-olds. The bitting rig is merely a skeleton harness with a check rein and side straps that may be adjusted to any size. The side strap fastens to the snaffle bit and to the back band at about the place where the shaft carriers ride. If one has a bitting rig, all well and good, and if he intends to break many colts it is a wise investment; otherwise, he may easily convert his breaking harness into a suitable bitting rig, by leaving off the breeching, if any, and the breast strap. The side straps may be made of any suitable straps that can be adjusted and should be fastened to the bit by spring snaps, for quick and easy loosening. The rear part of the side straps on a standard bitting rig, is snapped into a ring on the back band for that purpose. On an improvised bitting harness, they may be buckled into the shaft carriers, which are strapped down with the safety straps of the harness. I much prefer an open bridle with a side check; and when first starting the colt, I use only one snaffle bit.

We assume that the colt has been broke to the cross ties. The harness is now laid gently over its back, and the tail is very carefully raised and inserted into the crupper. It is a big help at this time, to have an assistant stand at the colt's head and caress it and talk gently to it, all the while keeping its attention. We must be sure that every single hair is picked clear of the crupper, as horse hairs are very coarse and hard and they will very easily cut into the tender skin underneath the tail, and will soon cause any colt to learn to kick. The back band is now fastened, but not tightly, as that will cause many colts to fight and sometimes to buck or throw themselves. They may injure themselves severely doing this. However, if one does throw itself intentionally, it must receive a couple of cuts of the whip while it is down and it must be taught to stand on its feet. This is a favorite defense of colts, and a large percentage of them throw themselves at one time or another. There is always a chance of a colt injuring itself while doing this, and therefore, extreme care must be taken not to do anything that may cause the colt to throw itself. However, if and when it does this, it must be punished before this develops into a habit. It must be done while the colt is still down, for if one waits until the colt gets up, he had better refrain from punishment at all for that time, for the colt in this case will attribute the punishment to meanness on the part of the trainer and retaliate. Any punishment of the colt must be directly associated with the act for which it is being punished. If, by chance, the trainer is unprepared, it is far better to forego punishment for that particular time, than to cause confusion in the colt's mind as to why it is getting whipped. Therein lies the secret of success, and all good trainers are always prepared for any unforeseen occurrence.

The bridle is now put on and adjusted. The colt should be tied with a strong halter, and for the first time one may as well put the bridle on over the halter. I prefer the braided rope halters for this work, when first starting colts or horses, as they are light and neat and strong enough so that they won't break. The bridle should be held in the right hand and the bit in the left, as in *Illustration III* in Chapter One. Held in this way, the thumb may be used if necessary to pry the mouth open, by placing it in the mouth on the bars where there are no teeth. After getting the bit in the mouth, the headstall is very gently placed over and behind the ears. One must be extremely careful with the ears, as they are about the most sensitive parts of the colt's anatomy. The bridle is adjusted so that the snaffle bit hangs just loose enough so that it doesn't wrinkle the lips. The colt will then be led outside, preferably into an enclosed ring.

The check rein is now adjusted just tight enough so that the colt cannot get its head down, but not tight enough so that it is restrained any. The side straps are also adjusted just loose enough that they do not restrain the movement of the colt's head. Too tight an adjustment, on either side straps or check rein, may cause the colt to throw itself. I like to have a light strap like a hame strap, with a free ring on it, running under the chin and fastened to the snaffle bit on each side. I then fasten the lunge line into this ring. The lunge line may be either rope, strap, or webbing. Rope is apt to burn one's hands if the colt pulls, and a strap will be too heavy to handle easily. For this reason, I prefer webbing. The lunge line should be about fifteen feet long. Unless the colt has been lunged as a weanling, the trainer will need an assistant to drive the colt around in the circle around the trainer, who will have his hands full trying to keep it circling instead of heading off at a tangent. A colt of this age can do some extremely hard pulling. The first day or two the colt may be allowed to walk, trot, or canter, until it gets the idea of traveling in a circle. It must be worked only a few times in one direction and then be forced to go in the opposite direction. If this is not done, it will very soon acquire the habit of going in only one direction and it will be almost impossible to get it to go the other way. It must never be brought to a stop twice in succession at the same spot on the circle. The horse is perhaps the easiest animal there is to become routined, and if stopped twice in the same place, it will want to stop there each time it comes to that spot. Instead, it must be stopped at many different places on the circle and never until it has completed the circle at least twice. If the colt has been circled as a weanling, it will remember, and can go ahead faster.

After the first couple of days, as soon as the colt gets the idea of traveling in a circle at the end of the rope, it must be taught to do nothing but trot. To do this, the trainer will snatch the lunge line every time the colt breaks into a canter, using no more force than necessary to exact obedience. At the command, "Whoa," the colt is brought sharply to a halt by making a quick hard pull, not a jerk, on the lunge line, bringing the colt's head toward the center and forcing it to halt. After a few times, the command, "Whoa," in conjunction with a lighter pull, will cause the colt to halt. This is the time to teach the colt that "Whoa," means to stop right now, and when one says to stop, he doesn't mean to slow down. If one wishes it to slow down, he should use an entirely different command such as, "Easy Boy," or any other distinct sound.

Each command must be clear, distinct, and different and with a definite meaning, in order to keep from confusing the colt. The colt must be taught to obey each command instantly, but must not be punished for its ignorance just because it does not know what a particular command means. Only a single command should be taught at a time, and as soon as the colt realizes exactly what is meant by that command, another may then be taught, continuing the use of the first, and so on until its complete vocabulary is established. Many men like to teach the colt to come to the trainer when it is stopped on the circle. This is permissible, *but* the colt must not be allowed to do so on its own initiative. Instead, when it is given the command, "Whoa," it must stop at the end of the lunge line and if it tries to approach the trainer, it must be forced back, with a whip if necessary. After it has come to a dead stop and has stood a few seconds, it may get the command, "Come Here," and be allowed or coaxed, as the case may be, to approach the trainer. In this case, the colt should have been taught the command, "Come Here," previous to this, perhaps during the whip breaking lessons so that he will not learn to confuse the command, "Come Here," with the command, "Whoa."

The command, "Get Up," is taught by the assistant, who carries the whip. When the trainer is ready, he signals the assistant, who gives the command, "Get Up," and immediately cracks the colt with the whip around the rump, with only enough force to cause the colt to move out. After a few times he will diminish the use of the whip until it is almost entirely eliminated, but he always has it ready for instant use in case the colt should fail to move out at the command, "Get Up." In this way the colt will soon learn to move forward instantly, at the command.

By the time the colt has learned these commands and will circle on the lunge at the trot, the services of the assistant may be dispensed with, and the trainer will continue, always having the whip with him, to compel instant obedience if necessary. This much work will probably take about a week or ten days to accomplish, working the colt once a day for ten to twenty minutes at a time. I see little use in working a colt twice a day on the bitting rig, as this kind of work is very fatiguing and the colt should never be worked until it begins to tire. It should be made to feel that this is play time and that the whole thing is a game. For this reason, I prefer to keep the colt up in a stall, so that it will be glad of a chance to get out and play. It will learn much faster in this way. The colt of this age is far too young to have excessive work of any kind. No attempt should be made to get either action or speed.

After the third or fourth day on the bitting rig, the check rein and side straps will be gradually tightened, never tight enough to cause any strain, but just tight enough to encourage the colt to a better head carriage. I always do this during, and not before, the workout. That is, I bring the colt out with the bitting harness adjusted exactly as it was the day before. Then, after working it that way for about five minutes, I tighten the check up one hole, if necessary. The following day, after working it about five minutes, I tighten up the side straps a hole, if necessary. Thus, it must always be done very gradually and the check is always tightened first. They must not be tightened until the colt has warmed up on the bit a little, and whenever the colt appears to be leaning on either check rein or side straps, it is due to too tight an adjustment, or to the fact that the colt is beginning to tire. The colt must not be asked to set its head higher, nor must it tuck it in more than its conformation permits. The man who intends to use his horse later to work stock, may dispense with the check rein altogether, as he will want his horse to have a lower head carriage than the man who is training a gaited horse. The man training his horse to be a jumper, may also dispense with the check reins and use side straps, in which there are light springs attached to one end. These should be fastened from the snaffle bit back to the turret on the saddle of the back band, rather than into the shaft carriers. They should be adjusted so that there will always be a very light pressure on the animal's mouth, but the more the animal sticks out its nose, the more pressure there will be. This type of side strap works very well with some gaited horses, but it must be so adjusted that when the animal tucks its head completely, there is no more pressure on the mouth. About this time, I prefer to add a secret bit, or small snaffle, to which is attached the check rein, the side straps remaining fastened to the large snaffle. This, of course, is only for the horse that will later wear a double bridle.

I prefer to continue work in this way, until the colt has learned a proper flexion. The check rein and side straps must never be adjusted tight enough to hold the colt's head in position, but rather they should merely encourage it to hold its head in the proper position of its own accord. Colts never get too much of this kind of work, and the gaited horse will probably be worked a day or so a week in this way, all its life. The bitting rig may also be used on older horses with success in curing certain faults, such as pulling their heads, boring, or getting behind the bit.

The command, "Back Up," may now be taught, while the colt is wearing the bitting harness. It will help to teach the colt to back in form and in a straight line. The colt is led to a level place with a wall on one side, if possible, to encourage it to back in a straight line. A short lead strap is fastened to the bit and the trainer gives the command, "Back Up," at the same time giving a sharp backward pull on the strap. He should be standing directly in front of the colt and reach his hand out to do this, at the same time moving toward the colt. It must only be asked to back one step at a time and never be allowed to back further of its own accord. After it will take one step backward, it should be taught to take two or three, or as many as are asked of it; but never one step more than is asked of it. Some colts will learn to back very readily, while others will stubbornly refuse, in which case more pressure may be applied. If necessary, the colt may be tapped on the nose with the butt end of the training whip, or it may receive a light crack on the knee, and when it lifts its foot it may be pushed back a step until it gets the idea. In exceptional cases, it may be necessary to use a pointed stick and jab the colt in the chest with it.

Many colts are very stubborn about backing, and it may be necessary for the trainer to use his ingenuity to the utmost in order to get it to back. In some cases, if one can make the colt lift a leg and get it slightly off balance, he may cause it to back a step by a sharp pull on the bridle rein. As soon as the colt begins to get the idea, it should be backed a few steps on a straight line, about twice. Too much work will soon sour the colt on anything and especially on this. It may be done twice, two or three times a day, however. It should then be taught to back freely a few feet. There is no point in teaching a colt to back any great distance. The colt or horse must never be allowed to back even a single step more than is asked of it. Fillis says, "The horse must keep the forward movement even when backing." In other words, the horse must always be up on the bit and ready to move forward at any time. In order to keep this forward movement, the colt must always be led a step forward immediately after it is backed and before it is brought to a complete halt. Later on, when asking the colt to back under saddle, the same rule must be observed.

BREAKING TO DRIVE

The colt is now ready for its actual training as a driving horse. I use the bitting harness, with the side straps, and use a long pair of reins. For the same reason as previously mentioned, I prefer web reins. In fact, it is one of these reins I use when lunging the colt. One should have reins that are long enough so that he can stay far enough behind the colt so that he cannot be kicked, and that means he will need a long, light whip also. The reins are run directly from the snaffle bit, through the shaft carriers or large rings in the bitting rig placed low on the back band. They must be placed low, so that the trainer can always keep the reins low around the colt's hips to prevent it from turning. At the command, "Get Up," the colt receives a crack around the hips, just hard enough to cause it to move out. A very wise precaution is to begin this training in a ring or riding hall, in order to get better control of the colt. It is driven this way from the ground each day for fifteen or twenty minutes, at times turning in different directions and stopping now and then at the command, "Whoa," accompanied by a pull of the rein. This pull should not be a steady, straight, back pull, but rather a sharp pull, first on one rein, then the other. One will find that this is far more effective than any straight, back pull, but of course it must be diminished in intensity as soon as the colt shows any inclination to obey the command. It should be taught to stand still for various lengths of time, keeping its head forward and ready to move forward when asked to do so. It must not be allowed to back.

This is really the colt's first introduction to the reins as a means of guiding, and it must be drilled carefully, yet thoroughly, in this phase of the work. It must also be taught to carry its head straight in front of it and to turn with its whole body, not just with its head. Most of this work will be done at the walk, for, if it is allowed to trot, the trainer soon tires and loses control, and it is not long before the colt will be running away and developing this habit. It can much easier be prevented from doing this if driven at a walk. Should the colt be too fresh, it may be worked a few minutes on the bitting harness, or turned out in a lot for a few minutes, to take the edge off it before starting to drive it. This is often a very good policy, as it makes the colt much easier to control and there will be less chance of developing a hard-mouthed puller. A word of caution to the budding trainer is that he must be careful to keep the reins very low around the colt's hips, especially if the colt has been in the habit of coming to the trainer, as such a colt and many others will try to turn towards the trainer and approach him. This, of course, is not wanted and one must be on the alert to prevent this and drive the colt ahead.

The colt should be taught to back, after it has been driven from the ground for a day or so. This will seldom be a hard task, if it has been taught to back previously. This driving from the ground may continue from three or four days to a couple of weeks, depending upon the colt, how it is taking to it and how much previous work it has had. It is not very likely that it will get too much, however, as most men are anxious to go ahead too fast and rush things a bit, rather than go too slow. At any rate, it is well to remember that the better a horse is broke to drive from the ground, the easier it will be to control after it is hitched to the breaking cart and the less chance there will be of an accident to the colt or trainer.

We are now ready to put the colt to the break cart. Most writers and instructors advise putting on kicking straps at this time. I, myself, advise all inexperienced men to do so, yet I never do it myself unless events prove that I must. Kicking straps may prevent having a runaway and many a broken cart, but they don't break a colt from kicking. However, in most instances, they do prevent it from doing much harm. In my opinion they often teach a colt to kick, which is my reason for leaving them off. I feel that by being watchful I can tell when a colt is ready to kick, and by snatching it I can prevent it from doing so and break it of the habit. This is one time I do not practice what I preach; but then, I am often instructing students who have not had the experience, nor the knowledge along this line that I have gained through the years. Other trainers of similar experience have developed their own particular ways of breaking colts and it would be foolish for me to try to change them even if I could. They have developed their own ways, which for them might work better than any way I could possibly teach them. All trainers follow about the same fundamental rules, but each develops a distinct type and method for himself, and who is to say which is the best. Each man's way is best for himself. The novice, however, has not developed his own style, and it is better for him to follow one particular way of doing things until he has had enough experience to be able to judge for himself by which method he can secure the best results. I therefore strongly advise the novice to use kicking straps on the colt for the first few times that it is harnessed to the cart.

Some colts will do better with a blind bridle, and some with an open bridle. I personally prefer to use an open bridle, if possible. I believe the colt should become accustomed to seeing things. However, some colts are extremely timid about a cart rolling behind them, and it is far safer to use a blind bridle on such a colt. It should first be led up to the cart and allowed plenty of time to feel all parts of it with its nose and to see it from every angle. Before hooking to it, I like to drive the colt a short while with long lines, and have the assistant pull the cart along just behind the colt, first on one side, then on the other. One can easily make use of two assistants on the first day he hitches the colt to the cart. One of them should snap a lunge line to the bit, then stand directly in front of the colt and hold it with both hands, one on either side of the bit. The trainer and other assistant then draws up the cart carefully and quickly hooks it to the colt.

The man who has been holding the colt's head, now moves toward the center of the ring with the lunge line and attempts to stay beside and slightly in rear of the colt's head, about twelve to fifteen feet away. He must allow some slack in the lunge line, so that the colt is disturbed as little as possible, but he must be prepared to help hold the colt and force it to run in a circle if it seems to be getting out of control. At the same time, the trainer and the other assistant move to the rear of the cart. The trainer climbs in, attempting to hold the colt still, and the assistant stands directly behind the cart in order to help push the cart and start the dead weight rolling when the trainer gives the command, "Get Up." This precaution will often prevent the colt from ever learning to balk.

This is the first time the colt ever pulls anything with its chest, and the more gradually it begins to learn to do this, the less chance there is of teaching it to become a balker. If the trainer has only the one assistant in the center with the lunge line, then he must walk behind the cart and help start it rolling and drive from the ground until the colt gets the idea of pulling the cart itself. If the colt becomes frightened or attempts to run away for any reason, the trainer can usually control it, if it has previously been thoroughly schooled in driving from the ground. A sharp snatch, first with one rein, then with the other, will be found to be far more effective than any straight back pull. If such a thing as this occurs, the man in the center with the lunge line must do nothing unless he is told to do so. He is merely there in case of an emergency to prevent a runaway. The colt must learn to be controlled from the cart, not from the center. If however, the trainer finds he cannot control the colt, he will then give instructions to the assistant to circle it, thus preventing an accident.

In case the colt throws itself and gets all tangled up in the harness, two assistants are invaluable in helping to extricate it. While it is entirely possible for one man to break a colt alone, the use of two assistants the first few days will pay big dividends in the long run, by cutting down on the number of accidents and speeding up the breaking process. After about two or three days, one of the assistants may be dispensed with and the other will only have to hold the colt while it is being hitched, after which he will no longer be needed, either.

The colt should be driven once or twice a day for ten or fifteen minutes every day, until it will stand quietly to be hitched and unhitched, and will drive readily, starting and stopping easily on command. It will now be taught to back, which should not be difficult if it has been taught previously to do this. The first few times, it may be necessary to have an assistant help back the cart. It may even be necessary to have another assistant to help back the colt from the head, until it gets the idea. After it learns to back, it will need to learn to pose in harness. An assistant will probably be advisable for this work also. He will lift the colt's head with the bridle, while the trainer coaxes it with the reins and perhaps taps it on the shoulder with a long whip. This work will have taken up the greater part of the fall, and as soon as the colt is well schooled in these things, it may as well be turned out for the winter.

As soon as the weather turns nice, in the spring of the colt's two-year-old form, it will be time for the colt to go to work again. The owner of the stock horse or the jumper may wish to wait one more year, or he may wish merely to review the colt's former training and then turn it out for another year. The owner of the hack may do the same, but this will be a big year for the gaited horse. All previous work will first be reviewed, after which the horse will be driven every day for very short periods until it begins to harden up. After it begins to get hardened, the jogging periods will be increased to about one-half hour a day. It will be given short bursts of speed about two days a week and will be worked on the bitting harness one or two days, instead of being driven. It will gradually be taught to carry itself in form and primp itself in harness. I generally alternate by primping the colt one day, working on the bitting rig the next day, and giving short bursts of speed on the third. Then I repeat the process.

Breaking to Saddle

Gaited horses will generally be started under saddle about early summer in their two-year-old form. Others may be given light work under saddle about this time also, as they will take to it far easier now than a year later, but there is no point at this time in going ahead with them any farther than getting them gentle to ride. The gaited horse, however, will be ridden lightly once or twice a week until fall, at which time the horse must be pretty hardened, as it will then be gaited. It must then be ridden every day.

To get the job done easily, one must remember that a colt generally bucks from fear. Therefore, the preliminary training should be designed to remove this fear from the colt. It will be saddled very gently, first allowing it to smell and feel the saddle. It is cinched very loose and bridled with a snaffle bridle. It is then led around the ring several times both ways, allowing the stirrups to dangle. It may then be ridden from the ground. That is, the reins are placed over the colt's neck and the trainer runs along beside it, rather than leading it. It should be worked with the trainer on one side, then the other, to accustom the colt to seeing the trainer from the rear. After a day or two of this, the colt will be brought to a halt alongside a wall, so that it cannot turn away, and turned over to an assistant to hold. He does this by standing directly in front of the colt and holding it with both hands, one on either side of the bit. The trainer now draws up a chair or a bench, at about the colt's mid-section. He then mounts this bench and proceeds to talk gently to it and caress it. He pats it all the way from the head to the rump and now and then leans some of his weight on the saddle; all this time he is talking gently to the colt. It is then turned the opposite way and worked quietly from the other side in the same way. The reason for this is gradually to accustom the colt to seeing the trainer in the approximate position that he will be in when riding.

An object may be very familiar to a horse from certain positions and yet the same object will frighten it, if viewed from a different angle or position. Most of us remember back in the days when we used driving horses, how often an old, gentle, family horse, that had been used to seeing street cars without number but generally on only one side, would, if seeing a street car from the opposite side, become violently frightened. A familiar dog suddenly approaching from the rear will nearly always frighten a horse, no matter how often the horse has seen it before. A horse can easily be broken of this fear, but I am trying to show that this fear of even familiar objects, at unfamiliar angles, is almost universal and perhaps instinctive. The time to teach the colt not to be afraid of the trainer in the position he will be when riding, is before he mounts it. In this way, not more than one colt out of a hundred will ever learn the bad habit of bucking. The process described above should be repeated several times a day for two or three days, before the trainer attempts to mount.

ILLUSTRATION X

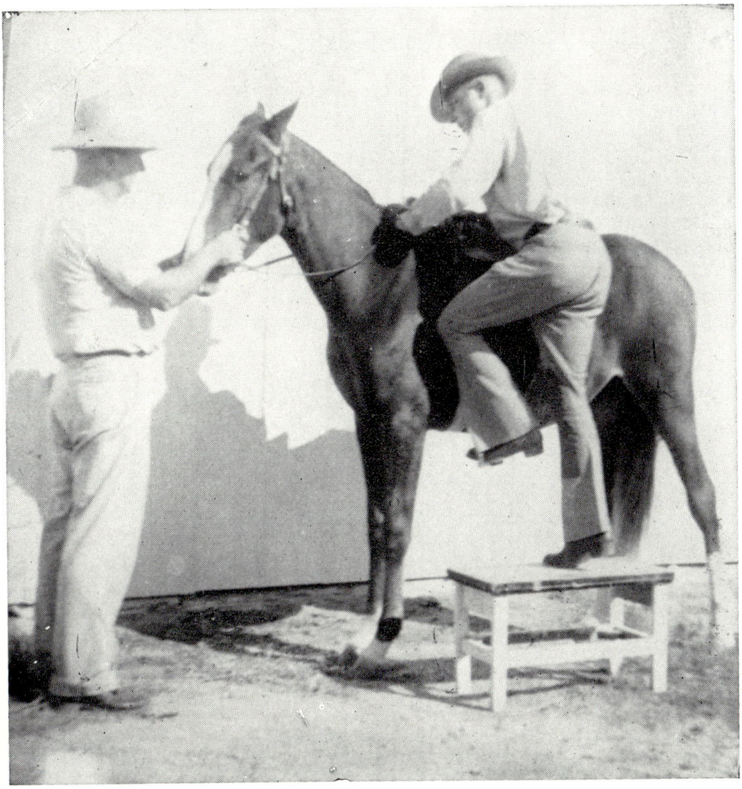

Showing correct way of holding and mounting colt for the first time.

ILLUSTRATION XI

Wire wheeled jog cart. This cart is lighter than the woodwheeled cart, not as suitable to be used as a break cart, but far better for jogging colts and for working gaited horses when one is trying to develop speed at the trot. These carts are remarkably well built and will take far more punishment than their appearance would suggest.

The Houghton Fine Harness Show buggy, used to display the five-gaited horse in the show ring when shown as a fine harness horse, or as a combination horse, also often used in the three-gaited combination class.

Wooden Wheeled Jog Cart used both as a breaking cart and as an exercise cart. This cart is quite light in weight but remarkably strong and is ideal for breaking two year olds, at which age most saddle horses are broke to harness. A heavier cart is generally unsuitable for these youngsters. Photos by courtesy of The Houghton Sulky Co.

The cinch will finally be tightened, and the trainer will begin climbing on and off the colt, from the bench. Soon, he will ask the assistant to lead the colt out a few steps, then gradually move out of the way. He will ride only at a walk for about five minutes, first one way, then another, until the colt relaxes a bit. Then he will ride back to the bench and dismount for that day.

All this sounds very easy, and in most cases it is. However, the man who attempts to break a colt to saddle should be a strong rider and should be able to stay on, no matter if that colt happens to be that one in a hundred that does do something. I well remember, that perhaps the most gentle colt I ever broke and one in which later events proved I had too much confidence, threw me twice the first day I rode her. The trainer should ride in perfect balance and with a loose rein, so that he does not disturb the colt. He must, however, be ready to tighten that rein in a hurry, if necessary. He should not ride long the first few days, in order to make the colt think it is play, rather than work. For several days, the trainer should have an assistant hold the colt for him to dismount, and he should use a bench or mounting block for dismounting, as well as for mounting, until the colt is fairly well broke.

The colt should be ridden each day from five to fifteen minutes, but not long enough to tire it. About the third to the fifth day it begins to get the feel of things and gets the hump out of its back. It is at this time that the trainer must be especially on the alert, for it may make a few jumps then, if it is ever going to do so. It must not be permitted to do so—must be stopped instantly. If the colt is broke in this way it will never learn to buck, and in later years it may be left in the stall several days and will not come out bucking. It will then truly be a saddle horse that one can depend upon, or sell with confidence to a friend, or allow ladies to ride. Even stock horses are broke this way on large ranches nowadays, as it is cheaper in the long run. There are less accidents and horses broke this way do not have to be "topped off" every morning, taking up a lot of time and energy. After being broke gentle, the gaited colt will be ridden only one day a week until fall. The stock horse, polo horse, hack or jumper, may be turned out if only two-year-olds, or they may be ridden very lightly a few days a week, as is desired.

THE UNUSUAL OR MEAN COLT

Once in a long while one will get a colt that does not seem to respond to ordinary methods of breaking. It may be actually mean, or it may be extraordinarily nervous, or perhaps it has been mishandled earlier. In any case, I am not going into too much detail about such colts, as each requires very specialized and individual treatment and is always to be handled by a professional. He has both the experience and the equipment necessary for such cases. The novice had better send such a colt to a professional rather than take a chance on having a serious accident. The best of us can have bad accidents at times, and there is no excuse for taking unnecessary risks. Some of these colts under proper handling, may turn out to be perfectly reliable. I well remember one such case which was brought to me. To all beliefs, it was just plain vicious. It would bite, strike, kick, or run away at the slightest opportunity. After some difficulty we got a combination throwing rig and bitting harness on it. At each outburst we threw it, and in a few days we had it driving to long lines fairly well. When first hitched to a cart, we had the same thing to do all over again. By the time we were ready to break it to saddle, it had become perfectly docile and took to saddle work as easily as any colt. I had the colt two and one half months before returning it to the owner. About a year later I stopped by to see how they were making out with it. A nine-year-old boy was riding it, and the owner said that anyone could work with it in the stall, or do anything necessary with it, as it had become perfectly gentle.

I had another case that didn't turn out quite so well. She was a gray mare and was about five years old before we attempted to break her. The longer she was driven, the worse she got. She was a confirmed balker and always hated a cart. However, she became perfectly gentle under saddle, and was ridden in a parade by my wife, about a week after I started riding her. She became my wife's favorite saddle horse until she was sold. The people who bought her wanted her only for riding and were very well satisfied, as she was gentle in every way but driving. It has always been my opinion that she had been spoiled when younger. Sometimes such a colt may be broken by being hitched up double with a heavy draft horse that is gentle and well broke. Perhaps some horses just resent being driven. Who knows?

Throwing is perhaps the surest way of demanding obedience from a mean horse or colt. It is also about the surest way of breaking a horse's spirit and making it lose its individuality. Some trainers go through life without ever having to throw a horse. Even so, in my opinion, it is still

done far too often; however, as a last resort, it may work when nothing else will.

Perhaps the easiest way to throw a horse is with the use of a W, that is, a surcingle with rings and separate hobbles around the fetlocks, each with large rings. A strong rope is run through a ring on the lower part of the surcingle on the near side, then down through the ring in the hobble, back up to the surcingle through another ring, down again through the ring in the other hobble and back up to the surcingle.

For this work one must be very sure to pad the knees very well. Many horses will fight this quite hard and will pound their knees. If they have not been well padded the horse may ruin its knees for life. The horse should be taken into a large lot, preferably one that has been plowed up so that the ground is not hard, and the bridle may as well be removed as it is just in the way and all control is transferred to the throwing rope. As the horse moves out the rope is pulled hard which pulls first one foot then the other up to the animal's belly. This is when the horse will fight and often fight very hard, going around on its hind legs, and incidentally putting great strain on its hocks and stifles. It will often beat its knees on the ground. All the trainer can do at this time is stay out of the way, not get hurt, and keep the rope tight, move around to keep from getting tangled up and never slacking off on the rope. How long this will continue depends upon the strength of the horse and its vitality and will to fight. Eventually it will come to its knees and stay there, but the trainer must not push it over. He must wait until the horse gives up and falls over on its side of its own accord. The trainer then bangs pan lids together making all the noise he can; he rattles newspapers, throws them at the horse, even cracks a whip, but never touches the horse with a whip. Naturally the horse will attempt to rise and start fighting all over again. The trainer continues to offer but passive resistance, always keeping the rope tight. This process goes on and on until eventually the horse gives up completely, and allows the trainer to walk all over him banging pan lids together, dropping newspapers all over him even around his head, anything except hurting the horse in any way. It must not be turned loose until it has given in completely whether this takes two hours or six the first time.

There may have to be a repeat performance the following day, but this won't take near as long as the first time. The horse may then be hitched to a break cart and driven in this lot, still with the W in place and an extra man working the rope. At the first sign of disobedience, the horse is thrown and while down, the cart is removed and the whole first day's performance repeated. In some cases one may want to put a throwing rig on over the saddle and get on to ride. Again the animal is thrown at the first sign of misbehavior. After a horse has once been thrown it is generally quite simple to throw it again even from his back. Of course, as soon as the animal goes to its knees the trainer dismounts and continues from the ground.

When a horse has been thrown a few times and has completely given in, especially if it has been thrown both while in a break cart and while the trainer was riding, it is pretty apt to be a broke horse. I mean broke in all sense of the word, broken in spirit, its individuality shattered, and even possibly a broken bone or a knee banged up so badly it is ruined for life, or maybe a stifle thrown out or a pair of curbs on the hocks.

Although it is one way of breaking a horse it is definitely not a job for an amateur, nor even for a professional unless all other means have failed. The only reason I am including this is that I have received quite a lot of questions concerning this method of breaking horses. It is not a new method, having been used at least a hundred years. Back in the old days when horses were cheap and when all one needed in most cases was a phlegmatic general purpose horse that was not apt to be frightened by anything, this method was in more or less general use. Today we need a different type of horse and horses are too expensive to use such drastic methods.

CHAPTER IV

TRAINING UNDER THE SADDLE

THE POLO AND STOCK HORSE

Up to this point the training of all types of riding horses may progress in much the same way; but from now on, the work becomes more specialized, such as hunters and jumpers, stock horses, polo horses, and gaited horses. For the most part, all trainers specialize in one or another phase of the work, although on certain jobs they may at times be asked to do some work on different types. I particularly like three- and five-gaited saddle horses, which are the only types I shall dwell on for any great length of time. The show horse of any type is only that particular type brought to the peak of its perfection. Thus, the gaited pleasure horse is bred and trained the same as its show brother, but for some reason lacks the quality that makes a show horse. At one time or another in my career, I have been called upon to break horses to jump, and to rein and work like stock horses and polo horses. I will endeavor to give hints to my readers who wish to train their horses for any of these particular uses. For more detailed instructions, one may find any number of books and articles on the training of any of these types with the exception of gaited horses. For some reason, the gaited horse is about the only type of riding horse about which volumes of literature have not been written.

In many parts of the country, especially the Southwest and the far West, when a pleasure horse is spoken of, one generally means a horse broke and trained like a stock horse, for use with a stock saddle and some variation of

ILLUSTRATION XIII

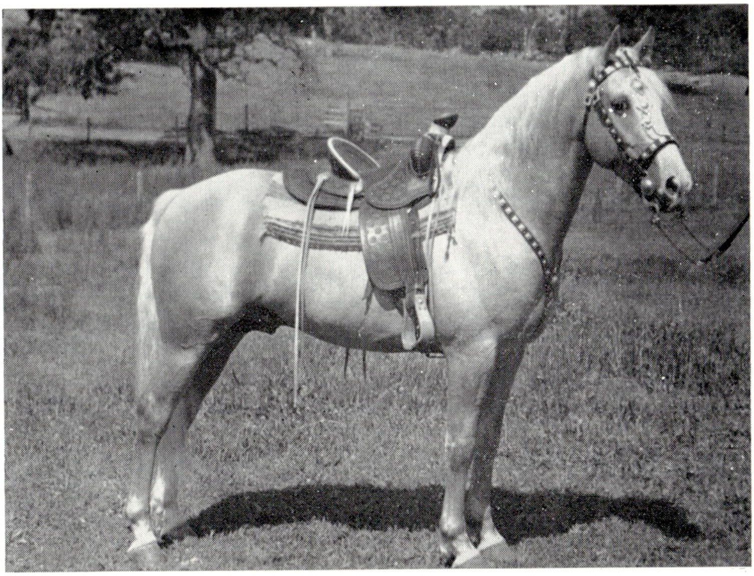

SPOTLIGHT DILLON

P.H.A. 408 and Part Blooded Registry S-394

This picture shows near perfect conformation and coloring of the stock horse type Palomino. In 1940 and '41 he was the winner of 19 firsts and 9 championships. Owned and standing at Pal-O-Mine Rancho, Brown's Valley, Calif.

Mexican bit. They are divided into two distinct classes, one of which is the trail horse, used primarily for horseback trips, which are about the counterpart of the true stock horse. Many are quarter horses or carry a percentage of Thoroughbred blood. They are compactly built, well muscled, and are able to run very fast for short distances, carrying considerable weight. Some of this type also carry the blood of the smaller Morgans, or Arabians, and even some of the American Saddle Horse that happens to be of the type desired. The latter breed is generally too fine to be desired for this type of horse.

The second type of pleasure horse in the West is what is known as parade horses. They are apt to be Palominos or pintos, although solid colors may be used. They must be tall and must have a fairly good head and tail carriage. This type generally carries quite a large infusion of Thoroughbred, or American Saddle Horse blood, the latter being most desired, as horses carrying this blood will generally have better head and tail carriages than those carrying Thoroughbred blood, although Thoroughbred blood produces the size desired. In the main features, the above horses are broke in much the same way, with the exception that the stock horse wants a low head carriage, and the trail horse may or may not have one. The parade horse, however, wants a high head carriage. All are taught to rein, to canter slowly, and to do a slow trot that one can sit, or a singlefoot. The stock horse must be able to stop and start instantly and must not be afraid of a rope swinging around its head. It must also be trained to cut cattle, to stop instantly when a catch is made, and to hold the catch as long as necessary. All this work with cattle takes actual practice with them, although the horses may be started on a sack, instead of a calf, until they get the idea. Anyone who is familiar enough with the actual roping and working of cattle, who needs or wants such a horse, will also know how to finish his mount for his own requirements. As with the exception of working cattle and holding a roped animal, the polo and stock horse are required to have approximately the same training, so we may as well consider the two at the same time.

Western horses are generally not broken until they are three or four years old. If the reader wishes he may follow the directions in the preceding chapter for breaking the colt to harness, then to the saddle, however, should he wish to omit the harness work, he may obtain good results by following the procedures used at most of the larger cattle ranches of today, which have well bred horses and handle them sensibly.

The colt is handled several days before any attempt is made to saddle it. It is taught to lead willingly and have its feet handled as it gradually loses its fear of humans. Not until this result is accomplished should the blanket, then the saddle, be gently placed on the animal's back and the girth drawn up just snug, not too tight. The colt is then bridled with a large easy snaffle bit and is led around for awhile. At this time I like to drive it with long lines passed through the stirrups which have been tied down by means of a strap from one to the other, under the animal's belly. This long line process is done exactly like explained in the preceding chapter, but in this case instead of preparing the colt to be driven to a cart, we are merely teaching it to turn by responding to the pressure of the reins. We will find that this will greatly simplify breaking later. If the colt is going to fight the pressure of the bit on its mouth when asked to turn, it had just as as well do it while the trainer is on the ground where he has more control.

After perhaps ten minutes of long lining, the colt is brought into a small strong enclosure about thirty by forty feet. A couple of grain sacks about half full of straw are tied to the saddle horn, one on each side. The reins are then tied to the saddle horn, short enough that the colt cannot get its head down but no shorter. The colt is then turned loose in this enclosure. It is allowed to play or attempt to buck as long as it wishes. It can do very little without its head down anyway. The colt will in this way get over the inclination to buck and at the same time learn to flex or give to the pressure of the bit.

When the animal quiets down it may as well be brought in, patted and unsaddled; its lesson being finished for that day. The same lesson is repeated for a few days until the colt learns to carry a saddle and turn willingly. During this time many horse breakers hobble the colt while they saddle it. This teaches it to stand still while being saddled. A gunny sack tied first around one ankle, then the other, serves very well for this purpose. While the colt is still hobbled, a sack partially filled with straw may be passed over the rump, shoulders, neck, legs and even the head until it will stand for this treatment without fear. After a few days of this preparatory treatment, one may then begin preparing the colt to be mounted, by following the steps as explained in the preceding chapter. If one is working alone, he may use the hobbles to hold the colt still, instead of having an assistant.

Each day before the colt is ridden, it is a good idea to turn it out in an enclosure for a few minutes, with the reins tied to the saddle horn. If necessary it should be chased around during this time. This will serve the double purpose of taking the excess play out of the colt, as well as furthering its instructions in bending or flexing to the bit. Before riding the horse each morning one may profitably spend a few minutes flexing its jaws and neck. To do this one stands on the left side of the mount and grasps the bit in his left hand. He now coaxes rather than forces the colt to give to the pressure. At the same time he must be prepared to use the training whip if necessary to prevent the colt from backing up thus learning to get behind the bit. This should be done from both sides to keep from developing one side of the colt's mouth. Naturally when the trainer moves to the off side he must reverse the hands he uses for the whip and the bit. All this must of course be done dismounted and it is far better done at a walk, rather than attempting to do it while the animal is at a standstill. There is always grave danger in attempting to teach any horse to flex while it is standing still. Any but the truly expert—and not the self styled expert—is almost sure to teach the animal to get behind the bit if he should attempt this.

The reader will note that through this course of instruction I have advised a snaffle bit. Perhaps some of you have wondered why I did not mention the hackamore. It of course may be used for this work if one prefers, however in my opinion the hackamore is really more for the expert rather than for the novice. In spite of all one reads to the contrary, the hackamore may be an instrument of cruelty in the hands of the novice and if not perfectly adjusted may do far more harm than good. Too many novices do not realize the importance of the heel knot nor its correct adjustment. The U. S. Army at one time had a hackamore with a patented heel knot made of wood covered with leather. It was adjustable by means of a thumb screw. To my mind, this type hackamore was far easier for the novice to correctly adjust than the regular Spanish type, however I have not seen any of these for many years and do not know where they may be obtained, if at all. I feel that a great many more horses are ruined by the misuse of the hackamore, than are made by its correct use and most horses broke with it must be broke all over again when the bit is to be used. The hackamore is directly responsible for so many western horses needing to be ridden with a tie down. In any but the hands of the expert, the hackamore teaches the animal to stick its nose out and feel for the pressure on its nose. I certainly feel that ninety-nine out of every hundred riders can progress faster, with less danger of spoiling a horse, by the use of a humane snaffle bit, than by the use of a hackamore. This is certainly intended as no reflection upon those who use and know how to use a hackamore correctly. Still we must remember that in the hands of the expert, the snaffle bit has a wide range of effects and with it, the novice can do but little harm.

There are a number of methods used in teaching an animal to rein, that is, to guide by the use of the bearing rein only. If one asks the average cowhand how it is done, he will simply say that one crosses the reins under the neck, but the average cowhand is not my idea of a horseman. Of course in doing this, the horse will start to rein almost immediately, but it seems to me that the principle of the thing is all wrong, and that it would not produce a finished, reined horse. While reining the animal in this way, the mouth is pulled toward the side that the animal is to be turned and the pressure is placed on the neck on the opposite side, all with the same rein. When the reins are later put on the side of the neck for which they were meant, it means a drastic change of effects, and all training should be with the end in view of making each change gradual, and toward the final effect desired. In the army, all saddle horses are taught to rein simply by using both the leading and the bearing reins. Gradually, as the animal becomes used to it, the effect of the leading rein is diminished until its use is entirely discontinued. This fulfills all the necessary requirements of gradual change towards the final result, but is too slow for most people.

I have heard that some trainers ride in a fenced area along the fence, and that each time they come to a place where the horse must turn, they use the bearing rein, and thus teach the animal to respond to it. This method has many good points (if it works). What I mean is that I would be afraid that the animal would not respond when it was taken out of that enclosure. That type of training relies too much on outside mechanical aids. Mechanical aids are all right in their place, but when entire reliance is placed upon them, one generally finds that he has not taught his horse very much.

Personally, I prefer to use the army method, but speeded up a bit. I supplement the use of the bearing rein with a crop or paddle, that will make a noise as it is slapped against the neck. This, then, fills all the necessary requirements of gradual change toward the final, desired effect, with a little extra force being applied, and the desired result is accomplished in considerably less time. In a very short time one can, in this way, have his mount reining fairly well. I then like to ride it in a wooded area where much turning is required, and in a few weeks the horse will turn at the slightest touch of the rein on the neck. All this work should have been done at a walk, and no attempt should be made to wheel the horse at faster gaits, until it responds to the slightest pressure on the neck at the walk. If one then wants to teach his mount to wheel at a gallop, he may take it in a fenced enclosure (board or railed fences, so the animal can see them easily, and to minimize the danger of getting it hurt). It may now be taken at a slow hand gallop down the center. Just before reaching the fence the rider signals a turn, leaning with his weight towards the inside, as well as using the bearing rein. In this way, he can soon have his horse responding to the slightest rein pressure at any gait. A lot of work at a hand gallop, in short circles and figure eights, may be used to advantage at this time.

Many trainers advocate the use of the hackamore for teaching the animal to rein and there can be no objection to this. The hackamore should certainly be used when teaching the horse to stop suddenly. However, I use a snaffle bit for teaching the horse to rein and, at least for me, that works just as satisfactorily. I like either a large hunting snaffle with a big easy mouthpiece, and large rings that do not slip through the mouth, or a leather-covered snaffle, with leather cheek guards that buckle under the chin. Any snaffle may, however, be used. One must not work a horse too long at one time, as it will sour on this type of work very easily. A few turns, first one way, then the other, followed by short road work and then repeated, will usually give the best results. As soon as the animal begins to rein, I discontinue the practice of making a lot of turns just to be turning, but continue figure eights in the ring about a day or two a week. I like to take a young horse away from the ring for road work as much as possible, to avoid getting it soured in the ring.

While serious work with the stock horse will probably begin when it is three years old, it should never have undue strain put on its legs until it is at least four. By this, I mean that it should not be started into a full run from a walk, wheeled, or brought to a sudden stop from a gallop, until at least that age is reached. Waiting until the colt is five is much safer. The result of doing these things to too young a colt will very likely be bad tendons, curbed hocks, jacks, or some other form of unsoundness. Fast starts will then be taught by the use of spurs and a hackamore should be used when first teaching the colt to stop quickly, in order to preserve its mouth. The change to a bit should then be made gradually, by using a snaffle and hackamore, then the stiff bit and hackamore, and finally dropping the hackamore altogether.

Many trainers will want to begin using the spade bit, or a variation thereof, at this time. In capable hands, it need not be an instrument of torture, as so many people seem to think. The average rider, however, would be far better off and would have horses with far better mouths, if he never used anything more severe than a port bit. The man who trains polo horses will no doubt use the pelham bit, and he may make the change gradual by using the snaffle reins primarily for some time. It is, of course, merely a combination of a curb and snaffle and is a very good bit to use wherever a high head carriage is not necessary. The animal's head cannot be set as high with a pelham bit as with a pair of bits, as the use of the curb rein nullifies the effect of the snaffle, so that while it is a combination of both curb and snaffle, only one set of reins can be effective at any one time.

To get the animal used to a rope swinging around its head and body, a short piece is used at first, at odd times during road work, etc. The animal is kept well under control for this exercise. Gradually, a longer piece of rope is used, and meanwhile the animal will be asked to go at faster gaits until at last a full loop will be used without frightening the animal. The amount of time this will take will depend entirely upon the individual animal, but a whip must never be used during this course of training. Complete reliance must be placed upon the spurs for control.

The same procedure is used to teach the polo horse to be unafraid of the polo stick. A short crop is first used to swing all around the animal's body and head, and now and then it should be allowed to touch the horse's body, without hurting it. Later, a training whip or a longer stock may be used and finally a regulation polo mallet. I cannot emphasize too much the necessity of doing any of this type work for only short periods in order to avoid getting the horse sour.

To teach the stock horse to work a rope, a hackamore or nose band is placed under the bridle and to this is attached a light window sash cord, about twenty feet long. It is run through a pulley attached to the saddle horn. The reins are then knotted, so that when they are dropped over the horn the horse cannot get its nose down to the ground. A stuffed sack will then be roped, and as the trainer dismounts, he takes this coil of sash cord with him and snatches it lightly, causing a pull on the animal's nose and making it back. In this way, the horse is taught to back into the rope and keep it taut. After the horse has learned to work well with a sack, it will then begin to work with calves. While this is the most usual method of teaching the horse to work a rope, some trainers prefer to force the horse back with a whip, or by tossing pebbles at it. Oftentimes, a combination of methods may be used with success until the animal begins to get the idea. As I said before, anyone who needs a horse for this style of work, will have his own ideas of how he wants his horse broke and finished.

The trail horse and parade horse may be taught any of the foregoing that may be desired. However, there is no reason for quick short turns, fast starts, and short stops on any type of pleasure horse, and the less they are used on any horse, the easier it will be to keep that animal sound. All types of pleasure horses should be absolutely fearless, and should travel easily and freely at any given gait, with fairly loose reins.

THE JUMPER AND HUNTER

After the first lessons under the saddle, and when the horse has acquired a free way of traveling, and shows no fear or disposition to bolt or any of the other vices, it is ready to be broke to jump. The first lessons should be given on a lunge line, with the head perfectly free. The colt is circled in a large circle, at such a place where low solid jumps may be placed. I prefer such things as telegraph poles, or logs laid on the ground. If the horse refuses to take these low jumps in its stride, long wings may be put up and an assistant with a whip will follow and drive it over these jumps. The jumps must be low enough so that the animal will have no difficulty taking them in its stride, and they should be solid so that it will not become careless and bump them. If the horse hits a solid log a few times, it will soon learn to gather itself and take enough care to clear the jump. Low jumps must be used for quite a long period of time, as the animal must learn to gauge the height of the jump and the position from which to take off. Above all, it must not be allowed to rush any of the jumps, at any time. If the colt begins to bolt, or rush the jumps, while working on the lunge

ILLUSTRATION XIV

COL. ALEX SYSIN UP ON NASONIA LASS

Notice the position of rider's feet and legs as well as the unorthodox method of holding reins.

ILLUSTRATION XV

MRS. ALEX SYSIN UP ON BON NORMAN

This picture gives a different angle of a very good position over fences.

line, it should be brought down to a trot and made to take the jumps from a trot. This will help to teach the horse to jump from a collected gait, and now is the time to teach that. An aged horse which has learned to rush the jumps, is a difficult problem. The colt should only be worked over the jumps for short periods and only a couple of days a week. The other days, it may be given light road work under the saddle. The colt should be at least three years old before any of this work is given.

After it has learned to clear these low jumps easily and freely without the use of wings, it may then be ridden over them at a trot. The jumps must be kept low, as the horse now has to learn to balance its rider and to give enough extra spring to carry the extra weight over the jumps. Now is the time to teach the colt to gallop. It may be jumped at a trot about one day a week and the other days may be used for teaching the gallop and getting in plenty of practice at this gait. It should be started into it in the ring just when coming out of the corner. After allowing it to start in a free gallop, it will gradually be collected into a hand gallop. A pair of running martingales may be used successfully for this purpose. The colt should have several months' work at a hand gallop until it will take and hold it easily without attempting to go too fast, before it is ever taken over the jumps at a gallop.

After the colt will take the jumps freely at a hand gallop, they may be raised very gradually. I prefer to keep them solid, until the height of about three feet is reached. Whenever the jumps are to be raised, the colt should be put over them on a lunge line before being ridden over. The higher the jumps become, the more watchful the animal must be to gauge properly the correct place for the take off. This should be no closer than the height of the jump and no farther than the length of the animal. It can easily be seen, that as the jumps approach five feet, the space for taking off becomes very small indeed. By this time, other types of jumps may be tried.

such as the triple bar, the hedge fence, stone walls, and barrels. When the animal will take any of these types of jumps easily and consistently, one has a well broke jumper, which cannot be made in a day or a month. One should remember that consistency and perfection are to be striven for, rather than height.

Jumpers and hunters are seldom ridden on anything but a snaffle bit. They neither need, nor want, a high head carriage, and need not travel completely collected. They should have a good fast walk on a loose rein, a perfectly balanced trot, and should be able to move out about eight or nine miles an hour at that gait and a collected canter, as well as at a good free hand gallop. They may be ridden lightly at the age of two, but training over jumps should not start until they are fully three years old.

THE GAITED HORSE AND WALKING HORSE

As we have seen in the previous chapter, gaited horses are generally started under saddle a few months after they are two years old. As soon as they become gentle under saddle, this work will let up until the fall of their two-year-old form. During this time they will be jogged about four days a week, worked in the bitting rig about once a week, and ridden about once a week. This is just an average, of course, and may be varied to suit the individual. One or two of the jogging days will be work days, at which time the colt will be primped part of the time and asked for bursts of speed at other times. In the early fall, we will begin riding the colt a little longer and about two days a week, to begin hardening it up for saddle work and to secure a well balanced trot under saddle. After about six weeks of this hardening process, the colt should be ready to be started in its gaits.

The three-gaited horse will continue the work described above until late fall, when it will probably be turned out for the winter, but the horse that is to be taught five gaits will wear a saddle every day for the rest of the fall and will be worked quite hard. If the horse is strong-gaited, it will probably need its shoes changed, to make the job of gaiting easier. Up until this time, in most cases, the colt will have worn a fairly light plate in front and a light hind shoe with small heel caulks. I like to roll the toes of the front shoes and square the toes on the hind shoes on a colt, in order to help it learn to break over squarely. Other than this, I don't bother much with the colt's action, except in specialized cases. These will all be treated fully in the chapter on shoeing. Now, however, the strong-gaited colt will need heavy shoes behind, perhaps either side-weighted or toe-weighted. In front, it will want the lightest possible plates, made of half round iron; four to six ounces in front and twelve to fourteen ounces behind. The hind toes will be allowed to grow fairly long and the front ones should be trimmed as short as possible. No definite instructions can be given, as each colt must be treated as an individual, but this much can be said—that the stronger the trot, the harder it will be to break up and the more weight and length one will need behind, and the less in front.

The colt that does not have a strong trot and that has already shown a tendency to rack, may be shod the same as it has been up until this time, or it may need a little additional weight in front, to keep it from learning to pace. Only a snaffle bridle is used until the colt is well established in its gaits. I like a hunting snaffle with large rings, or a leather-covered snaffle with leather cheek protectors, that buckle under the chin.

In order to allow my readers to visualize the actual differences and sometimes the slight differences between the various gaits of the five gaited horse, I have had motion pictures made up of each gait. On the following pages will be found true photographs of the motions a horse's legs go through making one complete stride at each of the different gaits and in the order they are called for in the show ring.

The gaited horse trot, the slow gait (stepping pace), the rack and the canter.

This mare, *Blythe Fairy,* has won many stakes, open and junior classes on the west coast as well as in the Midwest. These pictures were taken at Woodside, California, where Doug Robb Jr. operates a public training stable. Doug riding in the following pictures.

Before going on with the gaiting process, let us consider what we are actually setting out to accomplish. While the rack is a forced gait, it is, nevertheless, natural to some horses. In the Saddlebred five-gaited horse, it is brought to the peak of perfection by a combination of breeding and training. Many will singlefoot along naturally, but it is only by forcing this gait that we can bring out the true rack. It is a singlefoot movement, with each foot hitting the ground separately, and it gives one an easy, effortless ride, with none of the up-and-down movement we get when riding the trotter. It is the gait half way between the trot and the pace. Race horses (i.e. trotting horses) that have been trained to both gaits, will often take a singlefooting gait, before hitting their stride. The old-time, double-gaited driving horses would generally hit a lick of the singlefoot, when changing from one gait to another.

To teach the rack, we must break up the trot, or begin as though we were going to force the animal into a pace, but halt it midway and hold that midway gait and then force it on in that gait. We must never allow it to slip on over into a true pace, as we can force a horse out of a trot into a rack, but we cannot force it out of a pace into a rack. Therefore, when the colt breaks its gait, as all colts will do, it should be reaching for a trot, rather than a pace.

Now to begin the actual gaiting process. We will try to give some of the different methods which may be tried. However, the saying that each animal must be treated as an individual was never more true than when talking

Illustration XVI

THE GAITED HORSE SHOW TROT

Note the diagonal legs working in unison. Both hock and knee action should be quite high with considerable extension denoting speed.
Photography by Elliott Dopking

ILLUSTRATION XVII

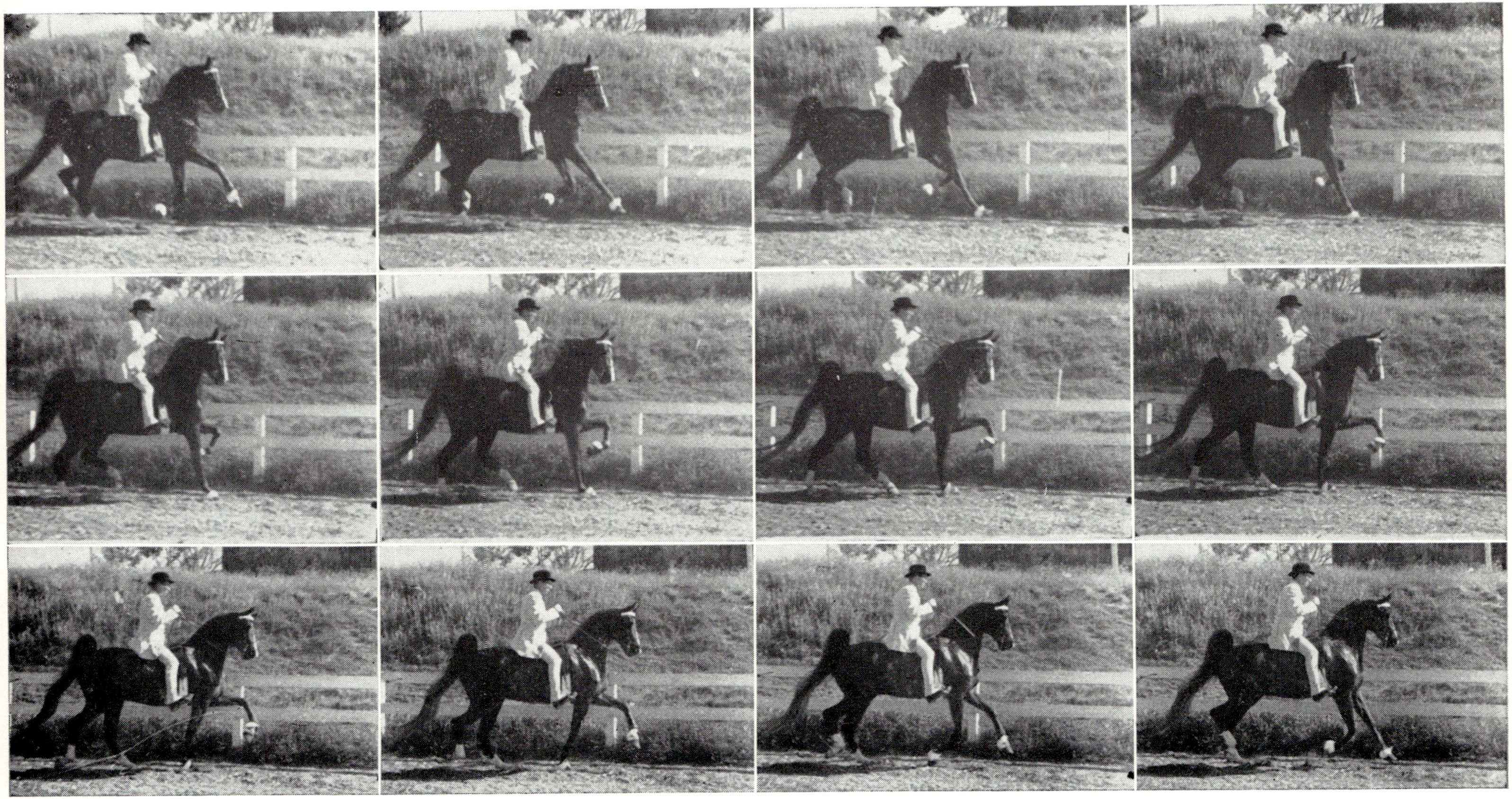

THE STEPPING PACE

Note, it is not a true pace wherein the lateral legs move in unison, rather it is a four-beat gait as the hind hoof on a side strikes the ground before the corresponding front hoof. It is slower and more collected than either the trot or the rack.

Illustration XVIII

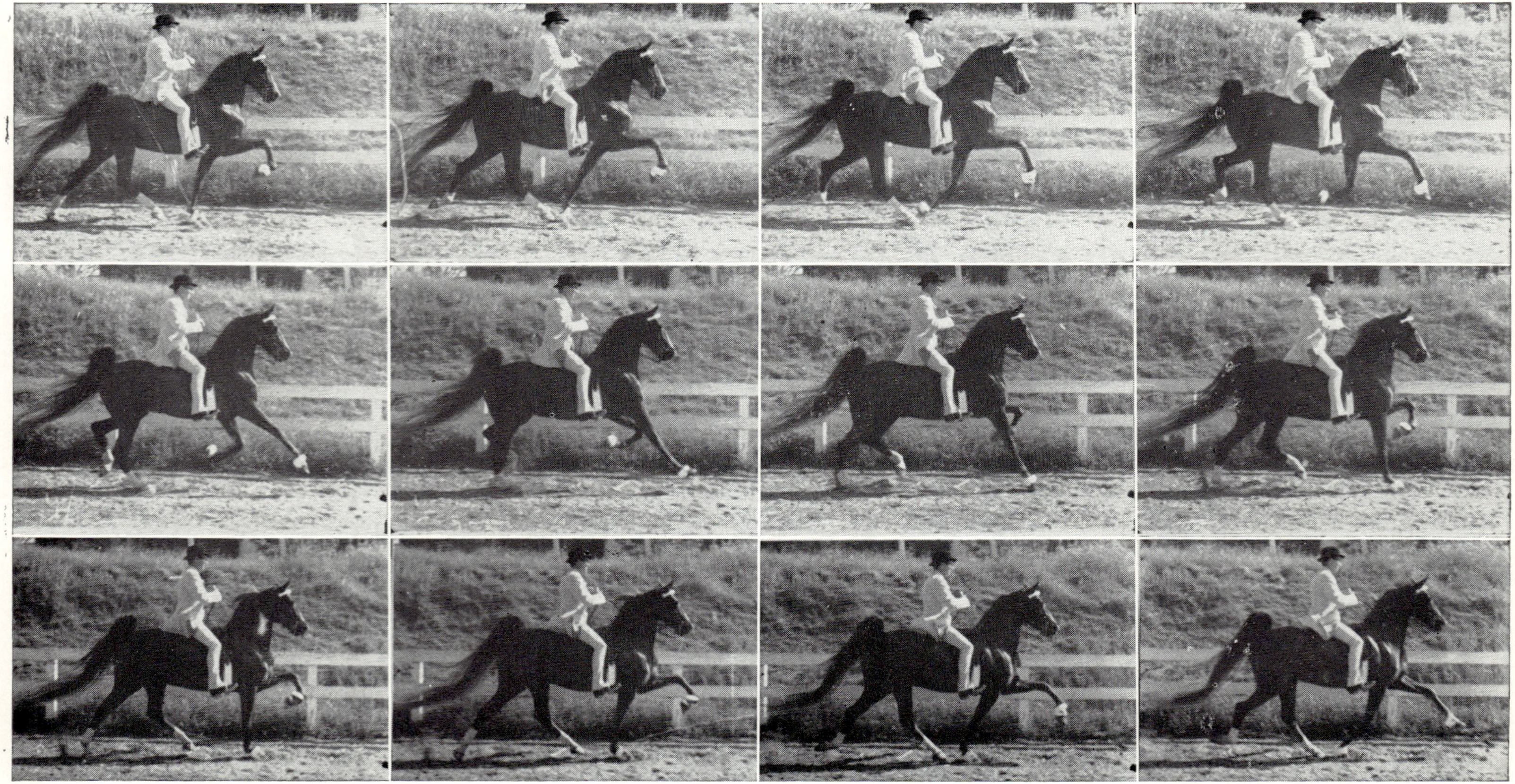

THE RACK

Truly a distinctive man-made gait, exhilarating to ride, beautiful and thrilling to watch, combining speed and action to an exceptional degree, a true four-beat gait with each hoof striking the ground in perfect cadence.

Illustration XIX

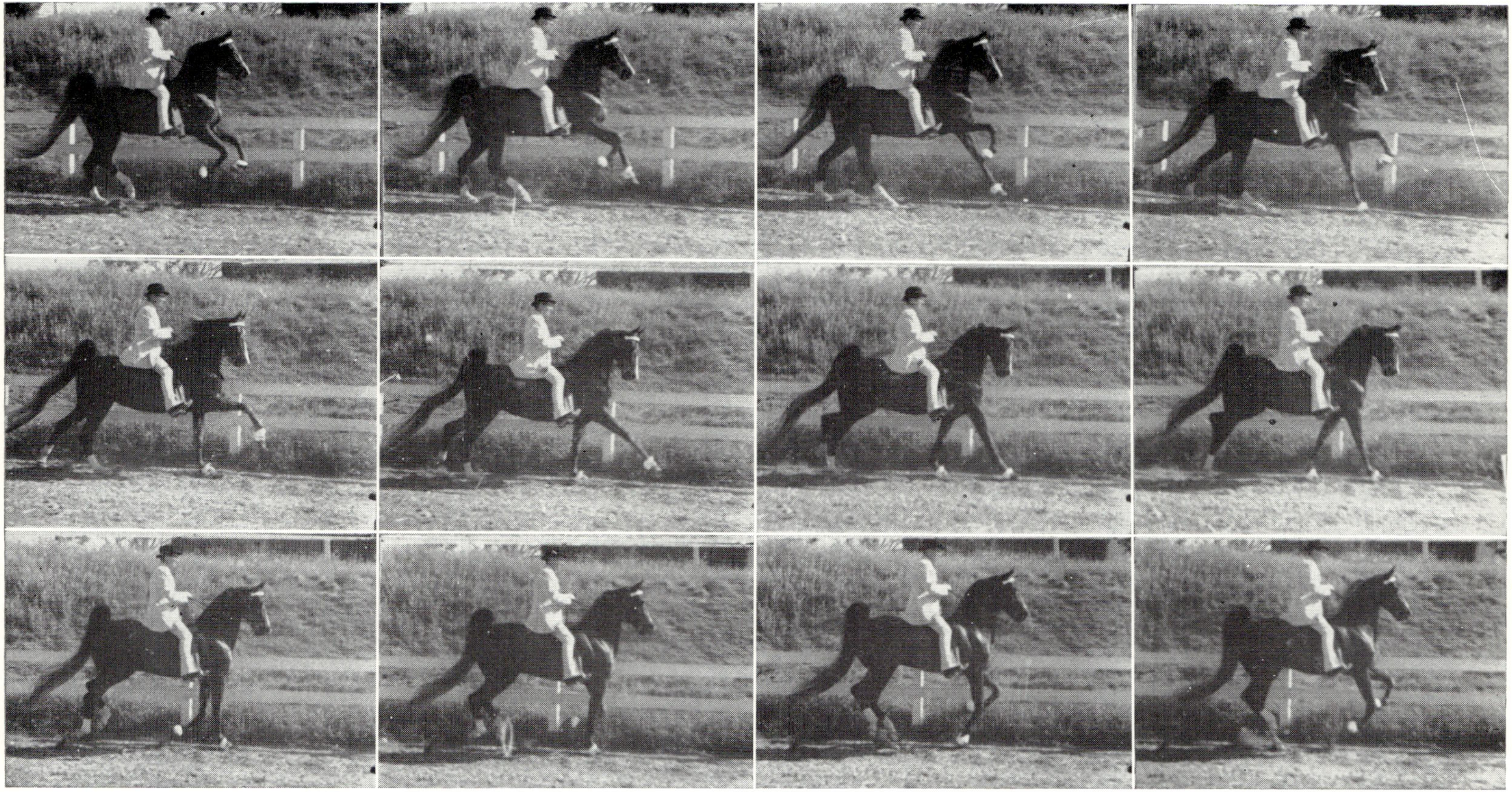

THE GAITED HORSE CANTER

A slow "rocking chair" like gait, a series of short leaps, performed smoothly and with considerable action.

about teaching the rack and slow gait. These explanations must be considered but generalities, and the wise trainer will instantly adapt himself to new conditions as they arise. Some horses will take the rack from a trot, some better from a walk, some down hill and toward the stable, while some may take it better away from the stable and some may take it better on the level. Some will need their heads up, others will want them down, but most of them will need them pulled from side to side. Some may be coaxed into it and some may be forced into it. The trainer must find out for himself into which class any particular colt may fall.

The usual thing is to lay up the colt at least one day before first starting it, in order to have it fresh and wanting to go on. It is then taken to an incline, headed for the stable. The trainer, in most cases, will need to carry a whip and wear spurs, to be used if necessary. Often, the training whip can be used advantageously by waving it back and forth, thus scaring the colt and causing it to want to go on. After the colt is turned at the top of the incline towards the stable, it is forced on and its head is shaken from side to side, in order to attempt to break up the gait and try to get it to take a step, or more, of the singlefoot. The colt may hit it almost instantly, or it may not hit it for weeks. In any case one must not work it until it becomes tired, and if it takes a lick of a rack or singlefoot it should be brought in immediately and allowed to rest on the idea. One can easily make the mistake of working it too hard, especially if it seems to be doing well. Make haste slowly. I allow the colt to take whatever variation of the gait it chooses at this time. That is, if the colt easily takes to it and wants to learn to rack first, I do that; otherwise, if it is more inclined to slow gait, I let it learn that first. Until the singlefooting movement is well established, I don't attempt to differentiate between the two gaits, nor do I try to force it along too fast, or hold it in too slowly.

In many cases, I might say in nearly all cases of older

horses to be gaited and with most colts, the neck of the animal will first have to be loosened up before the actual gaiting process commences. By this I mean the animal must be forced to give to the slightest pressure of the bit and swing its head from side to side as the rider pulls first one way, then the other. One may often get a horse that will stubbornly resist this and will refuse to swing its head more than once or twice; then it will set its head and tighten its muscles like a bull. This often calls for real fighting between the trainer and the horse. The trainer must keep at it day after day, pulling with all his strength, first one way then the other, until the colt will swing its head freely and easily. It is only after this result has been attained that the rider can begin to get the correct cadence to the swing to break up the trot and eventually develop the rack. Many colts will raise their heads too high during this process, in which case one should use the running martingale. In most cases it should be adjusted fairly long. A standing martingale should never be used during this period. As far as that goes, I personally see very little use for the standing martingale at any time. It certainly never teaches a horse anything good, but it will teach nearly all horses to continually force their noses out, feeling for the nose band. The wearing of a standing martingale certainly does not suggest a well broke horse.

If one finds he cannot get the colt to hit a lick by swinging its head from side to side, he may try raising its head, or try any other way he can think of to try to break up the trot. Generally, one will try racking it down the incline and allowing it to walk back up. If the colt is inclined to take to it too easily, the trainer must be very careful that he does not get it to pacing. He must never allow it to learn to hit a lick of the pace, for once it learns that, it will relieve itself any time it gets tired or leg weary by taking this gait. Consequently, at this time one must never allow the colt to get tired. He must keep it fresh at all costs, no matter how little he works the colt.

Just as soon as the colt learns to hit the singlefoot

movement whenever asked, it must be trotted occasionally. Otherwise, one of two things will be the result. Either the colt will get sour on the singlefoot and finally refuse to do it at all, or, if the animal is slightly inclined to do it, it will develop the habit of doing nothing but the singlefoot. Many novice trainers make this mistake, and soon have horses that will not trot a lick. This is really worse than not getting it to rack at all, for until the walking horse became so popular, that kind of an animal was almost impossible to sell. Now, however, if one does get hold of an animal like that, he can usually slow it down and get it to do a running walk on a loose rein and sell it for a walking horse. Many so-called walking horses do not do a true running walk, just as many so-called gaited horses have been spoiled and pace instead of rack.

Some colts will have to be continually snatched to keep them racking, while others will want to be just steadied slightly in this gait, as continual swinging of this type will throw them out of it. I cannot emphasize too strongly that one may have to try just about any means that he can think of to break up a strong trot. Colts of this type that are hard to start, however, often make very good racking horses once they learn, for they seldom go to pacing. Some colts will fight back quite hard, no matter how gentle they may be otherwise. Nevertheless, we must persist until they get the idea. I remember one little roan mare I had, that developed the habit of standing on her hind legs, then jumping straight into the air, every time I would ask her to rack. Yet, just as soon as she got the idea that I was not fighting her but was merely asking her to shake her head, she would start shaking it of her own accord, at the mere touch of the rein. She was soon racking along in fine style and was again as gentle as a kitten. Some horses that do not move freely in the shoulders will never learn to rack well enough to be really good five-gaited horses. The rack calls for complete freedom of movement in the shoulders. However, the shoulder action of this type of animal is often helped by gaiting the horse and working it considerably at a rack, before converting it to a three-gaited horse.

We must understand that all these gaits, such as the singlefoot, the stepping pace, running walk, and the rack, are nothing but variations of the same singlefoot movement. After one has his colt well enough started so that it will take whatever form of the singlefoot gait that is easiest for it to do and whenever it is asked and will hold it for perhaps a hundred yards, he may then begin to teach it the difference between the slow gait and the rack. To do this, I use the double bridle. I like a fairly large, easy snaffle and a curb bit with a short shank and low port that is easy on the mouth. After asking for the singlefoot, I try to produce as good a flexion as is possible with that particular horse, and at the same time I slow down the singlefoot, as slow as the colt will keep it. I keep this slow gait only a few yards, then jiggle the snaffle bit a little, release the flexion, and urge the colt forward as fast as it can go holding the rack without breaking. Real speed is not necessary at this time. All that one need really care about, is that the animal learns gradually to distinguish between the two gaits. True speed may be developed later, after the colt becomes letter perfect in its gaits, travels freely at the rack, and readily distinguishes between the rack and the slow gait. Both speed and form may then be developed. All training must be a gradual process.

I remember a good little sorrel mare I had, that was going along very well and beginning to do a very good job racking and slow gaiting, the latter being a true slow gait and not just a slow rack. She was not, however, well enough set in her gaits to begin to canter. Out of a clear sky, my employer decided to sell out, and this mare had to be taught to canter in a hurry, in order to get her ready for the state fair show just before the dispersal sale. This mare learned to canter very easily, but in so doing she completely lost her slow gait. Finally, she got so she would take it sometimes and at other times she would refuse.

In any ordinary case, I would never have consented to take such a horse to the show, but in this case, all one could do was to hope she would take it in the ring when called upon. As could be expected, she did not, and I considered myself quite lucky to be tied third in a class I could easily have won had she taken her slow gait when asked. The outcome was that a few days later, I discovered a new way of asking her for the slow gait, to which she would always respond; or perhaps it was just that she was coming to herself by that time. I guess it was a good policy in that case, as we managed to get her sold better than we would have had we not taken her to the show; but it definitely proved that one should only go as fast as the horse can learn, and it is utter foolishness to attempt to go faster.

Just as soon as the colt begins to differentiate between the rack and the slow gait, one must begin working it more in the latter gait, developing a perfect stepping pace rather than a slow rack, and gradually getting it to hold it for as long as it is asked. To get this perfect stepping pace, one must strive all the time for better and still better flexions, for it is only by obtaining complete collection that a perfect stepping pace may be established. This is the time to ask for action all the way around, by converting every bit of energy into action, rather than speed.

Neither the rack nor the trot must be forgotten, and we will begin calling for more speed at both rack and trot, at the same time keeping the colt well in form in the trot. By the time the colt has progressed about this far, cold weather will have set in, in most parts of the country. The colt's work will be lightened day by day, for a week or two, and then its shoes will be pulled and it will be turned out to rest up for the winter.

In the spring, the colt will be taken up and started at work on the bitting rig and in harness for a couple of weeks to harden it up before working it under the saddle. After it has begun to get hardened in, we may begin work under the saddle where we left off in the fall. At this

ILLUSTRATION XX

ENSIGN KIRBY 17526

A three-year-old Saddlebred stallion, after being worked by the Author about thirty days at a slow gait.

ILLUSTRATION XXI

THREE-GAITED SADDLEBRED MARE

Takodah's *Answer*, by King's *Genius*, has won many classes and stakes in the East as well as in the Midwest and on the West Coast. She is being ridden here by Mrs. Doug Robb Jr. of Woodside, California, whose husband manages a training stable there. Note the way the three-gaited horse is trimmed, instead of leaving a full mane and tail as on the five-gaited horse. Also note the rider's high silk hat which is never worn by riders of five-gaited horses.

time, however, the colt will be worked under saddle only about three days a week and in harness the other three days, or perhaps two days in harness and one day on the bitting rig, as may be needed. Speed at a trot will be asked in harness; and more speed at the trot and rack will be called for under the saddle. As soon as the colt is doing a good slow gait, a fairly fast trot in form, racking on quite well, and doing a good flat-footed walk under the saddle, this work will be further reduced to two days a week. We must never forget to keep the colt walking along at a good, fast, flat-footed walk, during all the time we are working with the other gaits. The walk is still one of the most important of all gaits and must never be forgotten. As we obtain speed in the rack, we will find that it is impossible to keep the colt as well in form at that gait as we can in the others. The two things just don't go together, but the colt must not be allowed to stick its nose out and get completely out of form, either.

The procedure for gaiting the Walking Horse is similar to that for the gaited horse; but the walking horse does not need to work under harness, as we need not develop a trot at all. Only the slow, singlefooting movement is asked for and this can generally be developed without the shaking of the head. The trot may be lost entirely. It is almost useless to try to make a walking horse unless the animal has shown some inclination along this line of its own accord, as the walking horse should not be forced-gaited, as is the five-gaited horse. It must be a normal gait to the horse, if it is ever to be developed correctly. Many Saddlebred horses will be found that are natural gaited, and these will often make very good walking horses. Both get their tendency toward the varieties of the saddle gaits from the same source, but the main difference is that while the gaited horse must retain its ability to trot high, balanced and square, the walking horse may lose its trot completely. Both types carry similar blood lines. Neither type is so fully established yet as a breed, that there are no throwbacks.

The Saddlebred horse having been registered much longer, will probably breed truer to type and conformation than the Walking Horse. The latter has been bred for those particular gaits as long as the gaited horse, but until recent years there has not been enough emphasis on conformation to establish it as a true breed as yet. It is claimed that it takes five generations of pure breeding to make a horse bred pure enough that there is little chance of a throwback, and that many of the papers on horses of both breeds will perhaps have only one registered dam. However, even with five full generations registered, we now and then have a throwback, as any breeder can testify. I know of a number of instances of Saddlebred horses looking enough like Thoroughbreds to completely fool any horseman. We have not overcome the tendency for many Saddlebred horses to be foaled natural-gaited. This is especially true in certain families, where this characteristic has been carried down with a great deal of potency.

The business of breeding gaited horses just right is a very delicate one, far more delicate than almost any other breed. In addition to breeding it for type, we must keep a very delicate balance in the saddling tendencies. We must have them, yet they must not predominate, or the horse will become natural-gaited and the trot be either lost entirely or become a saddling trot. In either case, such a horse will probably work out better as a walking horse than a gaited one. Yet, without these saddling tendencies, it is impossible to force a true rack. Surely none of us have ever seen such a true bred, straight gaited horse as a Thoroughbred, that could rack well enough to get anywhere in a gaited class. Perhaps if Saddle Horse breeders are careful enough in their selections of breeding stock, we may one day have the breed well enough established so that there will be no throwbacks either in gaits or in conformation. However, at the present time it remains a question of very thoughtful selection, plus a good amount of luck, to produce horses that carry that delicate balance of the two gaits, with a slight dominance of the trot, that is necessary in good five-gaited horses. It is necessary for the trainer to have a clear conception of the underlying causes and effects of this tendency of becoming natural-gaited in some animals if he is to truly master the art of gaiting horses.

As soon as the walking horse begins to take the singlefoot movement, all energy is directed along that line and the trot is completely forgotten. Speed is not necessary at this time. Instead, the animal is coaxed into settling into that peculiar walking gait, freely and easily and on a fairly loose rein. After developing this gait near perfection, and not until then, it is to be urged faster, but not so fast that it is likely to slip into a rack or pace. Light chains may be attached to the bit and left dangling, in order to encourage the horse to nod as it walks. We must not attempt to set the head high as we do the gaited horse; for if we did, we would soon get a stepping pace instead of a running walk. The animal must travel with a free head, and particularly so in the early stages of training. This gait perhaps more truly approaches the true natural singlefoot of a horse than any of the saddle gaits. The only other gaits the plantation horse needs are the flat-footed walk and the canter.

The canter will not be taught to the gaited horse until it is letter perfect in the other four gaits. The colt will next be taught to pose under the saddle. Perhaps the trainer will need an assistant the first day or two to get it started, after which the colt will learn very fast with practice each time it is ridden. To start the colt, the head will be lifted with the snaffle bit and one may poke it in the elbows with his toes. This latter practice should be discontinued just as soon as possible, as it is very unsightly and is only a means of starting the colt, not a means of asking it to pose after it has learned.

This is perhaps the time to teach the colt to back under saddle. It must be taught to back in a straight line, freely and easily. It is generally a good idea to have a wall on one side at first, to help keep the colt backing in a straight line. As soon as it learns to back fairly well, it must be taken in the open to be backed and kept straight by means of the lower legs only. To teach the colt to back under saddle, it must be well flexed and then asked to back with a give-and-take motion of the hands. This is a true give and take. The horse should be coaxed, rather than dragged back. If one begins yanking or dragging it back, he will probably have to continue to do so. Rather than resorting to anything like that, the services of an assistant should be obtained for a few days. One must remember that his legs are to be used on the animal to help gather it when it is asked to back. One sees so many riders attempting to drag their mounts back by leaning back and yanking on the horses' mouths and allowing their own legs to fly forward. In many cases of this kind, one will observe that making the attempt is about as far as this sort of rider gets. If the animal does finally take a few steps backward, it is all strung out and backs with an awkward sidestepping movement. Again, we must remember that the forward movement must be kept and the animal must not be allowed to back even one step more than is asked of it. As soon as it has been backed, it must be moved forward at least one step before coming to a stop, the same as in harness, to help preserve this forward movement.

Sooner or later we all run across the person who states that he does not want a horse that knows how to back, and that he perhaps knows of an accident that occurred because the animal backed when it was not asked to do so. If all horses were taught to back only when asked and as far as asked, and if all riders would remember always to keep that forward movement, we would never hear of such complaints. Such things are the fault of the rider, or of a previous trainer, who allowed the horse to learn to get behind the bit. All riders must remember that, whether they are riding a broke horse or not, they are continually teaching it new things, either good or bad. It is entirely up to the rider to continue teaching his mount the right things, rather than the wrong ones. So many spoiled horses are the result of careless riders.

Finally, when the horse has learned the above things and is letter perfect in its gaits, it is ready to be taught to canter. It should be brought into a fairly small, enclosed ring, if such a place is available. The horse is then taught to take the correct lead in the canter, from a walk. There are two principal methods that are used, both of which get results. However, the one is much prettier in execution and is really much simpler than the other. Saddle horses should be taught the use of the diagonal aids for this reason; but polo horses and stock horses may as well be taught the use of the lateral aids, as they are easier to use in that type work. It sometimes happens that a horse may be started more easily by means of the lateral aids, in which case they may be used until the animal begins to get the idea, after which one may switch to the use of the diagonal aids, if he so desires.

The canter is a perfectly natural gait of all horses and is therefore generally quite easy to teach. Spurs and a whip may be necessary for the first few lessons. As soon as the colt learns to go into a gallop, only the spurs will be necessary to help obtain collection. In using the lateral aids, the animal is brought to a sharp turn in an enclosure, and as soon as it comes out of the turn its head is pulled toward the center, both spurs are used, and the weight of the rider is thrown forward on the inside shoulder, in order to start the horse into a gallop on the inside lead. By using the aids in this way, the correct lead will at least be obtained in front. One cannot be so sure about the correct lead behind, when using this method. All that remains, is enough practice to get the horse to take the gallop each time it is asked and to make the movement more graceful. As soon as it is galloping freely, one begins slowing it down into a true canter, by means of producing flexions and bringing the horse together. The canter should be slow and rhythmic and ridden with the weight well back in the saddle.

We must start work on both leads from the very beginning, as a horse will very soon develop the habit of taking only one lead, if allowed to do so. If it once develops this habit, it is a difficult task to teach it to lead with the other foot, as it will have become supple going one way, but so stiff traveling on the other lead that it is actually hard for it to do so. Such a horse will also be hard to ride on the lead in which it has not been accustomed to traveling. The above method may become fairly smooth for any animal that neck reins. For all other horses, the use of the diagonal aids should be used.

In starting the gaited horse into the canter, one may find it necessary to use the lateral aids for the first day or so, as it is already confirmed in the other four gaits, and unless it is definitely forced into the canter, it will be very easy to get the gaited horse mixed up. Most other horses may be started right in by the use of the diagonal aids, which are smoother and perhaps a little more natural than the lateral aids, and the trainer will certainly have more control of the hind quarters. In this case, also, the trainer takes his mount into a ring or enclosure. As before, it is a little easier to start the animal just coming out of the turn. Instead of pulling the head toward the inside, it is lifted toward the rail or outside, and at the same time the rider's weight is shifted to the rear and outside. The outside spur is used well back, while the inside spur is used directly in rear of the cinch. All this tends to easily lift the animal into a graceful canter, and the outside heel forces the hindquarters in and makes the horse lead correctly with the hind leg, as well as with the foreleg. This is very important, for otherwise the animal may start cantering with the correct lead in front and the wrong lead behind. This is called cantering disunited and is very rough to ride. However, the horse will usually travel this way only a few jumps, and then will, of its own accord, switch either front or rear leads and again travel united. The trouble is that it generally switches the front legs so that they are leading the same as the rear, as it is actually the hind quarters that control the canter. When the animal does this, it will then be cantering false, or with the outside lead, which is the exact opposite of what we wish.

Too many people pay very little attention to the hindquarters, concentrating only on the fore-end, when in reality the hindquarters are the more important in the canter. They are the propelling power. Gradually, the horse will be slowed down to a slow, rhythmic, easy riding canter, well up on the bit and traveling in perfect collection. It must be taught to take either lead easily and gracefully, not only when coming out of a corner, but any place on the rail, or any place in the open where one may wish to ask his mount to canter.

This is truly a beautiful movement, if correctly performed and executed. One may, if his horse is well broke, finally get the canter just as slow as he wishes. It is also one of the principal high-school gaits; in which case the horse must change leads whenever asked, without making the slightest break in the movement. It may be taught to change leads at every jump. It is also taught to canter absolutely in place without gaining any ground whatsoever, and may go so far as to canter backward; that is, losing a few inches of ground at each jump. This requires an extremely high degree of collection, training, and horsemanship. The change is always asked for from the rear, on the silent beat.

The five-gaited horse cannot be expected to go that far with the canter, and for practical purposes it is not necessary. It is slightly harder to keep a five-gaited horse cantering slowly, as its muscles are trained in breaking up the trot rather than being perfectly balanced as is necessary in the schooled horse. All high-school work stresses perfect collection, perfect balance at both trot and canter, and perfect control. This is all seen in the various phases of the canter, the high trot, the Spanish walk, two-track work at the faster gaits, etc. The majority of so-called high-schooled horses that we ordinarily see, however, are in reality trick horses, and the gaits that they do are in reality tricks rather than under complete control. It takes five or six years for a skilled horseman to break a schooled horse correctly and to bring it under the perfect control that is necessary for the correct execution of the true high-school gaits, while the trick horse may be taught in as many months.

Perhaps this is a good place to learn the difference between the gallop, the hand gallop, and the canter. There has always been quite a lot of discussion on this subject. Fundamentally they are all but variations of the same gait, and where one lets off and the other begins is sometimes difficult to say. The gallop is the fastest of the three, being a series of long swinging leaps at the rate of about sixteen to twenty miles an hour. It can seldom be considered a collected gait, although the polo player, the cowboy, or the hunting man often keeps his mount fairly well in hand and ready to turn or stop fast, even when in an extended gallop.

The hand gallop should be performed well in hand always, with a definite degree of collection. The animal should work with its hind legs slightly under it and the rate of speed will be about twelve miles an hour. The hand gallop is a measured gallop, slower and in better collection than the true gallop. The gallop, either slow or fast, is a perfectly natural gait of the horse. Many riding horses are allowed to "lope" at about the rate of speed of the hand gallop, but it is a freer and more natural gait than the hand gallop, and there is little if any collection.

The canter, on the other hand, is a highly artificial gait. It should be done in full collection always, with the hind legs working well under the animal. Sometimes it is not quite as smooth a gait as the lope, as some horses climb a little with the front quarters. It should be done at a rate of about eight to ten miles an hour and may be done so slowly and with such a degree of collection that no ground is covered. The movement should be perfectly rhythmic. The head must be set with the nose completely tucked in, and it may be a trifle lower than is the case at the collected trot.

There is one thing more that all riding horses should be taught. That is to respond easily to the use of the lower legs. I have been talking all along about using the legs and spurs wherever necessary and if these directions have been followed, the horse should be pretty well broke to the use of the lower leg aids. They should be well enough schooled so that they may be asked to sidestep whenever necessary, and there are dozens of occasions in all types of riding when this is desirable. If the animal will not respond, it is simply because it is not under perfect control. In teaching the sidestep, both rein and leg aids should be used. It should be kept in mind that the horse should not be asked to step sideways, without also moving forward slightly at the same time. There are two reasons for this. First, to keep the mount up on the bit; that is, always to keep that forward movement, and second, to keep the animal from striking the front of the one foot as it raises the other to bring it across. At first there will be a greater forward movement than a side movement, but gradually the horse may be taught to move sideways in either direction, always keeping a forward movement too.

The gaited show horse will need extreme speed at both the rack and the trot. This is first developed at the trot under harness, after it is letter perfect in its gaits. It will be worked much like a road horse, except that it will be given bursts of speed for perhaps a sixteenth, then an eighth, of a mile. It need not learn to hold extreme speed for a much longer distance than that. It will have to learn to hold that speed on short turns, however. I like to use a light bike cart for this type of work, as it is much lighter than a break cart. After the horse has developed speed in harness, it should be asked for speed under saddle, first at a trot. If extreme speed can be developed at a trot, it is no trick to obtain it at a rack also, if the horse already has a perfect one-two-three-four rack.

The show horse will also need extreme action. Just how this action is achieved is probably the knowledge most sought after by all amateurs. If there were only some magic rule on how to obtain extreme action from all horses, how simple everything would be. One hears the question on all sides, "How can I give my horse more action?" Too often the novice thinks all that is necessary is to put on heavier shoes. Sometimes, however, this has just the opposite effect. Many horses cannot carry weight. Revel English, who owned *Edna May's King* when he was grand champion at Louisville two different years, has a saying, "The good ones all go light." Many horses, and good ones too, wear twelve ounces or less in front and eight ounces or less behind. I have even known good horses which worked their best wearing only eight ounces in front. Many horses just cannot carry weight, and lucky is the man who owns such a horse, as he will have much less tendon and ankle trouble than the man who owns a horse that needs twenty ounces to balance it.

No, my friends, there is no royal road to putting action on a show horse. If there were, all show horses and most pleasure horses would be hitting their chins. In the first place, real action cannot be put there. It is the same with true speed. Either the horse is foaled with a natural aptitude for it, or he will never have it; however, the natural action the animal has can be helped and increased, and this is one of the trainer's big jobs. Just how this is done varies with different horses. In order to get all possible action out of a particular horse it must first be thoroughly broke and be willing to travel in complete collection. This should be done before any attempt is made to obtain action. The next step is to fire up the horse. That is, scare it with the whip or by noise of any kind made by an assistant, such as waving or rattling papers or knocking tin cans together and perhaps giving the animal a cut of the whip around the front legs. It is then put to work while all scared up and anxious to go. Now its action is analyzed. This, of course, must be done by an assistant or ground man. He notes the action in front, behind, and from the side, how the animal handles its hind legs as well as the front ones. Then, and only then, can one begin experimenting with various types of shoes to correct certain deficiencies in action. The probable results of different types of shoes will be found in this book in the chapter on shoeing under the head of corrective shoeing.

After the horse's natural action has been observed, the trainer, the ground man, and the horseshoer hold a council of war and discuss which type shoe they think may be most likely to result in improving the action of the horse. After the shoes are made and fitted, the horse will be jogged a few days to get used to the new shoes, then the whole process of firing him up and working him under observation is repeated, and the effects of the new shoes noted. Often it will be found that this horse has reacted differently to certain changes than was expected. For instance, we may find that more weight in front actually has caused the horse to have less action rather than more.

Thus, by the trial-and-error method, we finally succeed in obtaining all the action possible with that particular animal; however, we try to avoid any extremes which may cause undue strain on the tendons or joints. Along with changing the shoes, the angle at which the hoof sets on the ground will also be changed and its effects noted. All these results should be written down for future reference. Along with the changes in the animal's action, the changes in its way of going must be noted, as we must keep the horse going correctly at all five gaits, because action in itself is of no benefit if the horse cannot do its gaits correctly.

One should keep in mind the way the top show horse should travel. The walk-trot horse must have extreme hock action with the hind legs working well under the body. It must also have extreme knee action and must fold its knees and ankles, but need not have the extreme reach which denotes speed. The gaited horse should also have extreme hock action with the hind legs working well under the body at the trot, but its front action must have quite a lot of reach with it, in order for it to attain the speed for which it will be called upon in both rack and trot. Both should travel with their front as well as their hind legs following a straight true line with no winging or paddling. These are the ideals for which we strive; however, oftentimes we cannot reach the ideal and must be satisfied with something less than perfection.

The gaited show horse is the Prima Donna of the horse world and like the Prima Donna of the theater, may be allowed a certain amount of temperament if he is good enough at his job. In other words, while we always strive for perfectly broke horses and especially is this the case in the show ring, nevertheless the judge does not tie on a perfect performance as so many people seem to think. Rather the horse that can put on the most brilliant performance with a lot of air, bloom and show horse personality, the one that captivates both audience and judge is the one that will get the nod from the judge regardless if he makes a little mistake here or there or has some minor defect in conformation. On the other hand, the horse that can just go into the ring and do a good job even if it is a perfect job (like a mechanical horse that has been wound up by a spring) if he doesn't have bloom, personality and show horse ways, will be tied down the line. Therefore, in making a show horse something more than mechanical, excellence is necessary. A horse with enough individuality and flashing personality about him to go into the ring and win, may be allowed certain indiscretions which would never be tolerated in the pleasure horse. For this reason, a retired show horse seldom makes an ideal pleasure mount.

I believe that this fact about the judging and training of show horses is probably less understood by the amateur and the novice, than any other and is no doubt the cause of so much discussion and unpleasantness after so many shows. One hears many people say, "Why my horse never made a mistake and he was tied down fourth, while the winner broke twice. This judge must be crooked" or "The winner was cow hocked or narrow chested, etc. This show must have been fixed beforehand," and many more comments in the same vein. What the owner or rider doesn't seem to understand, is that the judge is not trying to pick horses to pieces, nor to select the one which has the most mechanical perfect gaits, but the one which puts on the best show. These faults of course do not help the horse in question win, but they are too inconsequential to cause him to be tied down, under a horse which makes a less brilliant show. In preparing the animal for the show ring this thought must be kept uppermost in the mind of the trainer and its individuality and personality must not be suppressed if it is to become one of the truly great show horses.

I will never forget a show several years ago, where two champions met for the first time. The decision caused quite a lot of controversy, yet I could not see how anyone with half an eye could have tied the class any differently. True, the horse which was tied down second, had far more speed and action, which was what brought him on as far as he was; however, he moved like a machine rather than like a living thing. The mare which was tied first was not only beautiful with a long fine neck, the smartest pair of ears in the country and a big eye with lots of expression, but she walked into the ring like she owned it and everything therein, like a peacock preening its feathers. She looked at everyone in the audience and immediately captivated all of them and as far as I could see, had the class won before being asked to work. She then did her gaits perfectly and with a brilliance seldom seen. To my mind there was no horse in that ring worthy of being tied second to her that night.

CHAPTER V

STABLE MANAGEMENT

The prime requisite of a well run stable is the complete co-operation of the entire staff. It may therefore be worth while to make a few general remarks along that line. I confess I do so with the feeling that, "Fools rush in where Angels fear to tread," and without very much hope of doing a lot of good. Nevertheless, if I can help the personnel of one stable get along just a little bit better, I feel this shall have served its purpose. Dale Carnegie sold a number of books telling people how to get along with each other, so it may be that people actually are interested in trying to get along with each other.

We'll start with the owner and go right on down to the groom. The owner should realize that horsemen, and especially trainers, are generally a little bit, shall we say, strong minded, with a will of their own. If it weren't so, they wouldn't be trainers, as it is perhaps one of the hardest of all professions to break into, for it generally requires quite a lot of determination and stick-to-itiveness to last through the process of learning the business and finally trying to make enough of a reputation in order to get jobs which pay a living wage. By this time, they generally have had more experience with more horses under more varied conditions than the average owner has a chance to acquire in a lifetime. They therefore resent being told how to do things that they perhaps know far more about than the owner. If the owner has certain ways he wants things done, he will do well to use a little diplomacy in making the fact known and not go about it as if the trainer he has hired has never seen a horse before. The owner naturally has every right in the world to have things done the way he wants, if he is footing the bills. However, if he hired a man to break horses for him, he should have confidence in that man's ability to do the job correctly or he should not have hired him in the first place. This being the case, he should allow him to proceed in his own way; then, if he cannot get the job done, he should let him go.

A few general hints to owners, from personal observations, would be the following: Hire a good man, be particular and look around until one is found that is good. Pay him a living wage; otherwise, he may just take the job because he is out of work and will leave at the first opportunity of getting a decent job. Represent the job exactly as it is. Be sure that the man being hired is suitable for your particular job. For instance, a man may be a very good showman but may not be interested enough in mares and colts to be valuable on a breeding farm. I personally believe it is better for both sides, if possible, to give a month's trial before signing any contracts. This is long enough for the two to get acquainted with each other. If two personalities are going to work toward the same goal, it is necessary that they click and have the same general ideas. One buys and owns horses these days to have pleasure, recreation, and enjoyment. Therefore, he should not bother himself about details; that is part of the duties of the manager. If hiring a groom, expect him to know that part of the business, but don't expect him to know everything a trainer should know. If hiring a trainer get one that knows his business, and then allow him to proceed in his own way. Even though the owner does love horses and thinks he knows all about them, he seldom has either the training or knowledge along that line that the average trainer has. Horses are the business of horsemen and in order to make a living they must keep up with all new developments. The owner, on the other hand, has horses as a hobby and spends only his spare time with them. He has his own business in which he is no doubt successful or he could not afford to own horses, which means that his own business requires his time, energy, and knowledge. If these simple rules were followed, owners would have more pleasure from their horses and more pleasant relations with horsemen.

For the most part, trainers go into the business full of ambition, high ideals, and enthusiasm. Nearly all of them have a consuming love for horses. Many, however, as soon as they learn a little of the business of breaking horses, begin to think they know it all and regard any suggestion on the part of the owner as a personal affront. They should learn to take constructive criticism kindly, in the spirit in which it is given. None of us know it all or ever will. One fault of many trainers is that they seem to think a job is made for their benefit and enjoyment. They should realize that the owner has horses for his recreation and hires a trainer to keep them working correctly, break them, or prepare them for showing; whichever he wishes. Of course, the trainer who loves horses will enjoy his job, but he must not feel that the job is for his particular benefit.

A few trainers, generally youthful ones, seem to think they are too good to get their hands dirty. They should remember that the duties of a trainer extend farther than just riding horses. He is responsible for the whole upkeep of the stable, the tack, and the well-being and care of the horses in his charge. Even if he is not expected to do it all himself, he should be on hand to see that things are moving along smoothly. He should be ready to offer assistance to the grooms whenever necessary, and show them the easiest ways of getting things done properly. He should check on how the horses are eating and whether a change of feed may be indicated. Now and then he should take a look at a stall or a horse just to be sure that it has been properly cleaned, etc.

Little need be said about excessive drinking, as everyone knows that drink and work of any kind do not mix.

This fault often seems to be associated with horsemen. Why, I have never been able to find out, as in my opinion, there is as big a percentage of sober minded horsemen as there is in any other business. Excessive drinking does not necessarily go along with any particular profession. Some trainers make a lot of wild claims as to what they can do with their owner's horses, and when they fail to accomplish these results, it is, of course, worse for them than if they had been more frank in the first place. These so-called trainers are generally young fellows, or older men who are trying to make someone think they have had a lot more experience than is actually the case.

The trainer should be just as particular in selecting a man. I fully realize that in some cases he may be out of a job and have to take the first thing that comes along; but, if possible, it pays to try to select an employer whose personality and ways of thinking click with his own. He should realize that the owner has horses for the enjoyment he gets out of them. As soon as he fails to get pleasure out of his horses, he will dispose of them, not only letting the trainer out of a job, but making one less job in the country.

If I have seemed to be a little hard on young trainers, it is only from the desire to help them. The older ones are pretty much set in their ways, but the young ones can change for the better. The man who likes young people and understands them can usually secure loyal, honest, enthusiastic help from this source.

Of course, there will always be a few gypsies in the horse business, but what business does not have them? Doctors, lawyers, bankers, and business men are all plagued with a certain number of those who are unethical. Nevertheless, from the very nature of the saddle horse business as it is today, I really believe that trainers and horsemen as a whole have as high an average of men morally, physically, and ethically as any profession there is. On the whole, I believe they are a more hard-working class, with more real interest in their work and, for the most part, for less compensation for hours put in and time spent learning the business, than any other group.

If buyers or guests are expected on Sundays or any other holidays, both trainers and grooms alike are on hand, even though they may have planned to do something else. If a horse is sick, the trainer, or perhaps both he and a groom, spend many hours during the night with it, sometimes getting little sleep for several nights. The trainer or stable manager who goes out for the evening always stops in the stable, regardless of the time he arrives home, just to check up and see that everything is O. K., tail sets all on, etc. Many hours of sleep are lost during foaling season, yet the day work goes on as usual. At shows, especially night shows, both trainers and grooms are out to the barn by five o'clock in the morning and perhaps are up until midnight. Not all of it is hard work, it is true, but they just must be on the job. Is there ever any overtime pay? Horsemen never heard of overtime pay or unions. Most of them could make more money at almost anything else they would want to get into, but love of horses keeps them in the stable. Perhaps the only other profession requiring as much time to learn and as many irregular hours put in, is that of medicine, and for the most part the compensation is far different.

A gentleman once made the remark in a magazine article that perhaps all grooms wished currycombs had never been invented. I do not know how many grooms or what types of grooms he has ever had, but I do know that I have had quite a number work for me in different places and have known many others and have never received that impression. I know of few horsemen, grooms, or trainers, who would not willingly put in an extra hour's work in order to make a horse a little more comfortable; and I cannot say as much for many owners. I personally am proud to be a horseman and proud of most of my associates.

I can find less to say in criticism of grooms than of trainers or owners. The good groom takes as great a pride in his profession as the trainer does in his. He is proud of turning out a horse just right and proud of his part in producing a show horse; and it is no small part, either. The ones that do not measure up to standard are usually not true horsemen, but have just taken a job in a stable because there was no other work to be found. There are a few grooms who do not seem to realize that the owner has his horses for his pleasure; at least they act that way. Others seem to have little initiative and need to be told every move to make; but, on the whole, grooms are pretty much all right, and my hat's off to them for doing a good job and, for the most part, at small pay.

FEEDING

Feeds are so varied in different parts of the country that one can only generalize on this subject. All horses seem to do better if a percentage of their roughage comes from one of the legumes (alfalfa, lespedeza, or clover) or soybean hay. It will depend greatly upon what part of the country one is located in, as to which will be used. They all need to be well cured before being fed in any large amounts. Horses doing slow work or that are used for pleasure riding may be fed entirely on well cured legume hay, although it seems to me that they generally do a little better if they are also given some grass or grain hay. Horses doing fast work cannot be hardened or conditioned on a diet consisting primarily of legume hay. I personally like to feed a thin flake of alfalfa in the evenings along with the grain or grass hay.

The grain hays (barley or oats) or the grass hays (timothy or wild hay) should be fed twice a day, about eighteen pounds a day, depending upon the size of the animal and the amount and kind of work it is doing. I like to keep hay in front of my horses nearly all the time, except for those inclined to get pot-bellied, or before a hard workout, etc. I generally give a large feed at night, so that the horses may eat at any time they feel like it during the night and have a little left over in the morning. In this way they will learn to become night eaters and will have the edge taken off their appetites in the morning and will not gulp down their morning grain. In the morning, I try to feed just enough to last until early afternoon. Fed in this way, I do not believe they eat any more and they seem to do better than if the hay is rationed out. Of course, the gluttonous horse must have its hay rationed; and if one has a horse with a touch of heaves, it should be fed only about six pounds of hay a day, and that must be dampened. This horse should be fed more grain than the others and it, too, should be damp when fed.

One should remember that quite a lot of roughage is necessary to the well-being of a horse, as it has quite a large stomach and a large, short intestine. Therefore, concentrated feeds pass through without doing much good unless held by roughage. For this reason, horses need to be fed at fairly short intervals. The animal that wastes its hay will also have to have it rationed out. It should be fed about three times a day, giving it what it will clean up in about an hour and a half in the morning, one hour at noon and two hours at night. Grass is essential to the horse's well-being, as all kinds of hay loses a great deal of vitamin content. Whenever the grass is green, an effort should be made to graze each horse about an hour each day, either by turning it in a lot or holding it on a lead. If this is impossible, fresh grass may be cut each day and a good double handful given to each animal.

Grain forms a large part of the concentrated feed of the horse, and according to a bulletin from the United States Department of Agriculture, Bureau of Animal Husbandry, oats is the best all-around grain for horses. I prefer rolled or crushed oats, as it is easier assimilated.

Barley, corn, or even wheat, may also be fed. To the average saddle horse that I am working, I like to feed about a gallon of heavy oats three times a day, and about two or three quarts to the animal that is doing but little. To this, I add about one pint of bran for each feeding. Much depends upon the type of horse, the nature of his work, and his age. In the winter, I add corn to these rations, perhaps about three ears a day to be fed in the evenings. I prefer ear corn for adult horses and cracked corn for colts that are coming two. I never feed corn to colts under eighteen months of age. It is much more economical to buy good heavy oats even if it costs considerably more, as very light oats amount to little more than chaff. Barley or wheat is much hotter than oats, and only about half the quantity should be fed. Too much concentrated feed causes most horses to break out in little boils, or may cause scratches. If these things occur, the remedy is of course to cut down the amount of concentrated feed, and substitute bran mashes for a few days.

If the roughage the horse is being fed consists primarily of the legumes, less grain need be fed. This is especially true of soybean hay, which is very rich. It is the best hay I have ever used for keeping brood mares and colts in condition, and I like it very much for this purpose. In this case, however, they should have free access to a stack of oats straw.

If the animal is getting quite a lot of any legume hay, little bran need be fed. Otherwise, it is a daily necessity. I like to feed about a pint every meal to each animal, mixed in with the grain. They seem to do very well on this and do not actually need bran mashes. Nevertheless, a bran mash at intervals makes a welcome change of diet. This should be well steamed; if it is for a large stable, it may be made up in the morning, using about one-third crushed oats to the amount of bran being used, and a good pinch of salt for each animal. It should be well mixed with boiling water and covered with a couple of inches of dry bran and perhaps some burlap sacks, and allowed to steam all day. At feeding time, the dry bran is removed and saved, and that which has become damp is mixed in well with the rest and fed slightly warm, at least two gallons of the mixture being fed to a horse. In the small stable the mixture should be about the same proportions, and it may be put on the fire and stirred well until it comes to a boil, then allowed to steam and cool for about half a day before being fed.

Salt is a daily necessity, and salt blocks do not suffice. The simplest way to be sure that each animal gets sufficient quantities of salt, is to have small neat boxes built in each stall, perhaps on the tailboards, and keep loose salt in them all the time. They must be examined each day as the stall is being cleaned, as in some climates the salt will become hard and must be loosened up regularly and fresh salt replaced whenever necessary. I never put in more than a week's supply at a time. In many sections of the country the soil and water lack sufficient iodine, in which case iodized salt should always be used.

Iodine is as important to the animal's health as it is to the health of a human being. The soil and water in many sections of the country are deficient in minerals, and feed grown in these localities will also be found deficient. If one raises his own feed, he may, and should, remedy this condition of the soil, but if he buys his feed he will have to feed commercial minerals. These may be bought at almost any feed store or elevator, or from most veterinarians. The veterinarian can advise whether or not they are necessary. I find that the easiest way to feed commercial minerals is to mix them well with the loose salt in the salt boxes. If fed with the grain, a great many animals refuse to eat the minerals and allow them to lie in the bottom of the feed box and become sour. Grain boxes should be washed out a couple of times a month and a pinch of powdered charcoal should be placed in the bottom to keep them sweet.

I do not believe too much in sweet feeds. Many of them, especially the cheaper ones, are made up of the cheapest corn, oats, and alfalfa, some of which has often already started to spoil. However, there are times when a colt is not doing very well, or for various reasons, one will want to feed sweet feeds for a while. In this case, either buy good standard brands, or buy the various components and have them mixed. Any mill will do this. I mix about a thousand pounds of heavy, crushed oats, four hundred pounds of ground alfalfa, one to two hundred pounds of cracked corn, according to the season of the year, and about five pounds of salt, mixed with just enough molasses so that it becomes slightly gummy, about sixty or seventy pounds to the above recipe. This is a stronger feed than oats, and only about three quarters as much need be fed. Many horses refuse to eat sweet feeds, and I always thought that perhaps they knew more about what they need than the people doing the feeding. Too much sweet feed is, in my opinion, hard on the kidneys and bladder and helps cause worms.

Other roughage such as corn fodder, milo or cane, may be fed to brood mares during the winter when they are running out in the pasture. I personally prefer not to feed these in large amounts, as it has always seemed to me that mares and colts that are fed in this way are very liable to get worms and the resulting poor condition. When such feeding is necessary for financial reasons, the mares will do much better if they also have access to a good legume hay, or soybean hay and plenty of oat straw.

A handful of wheat may be fed once a day advantageously to both brood mares and stud horses during the breeding season. This is a natural and economical means of supplying the wheat germ. Brood mares should not get too fat, but should have plenty to eat to keep them in shape and should have extra rations during their last sixty days of pregnancy.

GROOMING

The horse should have a thorough grooming every day. Most people who own and take care of horses undoubtedly know how this is done, but for the benefit of new owners who plan to take care of their own horses, perhaps a few words of comment will be worth while. The animal may be merely brushed off before he is ridden or worked, for if the currycomb is used at that time, it will merely bring the dirt to the surface, and it will be hard to make the animal look well when it is taken out. In case the animal is going to be shown, it is thoroughly groomed several hours before showing. Then, immediately before showing, it is brushed well and rubbed with a good rub rag until it shines, but the currycomb is not used at that time. However, after the animal is worked it is completely cooled out and then given a thorough grooming.

To cool out their horses, trotting horse people give them a daily bath in warm water after every workout. They then rub them, blanket them with a woolen cooler, bandage their legs if necessary, and walk them until they are cooled and watered out. The horse is walked, until dry and cool to the touch, before being taken in and groomed. If one has a hard time telling whether or not his horse is completely cooled out, he may make use of a rectal thermometer and when the temperature gets down to about 100 degrees, the animal will be sufficiently cooled out to put away. If one wants to be very accurate, he may take the temperature of each horse in the barn while they are at rest, and thus determine that animal's normal temperature and record it. Horses' normal temperature may vary as much as 1.5 degrees between individuals. A good safe rule to follow is never put a horse away with more than .5 of a degree hotter than normal temperature.

The watering out process is done by giving only a few swallows of water at a time, every seven to ten minutes while the animal is being walked. When it will take no more, it is called watered out. When the horse is bathed, the legs should be bathed in cold water, and if the animal has been sweating, a great deal of the sweat underneath the fetlock joint must be washed out, and then the part thoroughly dried and powdered. The powder is merely an additional precaution to be sure that it is perfectly dry, as either sweat or water will cause the horse to break out in scratches.

The above means of cooling out a horse may well be used on the saddle horse also, when it gets very hot. However, the pleasure horse should seldom get hot enough to require that much treatment, and most show horse people believe that water used too frequently causes the hair to lose its luster and become dull. For this reason, few Saddle Horses are bathed regularly. Pleasure horses are generally walked the last ten or fifteen minutes of the ride and come in fairly cool. They may then merely have their backs rubbed with a little straw, have a drink of water and be turned loose until dried off, when they will be cleaned up. Show horses, on the other hand, are generally worked hard and fast enough to get pretty warm. They are brought in and rubbed with straw or clean dry rub rags and their legs are bandaged if necessary. Then they are blanketed, and walked and watered out. One thing that must be remembered is that sweating, or the lack of it, is not always an indication of inside heat. In humid weather a horse may sweat quite a lot without having an inside heat, while some horses have a tendency to dry up after they get hot. This type requires particular attention, and an effort must be made to get them to break out again. The warm water bath is no doubt best for this.

Rub rags may be made out of salt sack material. A full sack makes four good size rub rags, or one can buy them ready made up out of linen, or turkish towels make very good rub rags. Most homes have some towels partly worn out, which may as well be used for this purpose. Clean straw is about as good as anything for rubbing a warm horse. It dries well and loosens the dirt from the hide at the same time. As soon as the horse is completely cooled out and dried off, it should be thoroughly groomed before being put away. This cooling out process is to cool the horse slowly, instead of allowing it to cool rapidly and chill and perhaps stiffen up.

To groom a horse correctly, one should be equipped with a currycomb, preferably one of those made of rubber, a stiff brush made of fiber, a soft brush made of bristle, a soft wet brush, a sponge, a rub rag, and a hoof pick. In most cases, the feet will be picked out first, always picking from heel to toe. After a workout there will seldom be much to pick out, as the animal will have thrown out most of the dirt. Nevertheless, each hoof should be picked up and examined, to be sure that the shoes are all tight and that the animal picked up no stones during the workout. In most stables the hoofs are picked before the horse is taken from the barn also, primarily to prevent its carrying straw out on the floor of the stable. After the hoofs are examined, the currycomb is used over the entire body in a circular motion, loosening up the dirt and dandruff and bringing it to the surface. The stiff brush is then used, followed by the soft brush. The brushes are always used with the grain of the hair, in swift, deft strokes, making the hair lay, and brushing out all loose dirt and dandruff. This is followed by the rub rag, also used only with the grain of the hair and further laying it, and bringing out the natural sheen. Before entering the show ring, the groom will spend a long time, perhaps an hour or more, just with the rub rags in order to make the hair fairly shine. The wet brush is used on the small hairs on top of the mane, causing them to lay smoother and making the animal appear finer. The eyes, nostrils, ears, and dot are then sponged with a damp sponge. The hoofs may also be sponged off. Any grease or hoof preparation that is to be used, is applied. Any scratches or blemishes that are to be doctored, are taken care of, and the animal is ready to be put away; unless a tail set is being worn, in which case it is put on before the horse is put away.

When getting the animal ready for the show ring, the hoofs are neither washed nor greased, as this will cause dust to cling to them. Instead, they should be brushed off with a wire brush to clean them thoroughly, so that particles of dust will not cling to them. They may then be blackened by using a black sole dressing. I believe white hoofs look better when they are left white, but they should be thoroughly washed off early enough so that they will have time to dry completely. White socks or stockings should also be washed off a couple of hours before show time to allow them to dry thoroughly. When they are completely dry, corn starch may be rubbed into the white hair and then brushed out. This will make them perfectly white. Of course, in preparation for the show ring, all extra-long, straggly hairs are trimmed or singed. That is, the hair around the coronet, the fetlocks, whiskers, eyebrows, the hair under the jowls, and the mane, at the place the bridle covers, and the ears. The mane and tail are washed the day prior to showing and the tail of the walk-trot horse is generally braided up over night. The day of the show, both tail and mane are picked. That is, each hair is picked loose from the rest, using a slight bit of olive oil or brilliantine on the finger tips in doing the job. Very little must be used, as too much will collect the dust and make the tail and mane gummy, whereas just a little will hold each hair separate from the rest and make the tail look larger than it is, and it will shimmer and glisten. Of course, the walk-trot horse has its tail trimmed and its mane roached. This will take care of all the regular grooming the animal needs.

In all well run stables, the horses are kept trimmed up and looking neat all the time. Many stables have a regular rule that this must be done the first of each month or thereabouts. It takes just about a month for a horse to begin to look shaggy and that is about as often as they need be trimmed, in order to keep looking neat under ordinary circumstances. Having a definite time to do it, insures getting it done each month, rather than letting it slip by for six or seven weeks. If one is preparing to go to a show, those horses which will be exhibited will, of course, be trimmed just before showing.

The usual method of trimming is to use the regular horse clippers on the bridle path for a couple of inches; that is just where the bridle covers at the poll, under the chin, between the jaws, taking out those long hairs that grow there, around the coronet, all the back of the fetlock joint, and the stray hairs growing up the back of the leg. If the horse is three-gaited the whole mane is taken off as close as possible, and the hair around the outside of the tail for about a foot from the root. The clippers are then turned upside down, and the top of the tail is combed with the clippers in that position. This will thin it and shorten it; but will not take it too close making it look like a mule. The long hairs of the walk-trot horse's tail must be kept pulled, as it should not have too long a tail; but every effort is made to save all the long hairs in the gaited horse's tail. The ears are trimmed with either a pair of barber shears or small barber clippers.

CARE, BANDAGING, AND TREATMENTS

Beside the regular grooming all horses should have, there are some that will require special care at intervals for such things as cuts, scratches, bad legs, etc. The horse whose ankles have a tendency to wind puff, or whose tendons are slightly weak, needs to be bandaged immediately upon being brought in from a workout. Either a mild liniment, such as Absorbine or Dixie Rub, or a strong salt water wash, may be used on the legs and rubbed in well. One should never use a strong liniment under a bandage, as the horse's skin is very sensitive and his normal temperature is higher than that of human beings, thus causing the horse's skin to blister very easily. After the legs are well rubbed, the bandage is applied fairly tight over one full sheet of sheet cotton and left on from one to two hours, but no longer. Sheet cotton may be purchased at almost any department store. It may be used over and over again. Before using it the first time, one needs to split it and turn the glazed sides together, as the soft side will cling to the leg better, making a much neater bandage. The above is all the treatment this type of leg needs.

The animal with sore tendons will need a different course of treatment. If they are not too bad and one wants to continue working the horse, it may be done by wearing brace bandages during the workout. Brace bandages are woven with less elasticity than other bandages and they are applied very tight over one-half sheet of cotton, after a leg wash or mild liniment has been applied. They should extend only from knee to ankle, and not below it. They must be removed immediately after the workout and the legs should be rubbed again with a good bracer and the bandages reset. This time, however, the bandages should be set over two full sheets of cotton and wrapped just tight enough to hold. These are left on all night. In this way, it is possible to keep a horse going sound, unless the tendons become quite bad. In this case, they will need a mild blister such as Iodine, Anti-Firing, Savoss, Reducine, or Sloan's Liniment, and the animal may need to be laid up, with the hoofs cut as short as possible. I believe a mild blister repeated as often as necessary over a long period will do more good than one severe blister. Iodine need be applied once daily for three or four days, until a mild blister forms. Reducine, Savoss, or Anti-Firing should be applied according to directions on the bottle. Sloan's Liniment will cause a very severe blister if used too often or rubbed in. An Antiphlogistin treatment may work in many cases of bad tendons.

Splints often appear on colts for no apparent reason, and they usually come off of their own accord. However, when they do not, they may be treated in the same manner as other bony growths such as curbs, jacks, or other swellings due to bruises. A bruise is generally the cause of splints in older horses. Any of these swellings caused by bruises, such as big knees, hocks, and so forth, should first be treated with an ice pack until all the fever is removed, after which they may be treated with a counter-irritant, until a blister or scurf appears. In swellings from bruises, one may often secure good results in any time up to about six weeks. Bony growths may take much longer, sometimes lasting a year or more, and often they can never be removed.

Severe wire cuts or wounds had best be cared for by a veterinarian, if possible, as they may leave large scars or get badly infected. They can seldom be successfully sutured unless the part can be completely immobilized and covered. Otherwise, the sutures will certainly tear out or slough out, or as healing begins, it will cause itching and the animal will bite the sutures out, making a worse scar than if nature were allowed to take its own course.

If one must be his own veterinarian, wounds on the body should be washed out daily with a stream of cold water and treated with a drying, healing agent, such as sulfathiazole powder until a scab is formed, at which time an ointment may be applied to help the wound hair out and to make sure that the hair which does come in is the original color instead of white. Iodine with glycerine is a good healing agent and ointment combined for use at this stage. It should be mixed three parts of glycerine to one part pure iodine. Care should be taken to keep flies away. The best way, of course, is to keep the animal in a screened stable or stall which is kept sprayed. If this is impossible, one may apply a good repellent that will neither melt off nor wash off. K.R.S. answers this description and need only be applied once a day. However, it will blister many horses. If it does this, it may be diluted with mineral oil.

Wounds on the leg, especially below the knee and hock joints, will invariably produce proud flesh, unless they are kept bandaged with a pressure bandage applied over sheet cotton. The cotton should never be applied directly over an open wound. A piece of sterile gauze should be placed over the medication before the cotton and bandage are applied. The pressure bandage should be changed only about every third day, unless it becomes loosened. Healing will take a little longer when treated in this way, but there will be far less danger of proud flesh appearing. The treatment otherwise may be about the same as for wounds on other parts of the horse, except that the daily washings are omitted. Do not attempt to suture leg wounds. Cut off loose or hanging skin. At the slightest sign of proud flesh, it must be cauterized either with a hot iron, silver nitrate, or an acid such as carbolic. It is easy to recognize proud flesh by the angry fiery red color, whereas normal healing flesh has more of a pale color. If proud flesh is not cared for, it may often assume very large proportions, and cutting is dangerous, as the blood supply at these places is abnormal.

Scars are nearly impossible for the layman to take off. I have heard of good surgeons cutting out the scar tissue and sewing the skin together, using stitches very close together which, when healed, left very little if any noticeable scar. This is a tedious and very delicate operation, and would no doubt be very expensive. If radium is used correctly, it will take off scars, but it is impossible for anyone but a doctor to procure it. It cannot be bought and it is only rented to doctors. It is of course extremely dangerous to the user, unless he knows exactly how to handle it and is exceedingly careful with it. It is also a very expensive treatment. I have seen scars removed this way. After the treatment, one notices no effect for about three months, but after this, the scar gradually begins to disappear and is entirely gone in a few more months.

When the skin at the back of the leg under the fetlock joint breaks open, it is called scratches. It may become a running sore. It is quite a common ailment found in stables, and once the cause is determined and eradicated, it may be successfully treated by drying it with a good healing powder and then keeping the part well greased with a good ointment such as wool fat. Scratches are perhaps caused by a greater variety of things than any other ailment, but here are some of the principal things to look for. Horses running most of the time in mud, slush, or water, being brought in hot and sweating and the sweat allowed to accumulate without being properly cleaned out; being bathed and not having this part well dried; feeds that are too rich in proteins, or carbohydrates; excessive dirt, and other things on that order.

Horses often are afflicted with worms and need to be wormed occasionally. In most cases, this should be done by a veterinarian, as all parasitic medications are more or less injurious to the host, and many which may be given with comparative safety if administered correctly may be very dangerous if not properly given. Worm capsules for horses may be bought at most drug stores and given as directed. I like to keep on hand a worm powder containing nicotine and feed it occasionally for a few days in with the grain. This acts as a tonic and will keep the animal comparatively free of worms and is less toxic than most forms of worm pills generally used. The small owner may accomplish the same result by buying stale chewing tobacco and feeding about half a package a day for four or five days.

Bots are something else, and in sections of the country where they are prevalent, horses, especially those running out in pasture, need be wormed for bots about once a year. Horses kept in the stable are not apt to be bothered, as the botfly lays its eggs mostly on grasses and they stick to the animal's legs as it walks through the grass. When scratching the legs with the teeth the animal swallows many of these eggs, which then hatch out in the stomach and intestine during the early winter months. By the middle of January most of them will be hatched out, which is the time to worm. This should always be a job for the veterinarian, as the worm capsules used for bots should never be administered by an amateur.

Castrating is really a veterinarian's job, although many horsemen can do the job equally as well. Most veterinarians recommend that a dose of tetanus antitoxin be given at the time in order to be on the safe side. The after-care is, of course, the job of the horseman. If one has his colts castrated when they are yearlings, and in the early summer when the weather is warm and the flies have not become thick, he will seldom have any trouble. If he has a large pasture into which he can turn the colt along with other colts that will make it run and play, that is about all the care that will ordinarily be needed. In some sections of the country where blow flies and screw worms are prevalent and where animals must be kept in a fairly small space, they must have care while healing. This will consist of washing off the wound with cold water preferably squirted on with a hose, morning and night for a couple of weeks, or until the swelling has gone down and healing is well under way. After washing in the morning a little K.R.S. or other good fly repellent should be squirted on to prevent flies from accumulating and to keep the animal from getting worms and maggots in the incision. The animal must have exercise twice a day for at least two weeks, or until all the swelling has subsided. The more exercise they get the less they will swell, but the exercise must be forced, as the animal is too sore to take it on its own initiative. If the animal is a broke horse, it may be ridden at a trot morning and night about three or four miles. If a colt, it may be given its exercise on a lunge. Plenty of exercise will promote healing and greatly lessen the swelling, which will generally reach its peak about the fifth or sixth day. Older horses will swell more than colts and the swelling will last longer.

The male horse gets quite an accumulation of dirt in his sheath and a hard kernel on the end of his penis, which should be washed out regularly about once a month. Good warm water and soapsuds should be used, and it is not necessary to pull the penis out, as many people suppose. If one will run his hand through the second ring in the sheath when washing, he can do the job thoroughly and will not be so likely to cause the animal to fight it. After washing, it should be completely rinsed. I generally do this by running a hose up the sheath and giving it a thorough flushing.

To prepare a horse for shipping, its legs should be bandaged over one full sheet of cotton, from the knees down, as low as possible, and fairly snug. This will prevent many scratches, bumps, and bruises and gives added support to the legs. The tail should also be bandaged to prevent the animal from backing and rubbing it out, unless tail guards are worn. One may either purchase tail guards or make them from old three-ply leather girths. One girth will make about three tail guards. After the piece of girth is cut, three small straps with buckles are attached to fasten around the tail. A long strap is then sewed on the top, which buckles into a back-band and is adjusted so that it holds the tail guard in the proper place. If the horse is to be shipped for any distance in an open truck, its tail should be placed in a sack which is pinned to the sheet or blanket; otherwise, the wind is liable to whip it out. In nice weather, horses will generally ship better in an open truck, and they should be placed crossways, head and tail as close together as it is possible to pack them. In inclement weather a closed vehicle should be used, always allowing for plenty of ventilation without any drafts.

Loading horses many times presents quite a problem, due generally to the horse's fear of the unknown. I have read any number of articles on how to get the job done and have seen probably several thousand horses loaded and have loaded quite a few, perhaps nearly a thousand, myself and have yet to find a cure-all. However, I may be able to give a few general hints. First, have the conveyance as solid as possible, with as little incline as is necessary; second, always try to coax before resorting to force, as in most cases it is fear that causes the animal to refuse to load. Sometimes an animal may be backed into a vehicle that it refuses to lead into. Blindfolding the animal sometimes works. Oftentimes a cotton rope run around the animal's hindquarters will help it load. Use patience as well as your head.

TAIL SETTING

Here I am again sticking my neck out needlessly and no doubt fruitlessly. Nevertheless, I intend to clarify my position somewhat in regard to tail setting, as well as to try to give as much help as I am able to give on paper to those who wish to learn how to take proper care of a cut tail. I have been quoted and misquoted by those taking both sides of the question and have taken quite a bit of abuse and bad advertising, amounting almost to libel, from the powers that be, for my stand on this subject. It has been inferred that I could not and would not take care of tails myself, and that perhaps the reason I did not believe in cutting tails was because I was not born in Kentucky, or that other trainers and I who wished there were no set tails are too lazy to take care of them. Others have said that perhaps I had never been anyplace and did not know what I was talking about in the first place.

I wish to state, here and now, that I am not a member of the A.S.P.C.A. and that I do not believe in the position they have taken on this subject. Neither do I believe in any state laws for the abolishment of cutting or nicking tails; but I, as well as many other trainers, do wish that no such thing had ever been started and that some way could be found to do away with that whole part of the Saddle Horse business. I do not believe that cut tails contribute anything worth while, nor add to the actual beauty of the Saddle Horse, except that we have been conditioned to seeing Saddle Horses so presented. As far as laziness being a trait of trainers and horsemen in general, I have already had my say on that subject earlier in this chapter, but I will repeat that I do not think there is a harder working or more conscientious class of people anywhere than the average horseman. I know that some of the men who have discussed this problem with me were some of the best known and hardest working men in the business and that their whole concern was for the comfort of the horse. I am not mentioning any names, as I do not wish to draw any of my friends into this controversial subject against their wishes by some things which they have said to me in private. I was not born in Kentucky, it is true. I was born and reared in Ohio and am proud of that fact, and many good horsemen have come from that state, including the late Mr. Ross Long, the well known and respected Eli Long, Herbert Marks, Doc. Parshall, and many others. As far as that goes I never could understand the attitude taken by some people that one's birthplace has anything to do with his knowledge or ability with horses.

I have been around quite a little bit, having worked in about a dozen different states—including both Kentucky and Tennessee—and have been in about three-fourths of them. I have been cutting tails myself for over fifteen years. I have been taking care of cut tails and tail sets nearly as long as there has been any such thing, and will no doubt continue to do both as long as I live. As far as knowing what I am talking about, perhaps it is only the trainers and horsemen who get around enough to see the inside and actually know what is happening. I will give a few true cases to try to show why so many horsemen are opposed to setting tails; but first I wish to state that nearly all high-class stables employ competent help, who know their business, and therefore the horses in those stables have good tails, cut and taken care of correctly, with a minimum of trouble or discomfort to the animal. In small stables, however, the case is different. Many of these stables try to get by without the necessary finances. These stables are owned by the farmer boy, the man who takes care of his own horses, and the self-styled sport who either lacks the necessary money or the willingness to spend it to employ good help.

I was on a trip in Missouri to buy a truck load of horses a few years ago and went to see a nice little three-gaited mare. That is, she had been a nice mare until the farmer boy went to work on her tail with what, from the looks of things, was probably a corn knife. Her tail was swollen to at least a foot in diameter from infection. He asked three hundred and fifty dollars for the mare, which would not have been a bad price had her tail been untouched. As it was, I would not have given a ten-dollar bill for her chances of living, let alone keeping any kind of a tail. I know a stable in Ohio where I stopped to visit the day after a veterinarian had cut the tail on a nice little filly. She was getting the best of care. However that particular veterinarian had made a messy job of the whole business. He had cut from one side all the way across the other allowing a gap about two inches wide by about four inches across. How it possibly could heal in less than three months I do not know, besides leaving an open sore that big right under the tail to encourage infection. I will say that this was the sloppiest job I have ever seen done by a veterinarian.

I went to another stable in southern Illinois to cut some tails and was told of a number of them which had been cut by a so-called trainer the year before, none of which got the slightest care until they had all become infected quite badly, and the owner finally had to institute treatment which, while it may not have been according to Hoyle, was about the only thing to be done at that late date. One of the boys offered to bet me that my tails would also become infected. I offered him odds of five to one, and he backed out. When they were healed, he said, "Yes, but you took care of them," as if that were something unheard of.

I know of another case in Nebraska, where I got the story of the cutting from one of the boys who was on hand at the time. While I did not see the job of cutting, I did see the result, which was a complete necrosis of about three inches of one of the leaders in the tail, causing one of the worst looking tails I have ever seen. I was asked to recut it and I refused, explaining that I did not think that I, nor anyone else, could do it a bit of good. It was cut by a medical doctor who also did surgery. I'd like to have him cut on me, I'll bet.

These are only a few instances, but if anyone wishes to take the trouble to see for himself some of the results of poor tail cutting and poor care, he need not travel far. All he will have to do is to go to a few of the smaller shows in any part of the country and get back to the stables and watch (if allowed) the horses being prepared. Notice how many crooked tails, sore, raw tails, and cankered tails he will find. Almost all are the result of improper cutting and care. Also just notice the number of braces and wigs being used. Most of these horses are "has been" or "would be" show horses from small stables. Much of the trouble of sore and cankered tails comes from the decision of the owner, a week before the show, to exhibit his horse. He promptly has a pair of heavy shoes put on and puts on the tail set himself, draws it up tightly and is ready to go and compete with good horses. Then he is angry if he fails to win.

When it gets so that every farmer boy tries to work on tails with anything from a corn knife to a pen knife, and when all those who hardly know what a crupper looks like try their hand at setting and caring for those tails, it is about time for someone to say something against the whole practice. On the other hand, I'll agree with anyone that tails that are properly cut, with correct after-care and adjustment of the crupper, need only discomfort the horse a little. If anyone should quote me, I hope he will please quote the whole thought and not certain parts which make me appear to say things I did not say. To those who wish to learn how to care for the cut tail correctly, the following is directed.

The actual operation is simple, if it is performed by someone who knows his business and who uses a local anesthetic. There are still many who use no anesthetic, resulting not only in severe pain to the animal, but shock, followed oftentimes by severe illness. This practice should never be tolerated. Complete aseptic treatment should be followed throughout the procedure. One will need two knives, very small scalpels; a syringe (the glass hospital syringe is superior to the ordinary veterinary kind as it is so much easier to sterilize); two needles, in case one bends or breaks (they should be about eighteen caliber, as smaller sizes make administration of the anesthetic very difficult and larger sizes make too large a hole); and a pair of forceps will come in handy for removing instruments from the solution, etc. These instruments should have been completely sterilized, either in an autoclave or by boiling in a covered container for twenty minutes. One will also need a bottle of alcohol; a strong antiseptic such as iodine, Metaphen, or Merthiolate; an antiseptic for solution such as Haglogen or Amphyl; a large pan or basin; a small pan or dish; sterile cotton; some three-inch sterile gauze bandage; a little other sterile gauze; an anesthetic such as novocain; a pot of hot boiled water, and some adrenalin. The latter should merely be used in case of excessive hemorrhage. For the local anesthetic, I prefer two per cent Novocain in six c.c. vials with one to twenty thousand Suprarenin.

The tail should be washed very thoroughly just prioı to the time it is to be nicked. The horse is confined in the stocks, or with breeding hopples in a narrow place. A twitch should be handy for use during anesthetizing and actual cutting. Two assistants will be necessary; one to hold the animal, and the other to hold the tail.

The needles are placed in a small pan and covered with alcohol, and the knives are placed in the larger basin and covered with a solution of hot boiled water and Haglogen about two tablespoons to a quart of water. The under side of the tail is then washed with this solution, after which it is sponged off with cotton and alcohol. The novocain from one vial is then drawn into the syringe, and a cotton applicator is saturated in Metaphen. The horse is restrained with a twitch and the assistant holds up the tail. After the exact location for the incision is determined, the cotton applicator with Metaphen is first pressed against that spot and then the needle is inserted. The novocain is injected into all sections of the leader to be cut, as well as just under the skin. The needle is refilled with another six c.c. of novocain, another cotton applicator is saturated with Metaphen, and the same procedure is followed for the other leader. The twitch is now removed and the tail is allowed to drop. The animal is allowed to stand quietly about twelve minutes by the clock. This will give the novocain time to work. The horse is then restrained again with the twitch and the tail is lifted. The operator extracts one knife from the solution with the forceps, wipes off the handle, and rinses the blade in alcohol. Another cotton swab is saturated with Metaphen, and the place where the incision is to be made is wiped off with it. The original incision is made with this knife. This incision should be only as long as the width of the blade of the other knife and just through the skin. After this, the other knife is prepared and the leader is completely severed, the first knife having been placed back in the solution. The incision should be as near the base of the tail as possible, between two vertebrae. The leader is cut from the inside, leaving a hole only large enough to insert the knife blade. The reason for using two knives, is that it is impossible to completely sterilize the skin, which always has many germs and organisms on it, and if only one knife is used the danger of carrying infection into the wound is many times greater. Immediately after the first leader is cut completely through, the same procedure is followed in cutting the second.

The entire cutting process after the tail has been anesthetized will take only about five minutes or so, if everything goes well. Immediately after the cuts have been made, a compress soaked in alcohol is tied tightly over the incisions and around the tail. If the tail seems to be hemorrhaging, adrenalin may be used on the compress instead of alcohol. The horse is then turned into the stall and the compress is cut after about twenty minutes. The tail set is not put on until at least four hours are up, or until the novocain is completely worked out. I would rather allow the horse to rest all night without the crupper.

That completes the operation and in most cases the animal will make no fuss whatsoever. After four hours or more, the tail set is put on very loosely, barely holding up the tail, using plenty of clean cotton and a piece of gauze saturated in alcohol directly on the wounds. In the correct adjustment of the crupper, at this time, lies ninety per cent of the success or failure in the results which will be attained. It must be loose. The animal should not be worked hard on the first day after the operation, but it may be jogged lightly, after which one must swab off the under side of the tail with a solution of warm, boiled water, slightly above body temperature, into which has been poured a tablespoonful of haglogen for each quart of water. After all blood and dirt have been swabbed from the under side of the tail, one must keep soaking each incision with a cotton swab which has been soaked in this solution, until each incision bleeds freely and one is sure that there are no clots. The crupper may then be replaced exactly as before. This treatment must continue morning and night, as long as it is possible to get the incisions to drain, which should be about three to five days. Each time one works with the tail, it should be lifted high to keep the leaders from knitting together. All this work with the tail should be done very carefully and gently, as it is extremely sore. Most horses will be perfectly amiable to it, if it is done gently enough.

After the draining has stopped completely, the crupper must still be changed twice a day for at least six weeks, which is about the length of time the leaders will take to completely heal inside. The crupper must be worn very loose all this time. No crupper attached to the driving harness should be placed under the tail while it is in the healing process, and plenty of clean, loose, soft cotton should always be used in the tail set crupper. The piece of sterile gauze need be used directly on the wounds only while draining is taking place.

After about six weeks, the crupper may be tightened up one hole, and after that can gradually be tightened as is desirable; but never to the point that it is pulling on the animal's tail. Oh! If I could only stress that point enough, there would be so many better tails in the country and so much less trouble. Plenty of clean cotton should always be used, but it need not be completely changed each day. I have found that if one secures some old, clean, ladies' silk stockings, no matter how badly they are worn, cut off the foot part and pull the leg part over the crupper filled with cotton and tie underneath, it will hold the cotton in place and save a lot of it. These stockings ought to be changed whenever they get dirty, approximately once a week, and the top, thin layer of cotton should be removed. The rest can be fluffed up and another stocking used.

There have been so many changes and improvements in tail sets the past few years that we have little trouble with horses getting them off any more. It will pay to invest in one of the later type sets, as they fit much better than the older ones did. Any type of harness that is preferred may be used, but the crupper itself should have a deep spoon, not too long, but long enough to support the root of the tail; good, big, well padded rump plates and preferably a top that will cause an easy break over. They should be as light as possible and should be made either of aluminum or airplane metal. Most cruppers are now made in three angles, which for some reason the makers advertise as being for walking horses, gaited horses, and walk-trot horses, respectively. This is misleading to the amateur and novice and often causes him to buy the wrong type of set for his horse. Actually, the angle set needed for a particular horse depends upon the conformation of that horse, rather than how many gaits it is to have. The horse whose tail comes out extremely high, right out of the top of its back, will need a high angle crupper. The horse that has a tail coming out low, will need the low angle set which will work better on it and get a better, higher tail on that particular horse than the high angle set will. The medium angle set will come closer to fitting a greater majority of horses than any other angle.

Remember that the angle of the set does not entirely control the height of the made tail; but rather, the correct fit, which means a crupper that properly supports the tail at the root, will produce the best tail on that particular animal. I particularly like the Barrett tail net, or a homemade affair on the same order, for keeping the tail in the crupper, but until the tail is fairly well broken over, it must not be tied down tightly. Tying the end of the tail down too tight impedes circulation and causes canker sores, which, when once started, travel under the skin and are very hard to cure. If additional help is needed to keep the tail in the crupper, a piece of three-inch gauze bandage may be tied around the crupper and tail net near the top. It must not be tied tight, just fairly snug, yet allowing plenty of room for circulation.

In warm weather, I find that cornstarch placed in a kitchen salt shaker and lightly sprinkled over the cotton before the crupper is placed on the horse will reduce irritation. Baby powder may also be used for this purpose if one desires. However, doctors often recommend cornstarch instead of powder for babies, and I find it is cheaper and works better, perhaps. In very hot weather the crupper must be removed during the daytime at least. In fly time, a light sheet should always be worn over the horse to protect it from flies and a net placed over the tail and allowed to hang to about the hocks, for this same purpose. I generally use a burlap bag, and split one side of it and pin it with three pins to the sheet. This works very well.

If the crupper has not been worn for some time, it must first be adjusted very loose and left that way for about a month before tightening it a single hole, after which it may be tightened very gradually, always loose enough so that there is some slack in the straps supporting the crupper. When the tail is setting quite high, the top straps should be loosened about two holes at night, as otherwise there is a strain on it when the horse lies down, and it may cause the horse to slip the crupper over its back and thus learn to get it off. Many of the later types of tail set harnesses have elastic in the top straps which support the crupper. This type need not be loosened at night, as the elastic will give enough to prevent the animal from slipping the crupper and will remain snug and comfortable at all times. The side straps are fastened snugly, but never tightly. The one big fault every novice makes in adjusting the tail set, is that he gets the crupper too tight. If I could only get the point across, that loosely adjusted cruppers make for good tails as well as high tails, when the crupper fits the horse, my purpose in this whole article will be served.

CARE OF STABLES AND STALLS

Stalls should be cleaned out thoroughly at least once each day, and in most cases they will be picked several times a day in addition. This picking takes but little time and saves much bedding and time in the morning when the stalls are being cleaned, as it makes the job easier. Many people who have but one or two horses and take care of them themselves, will not have time to pick the stalls several times a day. In this case, I would suggest that one try to break his horse to be clean in its stall with its droppings. Perhaps this sounds funny, but in many instances it is quite possible to teach a horse to be very clean with its droppings. I have not yet found a way to teach the animal to be clean about urinating. The method used in teaching the animal to be particular where it leaves its droppings, is to determine the corner most generally used and keep that corner free of straw. At first, one should examine the stall as often as possible to observe if the animal has made a mistake and, if so, he should move the pile to the corner reserved for that purpose. When the stall is cleaned in the morning a pile of fresh droppings should be left in that corner. Following these directions, one will often be surprised at how clean he can teach many horses to be in the stall, which of course saves both time and bedding.

The tail boards and corners of the stall should be swept down occasionally and kept fairly free from cobwebs which form overnight. Feed boxes and water fountains or buckets should be kept clean and washed when necessary. A pinch of powdered charcoal placed in the feed boxes will help keep them sweet and fresh. The entire stable, tack room and all, should be swept out at least once a day and kept straightened up and clean. There is no reason for allowing stables to get and stay untidy and dirty. Windows in the stable need to be washed occasionally the same as windows in the house do, and cobwebs and dust have no place in a well run stable.

The stable may be easier to keep clean and neat if one has a specified place for everything and everything is always returned to that place after being used. There should be racks for hanging forks, brooms, rakes, and other implements. Nothing looks quite as untidy to me as a fork hung up with several pieces of straw still attached to it. If anything is broken, it should be immediately repaired or replaced, or placed in some location where it will be remembered when the time comes for replacement or repair. It is cheaper always to keep things up in proper repair, than to let them go until the whole thing needs to be replaced. It is attention to these little details that makes the difference between a well ordered stable and an untidy one.

CARE OF TACK

One should have a different bridle for each horse, so that once it is adjusted properly it will stay that way. All tack should be cleaned after each time it is used. Generally the mornings are the busy times in the stables, and when the horse is brought in from a workout, a wet sponge should be handy to wash off the bits, after which the bridle will probably be hung in the work room until the afternoon when it will be cleaned. If the weather is warm and the horse has been sweating profusely, a damp sponge may be used to remove excess sweat from the saddle before it is placed on another horse, or hung in the work room to be properly cleaned. Harness is generally cleaned but once a week, but show harness should be cleaned after each time it is used. Break carts and jog carts should be washed off about once a week also, as well as tail set harness, halters, and lead straps.

If all tack is cleaned as often as stated here, it is a very simple chore requiring but little time. Excess dandruff or gummy dirt, such as accumulates where two straps rub together or where a strap rubs on the horse, may be scraped off with a dull knife, after which the piece should be thoroughly washed with pure castile or glycerine soap. If glycerine soap is used this will be all the care that bridles or tan leather straps will require. However, as glycerine soap is soluble in water, and saddles if left in this condition will spot if they get wet, they therefore require a saddle dressing of some sort. It is generally applied with a sponge or soft cloth and shined with another soft cloth as soon as dry. Only the seat and skirts need to be so treated. Black straps will require an occasional dressing with a black harness dressing, or they may be washed with a regular black harness soap which contains a black dressing. Patent leather parts, such as blinders and colored nose bands are probably best treated with vaseline.

Very little oil should be used on most leather goods. A little neatsfoot oil occasionally is no doubt a good thing, but too much will rot both leather and stitching. I like to use olive oil over the complete saddle, when first breaking in a new one. It will require about three coats, about a week apart. A very little neatsfoot oil may be used once or twice on new bridles, until they are slightly darkened and broken in, after which perhaps once in two or three months, a little may be used on that part which buckles into the bits and which is apt to get wet quite often. A little neatsfoot oil may be used on the harness a couple of times a year. Parts of the saddle may have an application of neatsfoot oil now and then; that is, those parts which are hard to get at with a sponge and are thus seldom touched. However, never apply it to the seat, as it will stain the rider's clothes and blister him; and never put it on the pad which touches the horse, at it will blister the horse also. Bits, stirrups, and other hardware should be washed and dried each day. This will keep them in pretty good condition. About once a week they will need to be polished with steel wool and soap, or any good metal polish.

If tack is kept up in shape all the time, it is easy to keep clean, but if one allows it to get in bad shape, it becomes quite a chore. Here again, repairs and replacements must be made immediately.

Chapter VI

BREEDING PRINCIPLES

In this chapter we shall not attempt to give an exhaustive treatise on Breeding Principles; rather, we shall give some of the general rules which have been found to be correct through long careful experiments and by keeping complete records over many thousands of cases by those who have devoted their lives to this subject. It is only in this way that any true facts may be ascertained. A few cases may seem to prove almost anything. We hope to arouse the readers' interest in Breeding Principles to such a point that they will give the subject further study.

The following are a few of the questions which we will discuss, the answers to which the breeder will do well to try to discover, before he wastes valuable time and money in blindly groping:

Can the effects of environment be inherited?

Can variations be directly controlled? To what extent is evolution a gradual process, and to what extent may advances be made suddenly, such as "sports"?

What are the proper standards for selections? How much emphasis should be placed on utility and how much on appearance?

To what extent is individual excellence a safe guide to breeding powers?

What part is played by the parents and what part by the more remote ancestors?

What is the relative influence of the sire and the dam?

Are they constant?

Does Telegony exist?

What are the advantages and dangers of close breeding? Are they real or only probable?

Will a family or strain finally run out?

Can breeding be made to pay?

Every individual is the product of three forces; namely, inheritance, environment, and training. The breeder is interested in training only from the standpoint of ascertaining the relative excellence of breeding stock. Thus, if he breeds to a champion performer, he knows at least that that individual has the ability within itself to perform correctly. Whether it also has the power to transmit that quality is an unknown quantity until the offspring has also gone through a course of training, which is designed to bring out these characteristics for which he is breeding. Training, of course, adds no new characteristics but only develops those already possessed. An individual which has not been trained may be just as good a breeder as the individual which has been trained, as training is an acquired characteristic, and no acquired characteristic can be inherited. However, the individual that has been trained to perfection has the advantage in the eyes of the prospective breeders of proving that it has the ability within itself to absorb said training.

It is now generally thought that Darwin placed too much emphasis on the environment of an individual. The individual can transmit only those characteristics which have been handed on to it through the chromosomes of the fertilized egg cell from which it was produced. Each sperm cell of the male or ovum of the female carries half of these characteristics, and when united they form the complete embryo. Here, then, is the only place that ac-

quired characteristics may be passed on. If the parent is in a weakened condition, it must affect these life-giving cells and be passed on. Therefore, colts should be sought from healthy, properly fed, and prepotent parents. More will be said later of other qualities to look for in the parents. If the colt is properly fed and cared for, then environment has done all for it that is possible.

I fully realize that the word "characteristic" as here used is used incorrectly and is being unduly dignified. What is meant, of course, is the intensity or lack of intensity of a certain trait. Thus, we say that one horse has speed and another has none. It is easy to realize that both animals have a degree of speed, but that one has a propensity for much greater speed than the other. While one may be noted for its swiftness, the other has not enough to call attention to the fact. Thus it is with all characteristics; however, as this usage is very general, I will continue to use it to avoid ambiguity.

One point for which the breeder must be on the alert is the fact that while acquired characteristics are not inherited, the predisposition for them are. While a colt does not have curbs, splints, jacks, and so forth at birth, it may be foaled with a weakness in that direction, in which case they may develop at the first opportunity. For the practical breeder there is little difference between an animal being born with a constitutional weakness and one being born with a predisposition in that direction, which at the first opportunity is almost certain to develop that weakness. Therefore, the breeder should seek colts from healthy parents. The one exception to that rule is the case where the parent has acquired an unsoundness under conditions in which any horse would have acquired it.

The final and highest basis for the selection of breeding stock is by the performance of their offspring. With young or untried individuals this, of course, is impossible; and here blood lines, performance, and individual excellence must be relied upon. Then, the trial-and-error method must be used in establishing a "nick." We now believe that long pedigrees are futile and that any ancestor beyond the third generation contributes so little to an individual's make-up, that it is not worth while to even consider blood lines any farther back than that, unless there is evidence of intensive inbreeding or close breeding. This, as we shall see later, may have the effect of carrying on all characteristics. The following is quoted with permission from the book "Genetics," by Donald F. Jones:

"Since any ancestors beyond the immediate parents can be absolutely eliminated from the hereditary make-up of any particular individual, something more than pedigree must justify an evaluation based upon the qualities of an ancestor which may or may not have been carried on."

In this connection it is interesting to note the percentage that each ancestor transmits to the offspring. It is generally believed that if all animals are equally prepotent, the immediate parents contribute fifty per cent, the grandparents twenty-five per cent, and so on down. In which case, each individual parent contributes but twenty-five per cent, and each grandparent but six and one-quarter per cent, etc. In this way we can see how quickly the blood or relationship is diffused. By the fifth generation each ancestor contributes less than one-tenth of one per cent. Of course, in any method of figuring percentages, we must remember that this is only making an average. In actual fact, due to each ancestor transmitting only half the characteristics, they may not be divided equally from the way they were received from the parents. One or the other probably had been more potent, making his characteristics more readily transmitted. In that way, one individual ancestor may soon be completely lost and another may contribute much more than its share.

To be a little more specific, let us suppose that A is the offspring from B and C, who supposedly have each contributed half of A's characteristics. But, perhaps B is more intensely bred than C and the offspring A has characteristics more like B. Therefore, he will likely transmit more

ILLUSTRATION XXII

OAKHILL CHIEF

Sired by Stonewall King, owned by Miss Jean McLean, Green Acres Farm, Portsmouth, Virginia. Grand Champion Five-Gaited Saddle Horse of 1943, need more be said. Lee Roby up.

ILLUSTRATION XXIII

BEAU GENIUS 15613

An excellent type Saddlebred stallion, sired by King's Genius, and out of Hazel Love, by Guided by Love, second dam by Rex Peavine. Notice the natural high all-around action and the near perfect Saddle Horse conformation, as would be expected from such breeding. Owned by Brandtjen Farms, Farmington, Minn.

of B's characteristics than of C's. Now, if he is bred to another individual tracing to B, the result is likely to be very much like B, and C's characteristics may be lost entirely. Variation within the race, of course, must be taken into consideration in this type of analysis. I have made these statements involving as little mathematics as possible for the non-mathematical reader, although any breeder should be a bookkeeper and a statistician as well.

An animal may have all the qualities desired, yet for some reason may fail to pass them on to his offspring; while another, not as perfect an individual, may produce better than himself. For this reason, when choosing breeding stock, one should demand: First, that they have good pedigrees, which means that the immediate ancestors were good individuals and produced excellent individuals; second, that the individual in question is of very good type and possesses as many desirable characteristics as possible; and third, and by far the most important, that he has proven himself a producer of the type of offspring desired. It is always wise to examine as many offspring as possible from an individual one is considering for breeding stock.

We shall try to explain partially why some animals may not breed as good as themselves, while others seem to breed better than themselves. We must not lose sight of the laws of variation of all living things, and with two excellent individuals there is still a difference. Excellence is in degree only. One animal may not be quite as well born as another, but may have had the very best of environment and training and thus be considered an excellent individual. In this case, he may not breed as good as himself, because he cannot pass on the effects of environment and training, but only those characteristics imparted to him through heredity. On the other hand, another individual may have been extremely well born, but may not have had quite the environment or training to bring out the very best within him, or he may have met with an accident which curtailed his progress. In either case, he may breed better than himself.

Again, one animal may be a good individual but, having his blood so dispersed, may not be able to transmit those characteristics regularly. For instance, I know a particular stud that we will call A, while he is an excellent individual, a glance at his pedigree shows almost every good horse in the book but absolutely no concentration of one type or family. For some reason, he has combined the best within himself but lacks the ability to transmit those characteristics. He gets about one good colt in two score, and all his colts look different. On the other hand, a mare I know of has the most pure Denmark pedigree that has ever been my privilege to see. There is not a single outcross for five generations. Result—all her colts look alike and all have been better than average. I doubt if there is a living stud that is bred strong enough to breed intensely enough to overcome her strong pedigree.

The foregoing partially answers the question as to whether the sire or the dam contributes the most to the offspring. All things being equal, many persons believe the mare will contribute the most, as the relationship is somewhat closer, and after foaling she sets an example for the colt for a period of about six months. She, therefore, influences the early environment also. On the other hand, all things are never equal. Mendelism, which we shall take up a little later on, has much to do with which parent contributes the most to the offspring. Parents whose characteristics are dominant are apt to have the most influence in that respect on the offspring. We have pretty well established the dominant and recessive colors in horses, but other characteristics may also be governed by Mendel's laws, and it is harder to determine which of these are dominant and which are recessive. Horsemen have long believed that the size of the foal is dependent primarily upon the dam. Recent experiments have proved this to be correct. It is now believed that some substance within the mare governs the size of the foal. Experimentally, Shires and Shetlands have been crossed both ways, and foals out of Shire mares by Shetland stallions were about three times as large at birth as foals out of Shetland mares by Shire stallions. Foals normally are approximately 7 per cent of the weight of their dams, with some variation with individuals.

Other than the above, the parent that is the more intensely bred will in most cases be the most prepotent. That is, a Thoroughbred stallion will ordinarily have a bigger influence over a colt from a cold blooded mare than she will have. As in this country we trace back the pedigree on the stallion's side and, as a rule, pay more attention to the selection of the stallion than we do the mare, a stallion is apt to be more intensely bred and, therefore, more prepotent.

Too many people do not consider the mare enough. One must remember that no matter how good a stallion is he cannot make up for deficiencies in a poor mare. Both parents must be considered and both must be good in order to get good colts. It is generally thought that they should complement each other.

It is, of course, much harder to choose the mare according to the performance of her offspring than it is the stallion. If she has been a show mare, she probably will not be bred until about ten or twelve years of age. There is nearly a year of pregnancy and three to five more years before we can see how good the colt will turn out. By this time, the mare is well up in years and will not be good for many more colts. On the other hand, the stallion may start breeding mares at the age of three and may have several colts a year instead of only one. In a few years this gives us much more of a chance to judge the average quality of his colts, rather than depending on only one or two, as we must do with the mare.

There has always been a round table discussion in breeding circles on the matter of whether a male influences not only his own offspring, but later offspring the same female may have. This is called telegony, or the influence of previous impregnation. Many experiments have been carried on to ascertain if this is true. While in some few isolated cases, results may seem to indicate that telegony actually takes place, due to the laws of variation of all living things, anything may happen in an isolated case and true results from many thousands of cases definitely prove that no such thing exists. Some few dog breeders still feel that a full-blooded bitch that once gets mixed up with a mongrel is forever after useless for breeding purposes. Most breeders and biologists now attribute these few cases that seem to prove telegony to atavism, or reversion. They declare that there is no such thing as telegony.

Believers in telegony must presuppose one of four things:

First, that the male exerts an impression on the nervous system of the female at the time of impregnation, that in turn affects the fetus of not only this but of later matings also.

Second, that the sperm in some way fertilizes the womb or some part of the female herself so that it influences later offspring. It was once thought that the female herself was fertilized; now we know that this is not the case and that it is the ovum only being fertilized by the sperm.

Third, that the sperm fertilizes not only the ripe ovum but in some way partially fertilizes the unripe ova that are still in the ovaries.

Or, fourth, that the sperm cells lie dormant for years in the womb, and when mating reoccurs again spring into life and aid in fertilizing the ovum.

In the first place, many people believe that the fetus is more dependent upon the mother than is actually the case. The fact is that the fetus is dependent upon the mother for nourishment only. There is no nerve connection between the mother and the fetus, and an impression upon the brain of the mother has no effect upon the growing embryo. This also disposes of the idea some people have—that a mother can mark the growing fetus during pregnancy.

The second supposition has already been taken care of.

For the third proposition, there is no reason to think

that the unripe ova are in any condition to be fertilized, even if the sperm could reach them in the ovaries. This, of course, is an impossibility even if the sperm could pass up the Fallopian tubes.

And, the fourth idea, that the sperm lies dormant is also preposterous beyond all reason. It is known that they are expelled after a short time, and in any case, they die within a few days. If they did not die, there would be a succession of births from a single mating. And, the idea that two sperm cells can be used in fertilizing one egg cell has been proven incorrect. Even in multiple births, such as swine, if the sow is served by two different boars at a single heat, part of the offspring will partake of the nature of one and part of the nature of the other, but none will give any evidence of having two fathers. Therefore, there is no reason for not breeding to a mare which has formerly been mated to a stallion of an undesirable type.

Now, we shall briefly study Mendel's laws. Mendel himself experimented with shapes and sizes of plants, and when his works were first published no one gave them much attention. Since the first part of this century, however, Mendel's laws have generally been recognized to be correct; not only as he discovered them, but to have a wider variety of application extending to all animals and plants. All scientific breeders today take these laws into consideration. These laws have to do with cases where there are two or more colors, shapes or sizes, and where one is dominant to the other. For instance, in horses it has been found that the color black is dominant to the color chestnut. Therefore, if a pure-line black horse is bred to a pure-line chestnut, the progeny will be black; however, it will carry the recessive trait of chestnut, although unseen. If two of these blacks mate they will, in all probability, produce three blacks and one chestnut. In small animals and plants, this ratio always takes place. In larger animals, the law of average will cause it to take place when a great number of cases are taken into consideration, but in a single instance, it is impossible to accurately determine just what the result will be.

Now, we shall see just why this ratio is true. In the first instance the result is always BC, a hybrid black. B black, C chestnut order color of the individual first. As black is dominant, the individual looks black and cannot be distinguished from a pure-line black, except by observing the behavior of the offspring. From the mating of two BC individuals the following can be expected: three blacks and one chestnut. The chestnut in this case is pure line, and one of the blacks also. The two other blacks are hybrid blacks and will behave as the former two. Thus,

Male B with female B – BB
Male B with female C – BC
Male C with female B – CB (BC)
Male C with female C – CC

This is the way the colors may unite and as BC and CB are essentially the same combination; B, the dominant, should be written first. We, therefore, get the ratio above which is three blacks and one chestnut. The diagram for this follows. It must be understood that this depends upon the laws of chance. In no single instance can positive predictions be made, but if we observe enough cases this ratio will be found correct.

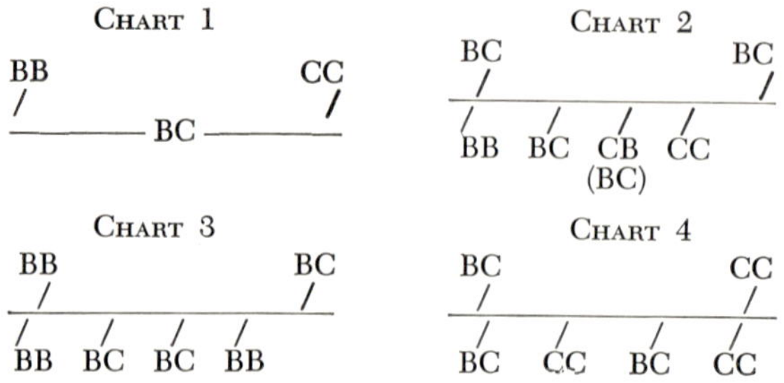

If the pure line unites with the hybrid, the result will be half pure line and half hybrid. For instance, if BB unites with BC the result will be all black horses, but two of them will be hybrid blacks (*Chart* 3), and if BC unites with CC the result will be two chestnuts and two blacks, the latter two, of course, are hybrid blacks (*Chart* 4).

Now, of course, in the case of colors in horses, there is such a variety that no accurate laws can be worked out to give the exact color of the offspring, but one may have more of an idea of what he may expect if he will remember that all recessive colors may or may not be carried within the chromosomes of the dominant individual. Chestnut is recessive to all colors. Gray and roan are considered dominant to all colors. Following in order are brown, bay, and black. From this we see that two chestnuts can only produce a chestnut. A black and a chestnut are almost equally apt to produce either a black or a chestnut, unless the black has a reputation of producing all black colts. Two blacks can produce only blacks or chestnuts. Grays and roans are liable to produce almost any color at almost any time. Few of them are pure line. We generally figure that a gray stallion will produce about fifty per cent gray colts.

Nothing but bays may be crossed for several generations and finally produce a black or chestnut. This is due, of course, to the fact that during this time hybrid bays have been foaled, carrying chestnut as a recessive trait. Constitutional weakness may be recessive and, in this way, be carried on for several generations without being seen before cropping out. In this case, the breeder can do nothing but look on helplessly. He can, however, feel sure that this sort of thing will happen but seldom.

All the older writers on breeding insisted on the fact that like begets like. We can see now that this may not always be the case, at least if visible characteristics only are taken into consideration. We should change that to, "Like begets like OR the likeness of a previous ancestor."

Here then is another reason for studying the pedigrees as well as the progeny of the animal one intends to breed to.

Darwin discovered that at times in plant, as well as in animal, breeding an almost new type to any one previously known springs up. These he called "sports." He paid little attention to them, however, and as he allowed them to breed back to ordinary types, they soon ceased to exist, failing to reproduce their kind. He considered the gradual process of evolution the only way for fixing types. Today, we have found that these "sports" or mutants, as we call them, are usually very prepotent and if bred for these characteristics closely, they will establish a new type. Both Gaines Denmark 61 and Justin Morgan have been called "sports."

Now, we come to the much mooted question, "To inbreed or not to inbreed." There has been much said and written on this subject, both pro and con. In earlier times most people were horror struck at the idea of breeding close relatives, such as brother and sister or parent and child. Most people did not even believe in breeding cousins, which amounts to the same thing in a lesser degree. This prejudice was, no doubt, started by the fact that it was noticed that inbreeding was many times followed by bad results, and, not knowing the laws of heredity, it was concluded that inbreeding was against God's laws. Because public opinion is hard to break, it was a long time before much experimenting was done along these lines. During the last century, however, many experiments were carried out on intensive breeding. The results at first seemed to show a greater percentage of loss of size, greater percentage of sterility, and abnormalities appeared. As these experiments progressed, using only the very best individuals, they seemed to be strong again, and healthy, and altogether superior individuals to those with which the experiments were started. Most of the bad effects lasted about four or five generations, after which they kept diminishing. We can see that by that time most of them were weeded out. If studied carefully, these experiments seem to indicate that these undesirable characteristics are recessive traits and crop out more frequently in the earlier generations. Later on, as we get more pure-line dominant qualities, there is less chance of recessive traits cropping out. By inbreeding, many of these recessive qualities may finally be lost entirely.

Thus, we can see that inbreeding is the way to purify any breed and it is nature's way to eliminate undesirable qualities. There is probably not a domestic breed of any animal today that has not been inbred quite a lot. This is the way all breeds and types are fixed. Inbreeding intensifies all qualities *good* or *bad* because the genetic constitution is fairly homogeneous. The breeder who practices inbreeding must be especially careful to weed out every single individual that is not up to standard in any way.

The practical breeder must remember that the above experiments were carried on primarily with guinea pigs or mice that are fast breeding. The practical breeder of horses must breed to make money, as well as improve the breed. Therefore, he must produce colts, the greater part of which will sell well the first generation. He must, for financial reasons, at times resort to outcrossing. Outcrossing generally only masks or covers up certain weaknesses. Outcrossing may produce excellent individuals in the first generation, but they probably will not be able to transmit those qualities to their offspring, or at least not to the greater percentage of them. The intensively bred individual is the one that breeds true and transmits his characteristics with regularity. It is possible that an endowed stock farm that did not need to bother trying to make money might be able to produce a race of super horses within a century. This, of course, would have to be done by the strictest kind of selection and inbreeding. These super horses should be able to transmit their qualities with remarkable regularity. Perhaps some day some wealthy public-spirited horse lover will endow such a farm for an experiment of this kind.

The following are the relative points of inbreeding and outcrossing for which I am indebted to Mr. Eugene Davenport from his book, "Principles of Breeding" (quoted by permission of Ginn and Co. Publishers, 1907). We shall use the numbers 1, 2, and 3 to denote the range of intensity of a single character. As for instance, speed in a horse: 1 denotes little speed, 2 denotes average speed, and 3 denotes extreme speed. Now, if we exclude inbreeding, we have three possible unions: 3 and 2, 3 and 1, and 2 and 1. If we also include inbreeding, we have three other possible unions: 3 and 3, 2 and 2, and 1 and 1. Now, which gives the best results?

OUTCROSSING

MATING	MIDPARENT	OFFSPRING
3 & 2	$\frac{3 \& 2}{2}$	2.5
3 & 1	$\frac{3 \& 1}{2}$	2
2 & 1	$\frac{2 \& 1}{2}$	1.5

INBREEDING

MATING	MIDPARENT	OFFSPRING
3 & 3	$\frac{3 \& 3}{2}$	3
2 & 2	$\frac{2 \& 2}{2}$	2
1 & 1	$\frac{1 \& 1}{2}$	1

From this we can see that by inbreeding we get the same means as with outcrossing but with greater extremes. Inbreeding is seen to have the wider range. By continually eliminating the inferior, we can easily see how quickly we can raise the average quality. We must remember that this is all we can ever hope to do. There will always be the law of variation, and some individuals will always be better than others. It is possible, however, to raise the average much higher than it is today.

True breeding with these ideals is very expensive, however; while mere reproduction is comparatively cheap. Man cannot afford the wholesale destruction of numbers that nature uses to accomplish her purpose.

The man who sets out to inbreed must not depend solely upon pedigree any more than any other breeder. Rather, he should be more particular than anyone else to select only excellent individuals who are proven producers, for this force works both ways. If unworthy individuals are allowed in the herd, the breeder is already foredoomed to failure. Many people suppose that inbreeding tends to a greater percentage of sterile animals. In this connection, fertility should be a prime consideration for the selection of breeding stock. Beware of the shy breeder for nature has already foredoomed that family to extinction. There is no reason, however, to suspect that a free breeding family will ever become extinct, no matter how rigidly inbred; rather, that should make them more prolific.

In breeding for hunters, a cold blooded mare of approved type is often put to a Thoroughbred stallion. This is a distinct outcross. With Saddle Horses we can make certain outcrosses without losing the right to register the progeny. We have three principal Saddle Horse families in the American Saddle Horse Registry: The Denmarks, Chiefs, and Highlanders. At first, they had little relationship; however, today they have been interbred quite a lot. Before the breeder attempts to cross these strains he should be thoroughly familiar with the type and quality of each of these families.

It may safely be assumed that inbreeding may be carried on much more intensely than is now being done by the average breeder. Some writers claim that the best way is once in and once out. They claim that this is the natural way a horse breeds in the wild state. I do not believe this claim can be substantiated. I believe, in the wild state, horses are intensely inbred. Horses, when found in the wild state, are in a very good position to support themselves and survive, but do not have those qualities that we require in them. They are not fine and are generally jug headed and stunted. This latter may be due to insufficient forage, as all such horses gain from two to three inches in height in the first generation when domesticated and properly cared for. However, wild horses are hardy and have good legs, feet, eyes, and wind. In other words, the essentials for them to survive are present. A thorough study of them in the wild state will, I am sure, reveal the fact that they are intensely inbred. They travel in herds or families with one stallion to the herd. He covers all mares in the herd, including his own daughters. He drives off or kills the young stallions as long as he is able. Finally one of his own sons becomes stronger and drives him off, and in turn becomes the leader of the herd. He, in turn, covers all mares in the herd, including mother, sisters, half sisters, and finally his daughters.

A few hints to the breeder. Do not breed scrubs. There is no longer a market for inferior horses, and they will not pay the cost of raising them. Do not breed two individuals which have the same general weakness or faulty conformation. Do not, if you own but one stallion, breed all your mares to him, regardless of blood lines. It is no reflection on your stallion for you to send mares to another; rather, it shows rare intelligence on your part. In the next chapter, we shall discuss care of breeding stock.

Chapter VII

CARE AND MANAGEMENT OF BREEDING STOCK

Owning breeding stock and conducting breeding operations is a very interesting and worthwhile hobby and may be profitable. However, in order to be entirely successful one needs to have a little more knowledge than merely being able to lead the stallion to the mare when she is in heat. Breeding stock requires a little less care and attention than horses in training, but the care they do require is specialized. It may be desirable to make a few general observations before proceeding with detailed instructions.

It goes without saying that one should attempt to breed only the best, as that is the only kind which will pay for the labor involved. It is no more costly to breed good horses than inferior ones, except for the initial investment required. One should exercise the greatest care in selecting his breeding stock, as even the best will produce a certain amount of mediocre offspring. Too many small Saddle Horse breeders breed down instead of up. By this, I mean that the general thought seems to run something like this, "Well, that mare isn't good enough to train, so I'll use her for a brood mare." I know this will be denied, but judging from the conversation of many small owners and an examination of their brood mares, this is the only conclusion at which one can arrive.

The laws of chance govern all breeding operations to a great degree, as from a single mating millions of variations are possible. The more intensely bred, both the sire and dam, the greater chance they will have of being prepotent and carrying on their desirable characteristics. Perhaps if it were economically possible to carry on breeding operations without regard to making them pay, we might be able to produce a race of super horses within about ten generations of very close breeding by completely breeding out undesirable characteristics. But, the fact that close breeding of any kind increases the force of both good and bad characteristics makes inbreeding an unprofitable venture in most cases. There are bound to be too many poor individuals during the first five generations. The practical breeder is forced to outcross, in an attempt to cover up certain undesirable qualities which are in the parent stock. Outcrossing merely covers them up in the offspring and they are liable to crop out in succeeding generations. For these reasons, we can never say with certainty what the offspring from any mating may be, but it has been found that the results are more apt to be those desired if a deficiency in one parent is counter-balanced by selecting a mate which is particularly good in that respect.

Here is an instance I know of that happened to work both ways. One man owned a nice little mare that was extremely fine in the head and neck especially but was slightly peaked in the rump and a little long in the back. He had a choice of two stallions to breed her to. The better known of the two stallions had these same undesirable characteristics and passed them on to his offspring, yet this mare was bred to him in order to get his name on the pedigree of the colt. The colt naturally carried on those faults, which were intensified. Later on another man, with more common sense, bought this mare and kept her in the same locality. He had the mare bred to the other lesser known stallion. This horse was slightly heavy in the neck but otherwise was very fine and well bred and particularly good in the back and over the rump. The colt from this mating, as was to be expected, was far superior to the one by the better known stallion and worth more money, in spite of being by a lesser known sire. Breeding to a stallion with a very good reputation is always a smart idea, but it should not be done blindly without regard to attempting to get a good cross also.

In my opinion, it will pay the breeder to select breeding stock and especially a herd sire whose colts have consistently been of high quality, rather than picking a horse that has a reputation of being a sketchy breeder; that is, one that produces a few exceptional colts and a large number of inferior ones. The breeder himself must depend upon high average quality rather than on one outstanding individual in many. Any good horse is liable to get an outstanding colt at any time by one of those rare but happy "nicks" or crosses. The breeder, however, seldom realizes the big profit from those exceptional individuals, as they do not show up as such until they are nearly matured. By that time, the breeder will, in most cases, have disposed of them at average prices.

CARE OF STALLIONS

The care of stallions is not at all difficult if one but uses a little common sense. Stallions are merely male animals and are not more naturally prone to be mean than mares. In fact, some of the meanest horses I have ever seen have been mares. Of course, some stallions do become mean, especially when boxed up in dark stalls, all alone, and seldom taken out except to breed a mare, and never allowed around a mare except at breeding time. Most men would become insane under those same conditions. Consider the cases of abnormality which take place in our prisons, where men are kept separate or cooped up together for a long period of time, without intercourse with the outside world. Our civilization has come a long way but we have not yet succeeded in finding the ideal way to treat criminals. This may seem a long way removed from the subject at hand, but I merely bring it up to show how nearly like criminals some of our stallions are treated; then we wonder why some of them become mean.

Instead of blaming ourselves and the treatment given some stallions, we believe that stallions are wild animals that cannot be thoroughly tamed. A stallion needs companionship, both human and equine, far more than a mare or a gelding does. He also needs a certain amount of sexual activity in order to keep perfectly healthy. The only place for a stallion is on a breeding farm or some place where he may be stood at service and used often enough to satisfy his actual needs during breeding season. He needs company all the time, particularly the company of mares. He should always be kept in a box stall, the sides of which should be open grill work or bars above the height of about four and a half feet. If possible, he should be kept between two horses, preferably mares. He should be ridden out with mares, both when they are in heat and when they are not. If this is done from colthood, he may be made as amenable as any mare or gelding and perhaps safer. A stallion is not so likely to become frightened, as is a gelding. It is possible to break a stallion just as thoroughly as any other horse, but one must use a little more finesse and must give him as normal a life as possible. If it is possible to turn young colts from a year to two years old out with a brood mare that is in foal and has had her colt weaned, is old enough not to be flighty and not mean, she will teach the colts to respect a mare without hurting them much. Mean mares or young mares may scar a colt.

The stallion must be made to respect the man handling him. He must not be allowed the slightest infraction of rules and yet the whip must be used with great care. A stallion will take just punishment, but will seldom stand for abuse or fighting without fighting back. When he is ridden, he must be taught to understand that he is being taken out for work, not pleasure. When going to serve a mare he must be kept under control. A special bridle should be used for this purpose, and it should never be placed upon the horse unless he is to breed or tease a mare. If just one particular place is always used for breeding mares and for no other purpose, the stallion will soon realize the purpose of that place. When a man takes a stallion out to serve a mare, he should always carry a whip and not allow any misbehavior at any time. Even a stud that is ordinarily quiet may easily get out of hand at this time, unless one is on the alert. This thing of a stallion coming out of a stall on his hind legs and rushing up to the mare is a lot of nonsense.

The stallion must be made to stand quietly, about six feet behind the mare, until ready, before being allowed to approach her. He should then approach her quietly and mount quietly. In some cases it may be necessary to allow him to approach the mare and nuzzle her to help him get ready, but this must not take the form of biting or chewing and should be continued only a few minutes at a time; then he is led away again. One must be careful that he does not kick the mare as he is led away. When breeding the mare, the stallion should be taught to stay there until the job is fully completed. Very often horses get the habit of dismounting too soon. I believe some of this comes from improper handling. Some men become impatient and pull at the horse as soon as they think the job is completed; instead, the horse should be encouraged or even forced to stay there for some time and be allowed to dismount of his own accord. He should never be pulled off. While the stallion is on the mare, assistants may take hold of his front feet, helping to hold him on and teaching him to stay.

The first time the young stallion is used, it may be necessary to allow a certain amount of nuzzling, both at the front and the rear of the mare, but one must be very careful that he does not develop the habit of striking or kicking. The first time, it may take quite a while to get the job done, and a certain amount of leniency may be necessary, but never to the extent that the stallion is in control rather than the handler. The handler must always keep complete control and use any means necessary to achieve and hold that control.

The age to start a stallion to breeding is much debated. My opinions on the subject are merely personal ones formed from personal observations. It seems to me that a well developed, slightly cagey stallion of two years will get along better, become more easily amenable, with less chance of forming the habit of masturbating, if allowed to serve two or three mares during the breeding season. At three years he may serve as many as one every other week and at four years he may serve as many as two a week during a short breeding season. Once a day is about the limit that any horse should be called upon, if he is to keep in condition, and less is better. A matured stallion requires about two services a month during breeding season to keep absolutely healthy.

The problem of masturbating will seldom be encountered if the stallion is kept in a stall between two mares, with bars between, so that they can nuzzle each other at will. It should be remembered that masturbating in horses, as in men, is a solitary vice. This treatment may effect a cure on a young horse that has already started the habit, but it will probably do no good on an aged horse, confirmed in the habit. A very young horse that acts as if it is beginning to learn to masturbate may often be discouraged by tying a stiff brush under the belly. In confirmed cases, it will generally be necessary to resort to the use of either the stallion ring or shield. The ring is placed around the penis just behind the head, quite tight. It must be tight enough to prevent an erection and must be taken off at regular intervals to be cleaned, as well as whenever the stud is to be used for breeding. The shield has sharp teeth on the inner side and is adjusted to hang just in front of the sheath. It is far handier and perhaps should be tried before resorting to the use of the ring.

The stallion's sheath should be washed at regular intervals and always after serving a mare, especially a strange mare, or any mare infected with leucorrhea, as he may become a carrier and infect the rest of the mares. All strange mares should be looked over carefully before being bred. It is true that the presence of durine cannot be positively detected without a blood test, but one should be wary of any mare with swelling along the veins of her belly, especially if accompanied by boil-like eruptions. One should refuse service to such a mare until she has had a blood test, the result of which should be shown to the manager of the stud before any service takes place. If the mare drags either hind leg, it may also indicate the presence of durine. Many mares show no signs of it at all. Little can be done in such cases, although the breeder need not be too concerned, as the U. S. Government has recently carried on quite an extensive examination of breeding stock for this disease, and all that were found to be carriers were destroyed. We may, therefore, expect to find it seldom, if ever.

The stallion should have regular exercise every day, especially during the breeding season. His feeding will be about the same as any other horse his size and weight that is kept up and worked, with the addition of increasing protein feeds during breeding season if the stud has a heavy season. A handful of wheat once a day is an economical way of feeding wheat germ during this time. If the stud is not to be kept up and worked, he should be kept in a large lot of an acre or more, with a shed into which the stud may go for protection from the elements.

BROOD MARES

The care of brood mares is a specialized business in itself and requires special training and knowledge. One should be careful to select brood mares not only for type and blood lines but also and primarily, for the quality of their previous offspring, as the future colts will depend at least as much on the mare as on the stallion.

Most brood mares will come in heat about the seventh day after foaling and stay in heat until about the eleventh or twelfth day. Many breeders advocate breeding in this heat period, claiming that the mare will catch better if bred in this period than in any other. Some believe in breeding on the eighth day, some on the ninth, and a few breed the mare back on the seventh. This practice may be all right if the mare is perfectly healthy, and if she foals late in the spring, and if one wishes the next colt to come earlier. In my experience, I have found that the mare will catch better if bred on the ninth or even the tenth day after foaling than at any other time in this heat period. Much depends upon the particular mare, but she should never be bred back in this heat period if there are any tears, if the mare's pregnancy lasted more than three hundred and forty days, or if there were any signs of a diseased placenta at the time of foaling. A placenta that was retained over one hour after foaling should also be taken as a danger sign, and one should have a veterinary examine such a mare before she is rebred in the first heat period. It has been found, by keeping a large number of complete records, that only about one-third of the mares rebred in the first period after foaling become pregnant from that service. If it is at all possible and practical, I much prefer to wait until the following period before breeding the mare back. This gives the mare more time to rest and more time for her organs to go back into place after foaling. Perhaps about sixty-five to seventy per cent of the mares correctly bred in the second heat period after foaling will catch at that time.

Most older authorities say that the mare will come in heat every eighteen days after the first heat period. This depends a great deal on the particular mare, but I have spent a good part of my life dealing with breeding stock and have kept fairly accurate records, and I find that the greatest majority of mares will go three weeks, rather than eighteen days, from the beginning of one heat period to the next. However, the mare whose records prove that she has been coming in heat every eighteen days will, no doubt, continue to do so; while the mare that has been coming in every three weeks will also generally continue in that way. In other words, there seems to be a greater variation between different mares than in the same mare. This variation may be quite a lot. Some few mares will be found that will come in as often as every two weeks, and some may go nearly four weeks between heat periods.

Many mares will discontinue coming in heat during the hot summer months, whether in foal or not. The fact that a mare does not come back in heat after being bred is not a sure indication that she is in foal. While it is the general rule to try mares back, as a means of determining whether pregnancy has taken place or not, it is not completely accurate. Some mares will quit coming in heat for several months and others only in the summer time, whether in foal or not; while a few mares will continue coming in heat even after they are in foal. Some of this latter type will continue to come in only for a month or so, while some may continue right up to the foaling time.

The only sure way of telling whether or not a mare is in foal is by palpation of the uterus through the rectum. This takes an experienced operator. However, anyone in charge of a number of brood mares, or one who is going to start a breeding farm and does not intend to hire competent help, should surely learn how this is done. The procedure is simple, but in order to become proficient one must have a great deal of practice. He must examine every mare possible, both those known to be in foal and those known not to be in foal, as well as during the different stages in the growth of the fetus. I have heard that some men can make a correct diagnosis after the mare has been bred thirty days, but there are really few men who have had enough practice to come close to that. In most cases it will take about ninety days before one can tell with any degree of accuracy. At any time after that, an experienced man should be able to tell definitely whether or not the mare is in foal. This is really soon enough, as until that time it will do no harm to rebreed the mare if she comes back in heat, even if she is in foal. On the other hand, if the mare is rebred after being in foal for one hundred days, she is liable to abort. By ninety days the fetus is about as big as a rat and can easily be felt by the man examining the mare.

I realize the difficulty one who is not a veterinarian experiences when trying to learn anything of this kind. I myself tried to get perhaps a half-dozen veterinarians to show me how to make this rectal examination before one finally consented to do so. It is seldom necessary to put breeding hopples on a mare to make this rectal examination, although if it is a strange mare, it is a wise precaution. One then washes the under side of the tail, the rectum, and the vulva, as well as his own hands and arms, leaving a good deposit of soap on his arm in order that it may slip into the rectum easier. He then puts his hand into the rectum and pulls out all the feces, cleaning the lower bowel completely. Replacing his hand and arm into the bowel, he feels along the bottom of the rectum until he feels the mouth of the uterus. If he will then follow the uterus along, he may feel each horn and easily determine whether or not the uterus contains a fetus. In this way, the chances of mistaking an ovary or a filled bladder for a fetus is minimized. The careful manager of a breeding farm will generally examine all uncertain mares after they have been bred for about three months. Unknown mares and irregular mares especially should be considered uncertain.

Many mares are very irregular in showing their heat periods. Some of these are in heat for a couple of weeks at a time and others only show in heat every few months. The latter will generally be found to be in a true heat when she does show; however, many mares of this type may not show at all during the breeding season. This is especially true of maiden mares, which may never show at all or at least very slightly. I have found that the best procedure in cases of this type is to examine the mare vaginally and, by careful manipulation, open the mouth of the uterus. Then place her in a stall next to a stallion. In most cases, this type of mare will then show in heat within a short time. More will be said later on about the general practice of opening up the uterus of mares before they are bred.

The other type, irregular mare, is the one that shows in heat most of the time or perhaps is in for about two weeks and then out for one, etc. In cases of this type, the mare may be bred several times without becoming pregnant. Actually, while such a mare may be mentally ready to take the stallion, she is not physically ready for conception to take place and is not in a true heat period during that time. There are two procedures which may be followed on this type of mare. She may be bred every other day all during the heat periods, hoping to catch her when she is in a true heat. This will oftentimes work but may prove fatiguing to the stallion, especially if he is a young horse or if he has a heavy stud season. The more accurate way of doing it is to examine the mare vaginally every other day and only breed her when she is in a true heat. The experienced operator can usually tell, by examination of the mouth of the uterus, whether or not the mare is in a true heat. If the mouth is either very tight or very loose, it is a foolish waste of time to breed her in most cases. The mouth of the uterus should be elastic enough so that one can insert his finger quite easily, but it should not be relaxed.

The mare that is hard to get in foal may be bred with capsules or by other means of artificial impregnation. Capsules are used in two ways: Perhaps the most usual way is to first breed the mare naturally, then insert the hand into the vagina, holding an open capsule, and attempt to scrape some of the deposited semen into the capsule. This is then deposited directly into the uterus. This calls for extreme cleanliness on the part of the operator and even so it may result in infection. No soap should remain on the operator's hand or arm, as it will kill the sperm cells. Rather, after the hands and arms are thoroughly washed in tincture of green soap, followed by careful rinsing in sterile water (either boiled or distilled), some type of vaginal jelly must be used for a lubricant. All dealers in breeders' supplies can furnish a powder which, when mixed with sterile water, forms a sterile, non-irritating, non-antiseptic, slimy lubricant; or one may go to the nearest drug store and purchase a tube of hospital K-Y vaginal jelly already mixed for this purpose.

The better way to practice capsule breeding is to place a breeding bag on the penis of the stallion before he serves the mare. This bag will catch all the semen. Immediately after it is taken off the stallion, it is placed in a container of water, which is kept at about 100 degrees Fahrenheit. The mare's rectum and vulva then is to be thoroughly washed and rinsed well. The operator must cleanse his own hands and arms completely and smear the vaginal jelly over the hand and arm that is to be inserted into the vagina. Meanwhile, an assistant partially fills a capsule from the bag, caps it, and hands it to the operator, who carefully inserts the closed capsule directly into the uterus. A number of capsules may be filled with one service of the stallion, and if the mares are all ready and the semen has been kept at body temperature, they may all be bred at the same time from this single service. I myself, have bred as many as eight mares at one time in this way and have always been more successful in getting them in foal by this method than with natural breeding. It is possible to keep the sperm cells alive for several hours in this way. I have personally kept them alive for about four hours, until such time as I could get to examine them under a microscope. How much longer they can be kept alive and fertile I do not know. It is claimed that for shipping the sperm, it may be quickly frozen and kept that way until time for use. I have never had experience with this. It is true that there is always a slight chance of infection resulting from capsule breeding, but in several hundred procedures of this kind, I have never had a single cause of infection. Primarily, it depends upon the cleanliness of the man doing the job. When practicing artificial impregnation of any kind, one should not take any chances of getting kicked and should always apply breeding hopples before attempting to insert the sperm, for many mares that are otherwise gentle will kick when in heat. I have never had to use a twitch.

One other method of artificial impregnation is quite common. Either the stallion bag or a mare bag may be used. If the former, it is placed in water and kept at about 100 degrees Fahrenheit, the same as before; but if a mare bag is used, it is left in the mare until all mares are bred. An impregnator syringe is used and the semen is drawn into it and then placed into the mare to be bred. In this case, one generally handles the syringe with his right hand and guides it into the uterus with his left. One must be very careful in inserting the tip into the uterus before the semen is expelled; otherwise, he may injure the uterus or fail to get it inserted into the proper place. This calls for the same precautionary technique as the former methods, with the addition that the syringe should be boiled at least fifteen minutes before it is used and between its use on different mares.

When breeding the mare the natural way, she should first be teased until she shows well in heat to insure proper lubrication of her vagina. This may be accomplished in a number of ways. She may be hoppled and teased directly, or if the stallion is in a strong stall, the mare may be led up to him and teased there, in which case, the man must be careful not to get kicked or struck by the mare. Sometimes the stallion may be led up to the mare's stall if it is very strong, and he may be allowed to tease her there or even over a strong fence. In any case, the man must be careful not to get hurt, as well as taking all precautions that neither stallion nor mare gets hurt. The mare must be bred only if she shows well in heat, as proper lubrication of her vagina is necessary to prevent danger of tearing.

The mare's uterus should not be opened up unless there is a very good reason for doing so. Too many stallion owners believe they have to open up every mare's uterus before she is bred. Many are not sure just what they are attempting to do, and others do not use proper cleansing precautions. It is very easy to introduce infection at this time, and nine mares out of ten would be better off if they were not touched. If it is necessary to open up the uterus, the same cleansing technique must be used as when breeding the mare artificially, and a vaginal jelly must be used to facilitate the entrance of the arm into the vagina. The mare is then tied or preferably held and hoppled. Then the outside of the vagina and rectum are washed and rinsed well. The type of hopple that passes over the neck and to a pulley through which a rope is passed and tied to each hock is, no doubt, the safest, from all angles. The hopple should be tight enough that the mare cannot kick with either one or two feet. Her tail should then be bandaged to prevent loose hair from getting into the vagina and to facilitate the stallion's entrance. Many men advocate the use of a twitch, but it has been my experience that very few mares that are properly in heat will need a twitch, and they will be more likely to stick if the twitch is not used. On some maiden mares, a twitch will be found necessary, but one will find that that is not the case with the majority of older mares which have had colts previously, except perhaps a few that are being bred back in the first heat period and are very foolish about their colts. I prefer to handle all mares with colts by placing the colt in a loose box stall and allowing the mare to put her head at the door or bars. When handled in this way, there is no chance of getting the colt hurt, and in most cases, the mare will be perfectly amenable while being bred if she is truly in heat.

The stallion must not be allowed to mount until both he and the mare are ready. The man leading the stallion will then pull the mare's tail out of the way, and it may be necessary for him to help insert the penis. This should never be done by pulling on the penis even slightly, but rather by pushing it back and guiding it into the vagina. After the mare is bred, different methods are used to cause her to draw up and hold the semen until some of the sperm cells have had time to find their way into the uterus. Some believe in splashing cold water on the vagina, others lead the mare around for four or five minutes and do not allow her to squat. We must understand that the semen is not deposited directly into the uterus, but rather into the vagina and from there some of the sperm cells must find their way into the uterus. For conception to take place, one of them must find its way to the ovum and fertilize it. As there are several millions of sperm cells thrown off each time and each carries half of the characteristics of the new fetus and only one may fertilize the ovum, we can readily see that it is pure chance which characteristics will be carried on. This, of course, is the reason for such a great variation between full brothers and sisters, etc.

In the care of the pregnant mare, the nearer one can approach the natural state the better. She may be ridden or worked up until about two months before foaling time, after which work must be lightened materially, and the mare should not be heated up after that time. Perhaps the safest but most expensive way of keeping brood mares is to have separate lots of about half an acre each and surrounded by a board fence. The mare should have a stall at least sixteen feet square, into which she may run at will, plenty of fresh water available at all times, as well as shade, and should be fed regularly if pasture is not sufficient. In most cases, especially if one has a large number of brood mares, this procedure is too expensive.

In Illinois, I had an ideal arrangement for a large number of brood mares, which consisted of a good pasture, about eighty acres of which was woods, with plenty of underbrush that the mares could pass through to brush flies and insects off. There was a good stream running through the pasture, but I also had a large cement watering trough, in which fresh water could be kept at all times. In the winter, I used a tank heater to keep the water slightly warm. The pasture was good enough to keep the mares fat all summer without additional feed. In this pasture there was a very large old barn about one hundred and forty feet long and nearly seventy feet wide. It was high and had doors on each end, which were large enough to drive through with a hay rack. We built two rows of hay racks the long way of the barn but allowed plenty of room on each end for mares to go around the racks. This left us a center aisle about thirty feet wide and two outside aisles about twenty feet wide. Thus, the mares could feed from any of four positions, which allowed plenty of room for timid mares and helped prevent the mares from fighting. I may add here, it is impossible to keep a large group of mares from fighting; however, if they are mares that have been together and have a lot of room to run in, certain ones soon establish their positions as bosses and others learn to keep out of their way. New mares should never be turned in with this group if they are heavy in foal, as a fight will almost always result, and very often several of the mares will abort, as the result of being kicked.

We had boxes for loose salt and minerals in each corner of this barn. In that country, it is necessary to feed additional minerals to breeding stock. We had large grain creeps out of doors for the colts, which could be converted into grain bunks for the brood mares in the winter time. There was a wooden corral in one corner into which we could run the mares to be caught or tested. The north end of the barn was closed in the winter time, and during a storm all mares could huddle together in one corner and keep much warmer than if they were in separate box stalls as they are in most barns. During a storm or blizzard, they will huddle together and stay that way until the storm abates, and there will be no fighting either. During the summer time, we left both doors open. This allowed a draft through. On warm days the mares would stand in the barn all day, out of the heat and away from most of the flies. They would come out to graze in the evening, at which time the colts would frisk and play for all they were worth.

Of course, an all wooden fence is by far the best and safest for horses, but a three-strand electric fence of smooth wire will work very well with but a slight danger of accidents once the mares become accustomed to it.

Any number of good arrangements may be made for brood mares, and they can stand quite severe weather if they have plenty of food and shelter from the elements.

The feeding of brood mares will depend a great deal on the part of the country in which one is located and other economic problems. In the South, lespedeza forms a very good all around hay and need be the only kind fed. Where it is available, soybean hay makes about the best brood mare feed I have ever been able to find. If this is fed, the mares should also have free access to a stack of oat straw, and a little alfalfa is desirable, but not necessary. In many parts of the country, soybean hay is not available. Whenever alfalfa hay is used, it should be cut after it is in the bloom and allowed to age about two or three months before being fed. If this is practiced, one will encounter no ill effects from feeding it, and it may form the principal portion of the brood mare's feed. Timothy hay or a mixture of timothy and clover hay may furnish a part of the brood mare's hay rations, the balance being alfalfa.

In the midwest, wild hay may be used instead of timothy, but timothy, wild hay, or Sudan grass is never sufficient in itself. Hay made from Sudan grass contains very little food value for the amount of weight consumed. Oat hay or straw may be fed along with any of the legumes, but it is not sufficient in itself. Many people feed a great deal of cane to brood mares; however, I am not much of a believer in sweet feeds, except in specialized cases or for a mere variation of diet. Cane especially seems to be hard on the kidneys of both mares and colts and will often cause worms. For awhile, horses seem to do very well on it, but they soon begin to show poor condition. If it must be fed, it should form not more than a third of the roughage, the balance being made up of one of the legumes and grass hay or grain hay. Corn stocks may be substituted for cane and in my opinion, are better.

On the whole, brood mares will get along pretty well on quite a large variety of feeds; the important thing is that they have plenty, especially in the winter time and during the last two months of pregnancy. One should also remember that the mare that has been bred back is actually eating to furnish nourishment for three—herself, her colt, and the fetus within her. The fetus gets the greatest portion of its growth during the last two months of pregnancy. If necessary, the brood mare should also have free access to minerals. I like to have at least two kinds of roughage for brood mares, one of which is a legume. Hay should be kept in front of mares at all times, in racks so constructed that the mares cannot pull the hay out and waste it. If there is sufficient pasture in summer time, that is the best food of all.

Plenty of oats, about two gallons a day per mare, should be fed during fall, winter, and spring. Crushed oats is always superior to whole oats. Corn should be fed only in the cold winter months, about four to six large ears of good yellow corn per mare. Grain need only be fed once a day. There should always be a plentiful supply of salt. If it is at all possible to keep it under cover, loose salt is by far the best, as horses simply will not get enough for their actual needs if block salt is fed. One should investigate his locality and find out if the soil and water contain iodine in sufficient quantities, and if not, iodized salt should always be provided. Lack of iodine varies a great deal in the same general locality, and the best way is to take a sample of the soil from the pasture and the water used and send it to the state college to be tested. At the same time, the mineral content of both soil and water should be examined in the same way. A deficiency in minerals causes weak bones and stunted growth. Any deficiency in the soil and water should be made up by feeding any of the commercial preparations. The veterinarian in any locality can generally supply one's needs along these lines. The mineral deficiency in the soil in pastures may be built up, and it is up to the manager to see that this is done. This is a good place to dispose of horse manure in the fall. If done during the summer, the horses will refuse to eat the grass around the places where the manure has been spread. If one has trouble getting the mares to eat sufficient quantities of commercial minerals, he may mix them with loose salt so that they will be taken at the same time the salt is eaten.

Leucorrhea is quite common in brood mares. It may be carried from one mare to another by the stallion, which is a very good reason for washing off the stallion's penis after he has served a mare. It is a whitish discharge and has no apparent ill effect on either the mare or the colt. It may often be cleared by a series of soda water douches.

The mare should be watched very closely as foaling time approaches and be brought into the stable or foaling shed at least two weeks before the colt is expected. The gestation period for mares is supposed to be three hundred and forty days, or a little over eleven months. This will come very close to average time, but individual mares may vary as much as a month, one way or the other. It is far better to have the colt come a couple of weeks too soon than to have the mare carry the colt much longer than the usual three hundred and forty days, as it should always be taken as a danger sign if the mare is late in delivering her foal. The mare should seldom vary much from her usual time in carrying her foal. The variation between mares will be found much greater than with any one particular mare.

In warm weather a good place for the mare to have her foal is in a foaling lot in which there is a foaling stall about sixteen feet square that the mare may run in and out of at will. There is less danger of infection if she foals outside on clean grass, but, if trouble occurs, it means that one will have to work with flash lights, as nearly all mares foal during the night. If the weather is quite cold, the mare should be provided with a foaling stall, either in the main barn or a good warm foaling stall in which she may be kept up at night as the time for foaling draws near. This foaling stall should be well disinfected before the mare is placed therein, and especially if that stall has been occupied by a mare which was in any way sick, such as having a cold or distemper. The stall should be kept extremely clean and bedded fairly heavy with short rather than long straw. After foaling, common cleanliness suggests cleaning it out entirely and burning or otherwise destroying the afterbirth.

Both colt and mare may be turned out in a lot in the daytime the third day after foaling if the weather is not inclement or terribly cold, as the colt will then be strong enough to get around with its mother and take care of itself pretty well. It is generally better not to turn them out in the pasture until the colt is about a week old. If the mare is to be bred back in the first heat, she may as well be kept up until that time. In all these things, a man must use his judgment as to condition of the weather and so on; however, even a young colt can stand quite a lot of cold if it is not both wet and cold. I can see no sense in putting a young colt to as much extremes as it can stand, and prefer to take a little too much care of it rather than too little.

Unless the mare is fed almost entirely on legumes or green grass, she should have a bran mash every evening for a week or so before foaling time. This mash should be made up of about a gallon and a half of bran, two quarts of oats, and a pinch of salt, to which enough boiling water is added to make a good gruel, but it should not be too sloppy. It may then be covered with about an inch of dry bran and some burlap sacks. This is allowed to steam several hours before feeding time, when it should be fed warm. If one makes this up about noon, he will generally find that it is about the right temperature at feeding time in the evening. When it is fed, the dry bran may be scraped off the top and saved and that which has become moist may be mixed with the mash.

The appearance of wax on the mare's teats may or may not indicate that she will foal that night. The common rule is that such a mare will foal during the night after wax appears on her teats, and this will generally be the case. However, I have had mares that had wax on their teats three or four days before each time they foaled. Others would never show a sign of wax up to the very evening of foaling, and some, on which wax would appear only a couple of hours before foaling started. Many times, one can judge when the mare is to foal by her restless condition during the day, while other mares will show no change whatsoever. Most mares will foal naturally without any help and get along fine; however, it is a good idea for the man in charge to take a look at the expectant mare about every hour or so during the night that he expects her to foal. He should stay with her as soon as labor commences. During this time, the mare may get up and lie down again and show unmistakable signs of uneasiness. The less she is bothered at this time the better. One should remain outside the stall but have a vantage point from which he can watch the proceedings. Soon thereafter, the water bag will probably break and the mare's vulva will dilate and the colt's nose or front feet will be visible. This may happen while the mare is lying down or standing up. Very often, she will stand up until the withers have come out, then lie down to expel the remainder of the colt. Once the colt starts to come, it must come quite fast if it is to be viable.

If there seems to be too long a delay, one may wash his hands well and examine to see if the head may be twisted around, or if a leg is down, etc. In either case, he had better push the colt back far enough to straighten out both forelegs and the head above them and then wait a short time to see if the mare is able to expel the colt of her own accord. Otherwise, it may be necessary to help her along by applying traction during pains. If he does not have enough strength to get the job done, he may call an assistant, who has been arranged for in case something like this should occur. If it should be necessary to apply a block and tackle, a veterinarian should always be called. All of these things should have been in readiness for an emergency. If the hind feet are first to be seen and they are not sticking out too far, one may push the colt back in and reverse it, then try to allow the mare to deliver it normally. It may be that the colt will have to be delivered just as it has presented itself, and one may as well get the block and tackle ready, as it will probably be necessary in order to help the mare at the time the withers and elbows are ready to come out. If the colt is coming along normally, nothing need be done until the job is completed. One should not be too anxious to help the mare deliver, as nearly all mares will deliver normally if left alone. Interference by inexperienced help may do a great deal more harm than good. If it is absolutely necessary to apply traction, it should be applied down and back, never straight back, and always with the pains.

There is one other thing that one needs to watch for. If the water bag has not broken of its own accord, one should break or tear it as soon as it presents itself. In this case, he must be on hand to pull it away from the mouth and head of the colt as soon as the head is out. He must then clear the mucus out of both the nostrils and the mouth, for the colt may smother unless this is cleared out. In a case of this kind, the colt may be covered with membranes when it comes out, and these membranes must be removed immediately.

After the colt is delivered, it may be allowed to rest a while, and the cord will probably break of its own accord, then bleed slightly before clotting. It should then be painted with iodine or metaphen. If the bleeding seems to be excessive, the cord may be clamped or tied off with a sterile string. If the cord refuses to break of its own accord after a reasonable length of time and after the pulsations in the cord have stopped, two ties should be made

—one a couple of inches from the body of the colt and the other an inch or two away from the first. The cord is then cut between the two ties and iodine is applied. One should not be in a hurry to do this, because if done too soon it may cause a blood clot in the colt. I prefer to wait about ten minutes after pulsations have stopped. Some veterinarians advise pulling the cord to tear it, rather than tying it off and cutting it.

During this time, the mare will probably have been lying quiet and resting, but about now she will either get to her feet or turn her head around and start licking off the colt. If it is warm, the mare may be allowed to do this herself; however, in cold weather, one should help her dry the colt as quickly as possible to prevent it from taking cold. Old burlap sacks make ideal material for this purpose. As soon as possible after the mare gets up, the stall should be cleaned out, or the mare should be placed in a different stall. One may wish to do this if he has a lot of mares and only one foaling stall. I have used one foaling stall three different times in one night. This seldom happens, however. If the mare is to be moved, perhaps the best procedure is to pick up the colt and carry it and allow the mare to follow. The mare may expel the placenta almost immediately. If she doesn't, one need not worry too much about it and may as well go back to bed. In the morning, however, one must be sure that the mare has cleaned out thoroughly. If all or part of the afterbirth has not been expelled, a veterinarian should be called to remove it. It should never be left longer than six hours.

CARE OF COLTS

The premature colt may often be saved if it is not too much premature and if it is given special care. True prematures will be too weak to stand up and will, therefore, require feeding from a bottle. They also will need additional warmth, unless the temperature night and day is above ninety degrees fahrenheit. This may be accomplished by having the stall well bedded to avoid dampness, and by wrapping the colt in woolen blankets, and perhaps placing hot water bottles or chemical heating pads around it, and wrapping the legs from the body down over the hoofs in woolen bandages.

The premature must generally be fed a formula from a bottle, as in most cases the mare's milk will not begin to flow for three or four days and maybe not for a week. The formula should be made up of diluted cow's milk. Jersey or Guernsey milk will need to be diluted about half, while Holstein milk need only be diluted about one-third. I prefer to use lime water for this purpose, as cow's milk is not as rich in lime as is a mare's milk. To obtain this, I place some lime into a bucket, about one quarter full, then fill with water and stir, then allow to stand several hours, and use only the top clear water. Lime to be of any value to a colt must be soluble, as a horse's stomach contains no hydrochloric acid. The formula must also be sweetened by the addition of corn syrup, about a tablespoon full to a pint of formula. This formula should be brought to a boiling point, but not allowed to boil, then cooled to body temperature before being fed. The colt should be fed at least every two hours day and night, but it will take only a few ounces of it each time. It should also be given about an ounce of linseed oil each day, especially the first day, to make it pass its feces. It is very necessary for the colt to get the mare's first milk as it contains a laxative, and when it doesn't, as is the case with the premature, it must have linseed oil or some other mild laxative instead. The bottles and nipples must be boiled each time before they are used, about ten minutes for the bottles and one minute for the nipples.

It is no doubt better, in the case of a weak premature, to take the mare away from the colt and place her in an adjoining stall where she can watch the colt, until it is able to stand. However, she must be brought back into the colt's stall at least twice a day, otherwise she may refuse to take the colt when it is able to stand. The mare's bag should be watched very closely, and her milk should be given to the colt instead of the formula as soon as it comes in. In this case, after the bottle is prepared, the mare is milked directly into the bottle, and it is given immediately to the colt. One should milk from one teat one time and from the other teat the next time, in order to help her milk come in. Any unused milk is thrown away directly after the colt finishes its meal. Formula should always be given at body temperature.

In cases of full-time colts that lose their mother, a formula may be prepared the same as for a premature, but in this case, the colt may be taught to drink from a bucket and be fed only every three hours during the day and about once during the night. The hours of six, nine, twelve, three, six, nine, and two will be found to be about correct for feeding time, as well as the easiest to remember. The colt will take about a pint at a feeding, depending on the size and age of the colt. It is often possible in cases like this to persuade another mare to adopt such a colt. This will facilitate matters considerably. It will take time and patience, but if a mare is a good milker she can easily raise two colts. On the other hand, I have weaned a four-months-old colt and persuaded its mother to adopt a two-months-old colt, whose mother had died. In this particular case, I had to hold the mare and force her to allow the colt to nurse each time for over a week, and finally when the two were turned into a lot, the colt would wait until it saw me coming before running up to nurse. The mare finally adopted this colt and treated it as if it were her own.

After the colt is about a week old, both mare and colt may be turned out in the brood mare pasture or wherever they are to be kept permanently. One may begin riding the mare a little by the time the colt is about three weeks old, if judgment is used not to over-ride her and not to get her hot. At this age, the colt should be allowed to follow alongside the mare if it is at all convenient. By the time the colt is three months old, the mare may be worked and the colt kept up in a box stall that is strong and in which there are no projections on which it can get hurt. The mare must not be turned back with the colt while she is hot but must be thoroughly cooled out first. The colt will get along if weaned at this time, and many have been weaned at this age; but, unless one has a very good reason for doing so, it should be left on the mare until as near six months as possible.

At any time after five months, the colt will be ready to be weaned. Six months is probably the ideal time. By this time the colt will have learned to eat grass with its mother, and it should also have access to all the crushed oats it will eat. On most breeding farms, this is accomplished by having grain bunks called creeps. There is a rail placed around the bunk, at a distance of about four feet from the bunk and low enough that the mares cannot get under, but high enough so that the colts can easily get under to feed. Crushed oats are kept in these bunks almost continuously. The colt will generally start nibbling at grass at about four to six weeks and will be eating a little hay soon after. If colts are brought up in this way, there will be no problem at weaning time. It is always wiser to try to wean two or more colts at the same time and put them together in large stalls, sheds, or pens. There must be ample space for them to eat or else the stronger ones will drive the others away. If one owns a single mare and colt, it will have to be weaned alone, of course. In this case, it had probably better be a gradual process, with the mare being placed with the colt for about half an hour twice a day for three or four days, then once a day for several days, and finally not at all. The mare's bag must be watched and perhaps a small amount milked out, if necessary, for a few days, so that it does not become feverish or caked. On a large breeding farm where several colts are to be weaned at the same time, they will probably do better if taken away all at once. In most cases like this, the colts will be eating well by the second day and will hardly lose a pound.

The mares will have to be dried up by hand. They will be milked twice a day, but only about a half cupful from each teat, depending upon the mare and how much milk she gives. It must not all be taken, yet there must be enough taken to make the bag fairly loose and to have the milk come freely. One can hurry the drying up process if, after milking, he will rub a little camphorated oil onto the bag. This is the safest procedure by far, as in this way one runs little danger of getting a caked bag. A caked bag is very serious and must be reported to a veterinarian at once. After a few days, one can generally limit the milking to just once a day and soon the mare will be near enough dried up that she may be turned out with safety. One must check up on her bag every day until it is completely dried up in order to avoid any chance of a caked bag, which, in almost all instances, is nothing but the result of carelessness or ignorance. During the drying up process, the mare should be fed entirely on dry feed and her water intake should be controlled. Probably half of what she has been accustomed to drinking will be sufficient. No legumes, such as alfalfa, or lespedeza, or soybean hay should be fed at this time.

Chapter VIII

CARE OF FEET AND SHOEING

In my former book, "The American Saddle Horse," I had a few comments on shoeing, which called forth so many questions that I feel there is a lot of interest in the subject and also that people are much misinformed. Hence, I have decided that a little broader treatment of the subject is desirable.

Colts

The hoofs of the young colts should be pared regularly at intervals of about two months, beginning about the age of three months. They should merely be pared and rasped level and the edges slightly rounded off to prevent breaking. If this were done on all colts, I believe we would have less nigger-heeled and pigeon-toed horses. Colts, of course, should be allowed to run barefoot while running out in pasture, and even while taking their first light work, until their hoofs begin to show wear, making shoes necessary. Seldom are shoes ever put on until the colt is taken up for work in its two-year-old form, and many are allowed to go barefoot until they are gaited. The condition of the track or work ring will have to determine this to a large extent, as a hard track or rough, hard ground will cause greater wear on the hoofs and thus necessitate shoeing earlier than if the track is fairly soft. In any case, the nearer to nature that we can keep the feet the better they will grow and the firmer they will become.

The young colt that is to be shown in hand in weanling classes or yearling classes will probably want to be shod for the show, as it dresses up the feet slightly and makes a better appearance in the show ring. Oftentimes, this is merely done in front, the hind feet being allowed to go barefoot, merely being trimmed just prior to the show. If the very young colt must be shod for the above reasons, the shoes should be very light plates with only four nail holes, two on each side. The smallest nails available should be used. The colt may be shod about a week before the show in order to allow it a chance to get accustomed to the shoes before showing, but they should be removed as soon as possible after the show is completed. Even light shoes on a very young colt cause some strain on both ankles and tendons, and if one wishes the colt to grow up with strong, well formed feet and legs, he will take good care of them while the colt is still young.

In the event that the colt is inclined to be pigeon-toed (toeing in from the ankles down), the hoofs may be trimmed so that the feet will sit straight on the ground, which will mean that the outside of the hoof will be trimmed lower than the inside. This actually causes a strain on the young legs. However, in many instances, if this procedure is followed and the colt's hoofs are kept trimmed in this way from the time it is about three months of age, at intervals of about one month, by the time the colt has reached two years of age its hoofs may be setting on perfectly straight. What has happened in this case, as one can easily tell by feeling the long pastern bone and the pastern joint, is that the bones have grown in a slight curve, making the colt stand straight. As we have said before, this has been a strain on those bones, which are at that period quite pliable, but I feel that the probable results are worth the chance taken, in that the shoeing problem later on will be greatly facilitated.

On the other hand, if the colt is inclined to stand nigger-heeled (toeing out from the ankles down), the reverse procedure may be used, causing the same result. That is, the inside of the hoof is pared lower than the outside, until the colt stands straight. The curve formed in the bones in this case is in the opposite direction. This practice is not without danger, as it may cause the colt to develop side bones or ring bones. Nevertheless, it is worth the chance, in my opinion, as one will not have a knee-knocker to contend with later on.

Notice carefully that I said, "if these defects were from the ankles down," this procedure will probably work. If they start at the knee instead of the ankle, there is little to be done. The above is perhaps the only instance in which the hoofs should not be pared level, and even then it may not always work, and one should recognize the danger involved before going ahead.

In most cases, the colt will be first shod soon after it starts work in the two-year-old form, or immediately before starting in its gaits, or perhaps not until after it is gaited. With the colt that has very little work until its three-year-old form, that will probably be the first time it will wear shoes, although its hoofs will still need regular trimming until that time. At this point, there should be no attempt at corrective shoeing, as all such shoeing induces strain of one kind or another, and the sole object now should be protection. This calls for light plates all the way around, without the use of any caulks. However, the toes may be rolled on the front shoes, which enables the colt to break over easier, and the toes on the hind shoes may be squared in order to help teach the colt to break squarely behind. The frog must not be pared away as it should come in contact with the ground. This is nature's way of forcing blood throughout the hoof.

It may be necessary to deviate from this natural way of shoeing colts in the case of the very strong gaited colt that is ready to be gaited. In this case, the front shoes will be left off entirely if possible. Otherwise, very light plates made of half round steel may be used in front, and the front toes may be pared quite short. In the rear, the toes will be left as long as possible and fairly heavy toe-weighted or side-weighted shoes may be worn. No heel caulks. By "fairly heavy," I mean twelve to fourteen ounces.

GENERAL SHOEING

The following directions will apply to broke horses as well as to colts, except where corrective shoeing may be necessary. The hoofs should be trimmed perfectly level before fitting the shoe, which should not be fitted hot. By this, I mean that a seat for the shoe should not be burned in the hoof, except in very special cases where it may be absolutely necessary. However, a warm shoe may be touched to the hoof without causing any damage. One cannot expect the farrier to completely cool each shoe every time it may be necessary to place it on the hoof to see if further alterations may be necessary. In other words, while one does not want hot fitting, he must be a little reasonable about such things. In this, as in most things, if one will employ a competent farrier, he need not watch every move made, as no doubt the farrier has had far more experience in that line than almost any owner, and if he is competent he may be relied upon to do the right thing. There is no reason for trimming out the sole or the frog, except for the sake of appearance. The dead sole and frog are usually trimmed out and may as well be, as they will soon be shed anyway. No further trimming is necessary; and, above all, the bars or that part of the hoof at the heel where the frog joins the outer wall of the hoof should not be pared away. To do this would definitely weaken this part and might cause the hoofs to become contracted. The hoofs should not only be trimmed level but at such an angle so that when the foot is set on the ground, the angle of the foot is natural to that animal. That is, there should be an unbroken line from the ground to the fetlock joint when viewed from the side. This angle will vary on different horses, but one can easily judge by his eye whether or not the toe is too long or the heel is too high, causing a sharp break at the pastern joint one way or another.

The broke horse may need a certain change from this natural angle, which will be dealt with later on, but even when necessary, the change should be as little as possible. Personally, I cannot see any use in measuring the angle on the colt's hoofs, as it will vary with different animals. One can better judge by his eye which is the correct angle for that particular colt, than by the use of a foot leveler and angle measurer. On the older horse, where it may be necessary to keep a specified angle that has proved to be best for that particular horse, then a measurement of the angle will be necessary.

I far prefer the use of shoes punched for three nails on a side to those punched for four, and practically all handmade shoes are so made. The use of four nails on a side puts them too close together, with the result that there is far greater danger of breaking off the shell of the hoof than if only three are used. This is especially true with horses that have hoofs with thin, brittle shells. Nails should be long enough that they may be driven sufficiently high to get a good solid hold and no larger, as larger nails than necessary punch holes that are too big. Most Saddle Horses will require a number five or six nail. A small line will be rasped under each nail before the nail is clinched; otherwise, the less the rasp is used on the outside of the hoof the better. The outside of the hoof contains a gummy substance which nature placed there to protect the hoof from drying out, and it should not be removed. In the case of the horse's hoofs, nature did a remarkable job, and the less it is changed or interfered with, the better hoofs the horse will have. Due to the artificial way of keeping horses, it is necessary to make some changes, included in which is shoeing; but these changes should be as slight as possible. There is no reason, except looks, for not using clips on the shoe. They will help hold the shoe more than an additional nail on each side. They should not be placed too far around the side, however, as this may cramp the hoof.

Care

The hoof contains natural oils which keep the hoof from becoming brittle and make it tougher and more elastic. These natural oils are in most cases completely sufficient to do the job; in other cases, it may be necessary to add certain oils. There are a number of preparations on the market for this purpose, one about as good as another. They should be made up primarily of animal fats, especially wool fat or neat's foot oil, which will not keep out moisture. Either of these are fully as good as any of the advertised products, in my opinion. The only places that oils of any sort will do any good are the heels, frog, and coronet, as these are the only live parts of the outside of the hoof. Oils may be used in the winter time or if the animal is to be kept in the stall most of the time, but if the horse is used outside in hot weather, the use of oils may cause burning and excessive drying and do far more harm than good. In my experience, in our eagerness to do everything possible for the horse, we have, as a rule, overused oils rather than underused them. This is probably due, in no small way, to the great American habit of paying too much attention to advertising. My father has been a farrier all his life and a specialist in the care of diseased hoofs. He fully believes that as much trouble is caused by the overuse of oils as is caused by any other factor. I know of cases of severe quarter cracks of very long duration being cured primarily by the absolute abolishment of oils and by using water and packing with clay instead.

Moisture is an absolute necessity if the animal's hoofs are to be kept healthy and elastic. The horse running out in pasture where there is dew on the grass in the morning and perhaps a stream that it runs through occasionally need have no special care of its feet other than trimming. This type of horse usually has hoofs which are hard, tough, and elastic and not brittle; however, when we bring them into the stable, it is often a different matter. A number of horse shoers have made the remark to me that we keep our stalls too clean nowadays for the animal's own good. We will notice that the hind hoofs seldom get dried out or contracted, nor do they develop quarter cracks. All these things generally happen to the front hoofs, if at all. We also notice that soon after the animal urinates or passes its feces, it will step into it with its hind feet. One may draw his own conclusions as to whether moisture is necessary. The hind hoofs seldom need much care, but the front ones should be sponged off occasionally, or better still, be packed in a good clay that will hold moisture. How often they need to be packed depends upon the climate, the soil, and the particular horse. If there is any doubt, a hoof that seems dry may be packed every night in most cases with no ill effects. If one uses ordinary clay he will generally have to pick it out in the morning, for if it is left in the hoof until it becomes dry, it will start drawing moisture from the hoof itself and do more harm than good. In a country where good clay is unobtainable, one may buy white rock. This will have to be powdered and placed in a bucket about a third full and then covered with water. As it absorbs the water, more water must be added. It will absorb a tremendous amount of water, three or four times its own volume. When packed in the hoofs, it will remain moist for two to four days, depending upon the climate. Most trainers add a little salt to the bucket of clay or white rock, which will help hold the moisture. If the hoofs are to be packed they should be picked clean first, then the clay is applied with a paddle. In most cases, it will hold without anything further being done. Sometimes, a little straw may be placed on top of the clay in order to hold it in. Some people prefer to cut pieces of paper about the size of the inside of the shoe and place that on the clay. This may be done if the clay doesn't hold of its own accord.

While some moisture is necessary for the preservation of a healthy hoof, it must not be thought that more will be better. It is a case where a little bit is fine, but too much is no good at all. Horses standing in unclean stalls develop thrush quite severely at times, and horses running out in pasture that needs continuous irrigation develop soft spongy hoofs, as well as severe cases of thrush. On the other hand, horses that have been raised in desert countries for more than one generation seem to develop a resistance to lack of water, needing none except that supplied by their own bodies. Their hoofs become hard and flinty, but not brittle. The above will be found to be about all the care the normal healthy hoof will require.

Diseases of the Hoof

Thrush is probably one of the most common diseases of horses' hoofs. It may be caused by too much water or moisture, whether the water be dirty or clean; however, one seldom encounters a very severe case of thrush except where the animal's stall is not only extremely wet but actually rotten. The groom is generally blamed for this condition, and it is thought that it comes from a stall that is not being properly cleaned each day. On the whole, this is a popular misconception. I have known places where stalls were cleaned only once a week and no semblance of this condition existed. In some others, where the stalls were cleaned very thoroughly twice a day, the stalls had rotten holes in them in a very short time. In this case, a month after a horse was placed in the stall these rotten holes would appear, necessitating continual digging and reclaying of the stalls. I have seen brood mares running out in pasture with severe cases of thrush. On the other hand, I have never seen either a severe case of thrush or this rotten condition of the stalls, without an attendant case of kidney condition. This leads one to the conclusion that all these severe cases of thrush are indirectly the outgrowth of a kidney condition. If the kidneys can be cleared up, the stalls can be reclayed, and one can clear up the case of thrush and have little or no more trouble.

Clearing up a severe case of kidney condition is a job for the veterinarian; but in many instances it is directly due to the lack of enough salt. No matter if block salt is kept in front of the horse at all times, it will not get sufficient amounts, as block salt is made primarily for cattle whose tongues are far rougher than the horse's tongue. Many times the only remedy necessary to clear up a case of kidney condition that is not too severe is to make loose salt available at all times. The horse that has been used to going without proper amounts of salt will have to be encouraged to eat more by placing a pinch of salt in its grain at feeding time for several months. It will eventually develop the habit of taking salt in sufficient quantities. Getting the animal's kidneys in proper condition will probably take six months or more.

As to the treatment of the thrush itself—in simple cases it may be cleared up by the use of almost any drying antiseptic. Even table salt packed in the hoof each day will soon clear up these cases of thrush. Many people use iodine which will do all right on simple cases, but if they are a little deeper, the iodine will merely dry up the outside but will not penetrate. Because of the crust formed one will think he has killed it, while in reality it is still working deeper and will soon break out worse than ever. In severe cases, I prefer to trim away as much of the rotted frog and sole as is possible, then apply carbolic acid. This will penetrate and kill it instantly. One must be very careful when using carbolic acid not to spill any either on the horse's leg or on one's self, as it will cause a very deep burn. We must remember, however, that this treatment is very drying and one will need to start packing the feet almost immediately after this treatment is used to avoid allowing the hoofs to dry out.

While thrush is caused by too much dampness, most other hoof troubles may be directly attributed to lack of moisture. Contracted heels are one of these common ailments. To correct this, one must first restore the moisture content of the hoof in order to make it more elastic. This is done by standing the animal for about a half day in a wooden tub filled with water deep enough to cover the hoofs, or by tying it so that it must stand in a good mud hole for about a half day. The mud should be very wet and deep enough to cover the hoofs. After this, oils, water, or clay packing, or a combination of these should be used regularly. Felt swabs may be purchased, which buckle around the hoofs after being soaked in water. They will generally keep moist for about twelve hours, and the water content may easily be restored without removing them. Without first getting the hoofs elastic, no other treatment will do much good. After this is done, if one can spare the horse and turn it out, it may be shod with tips or half shoes. They are very light and come only half way around the hoofs and merely protect the toe. The tip is sunk into the hoof so that it sets level on the ground after being put on. The horse may be worked lightly with tips on very soft ground, but if the ground is firm it will soon wear the heels down. The whole object of these tips is to give plenty of frog pressure. As the hoof grows out, it will come back into shape if kept moist.

If the animal must be used, bar shoes giving plenty of frog pressure, will work just about as well. They must be made a little wider than the hoof at the heels to help the hoof spread, and the web must be wide enough to allow a good bearing at the heel. In a case like this, I generally have a bar shoe made with plenty of frog pressure and have the web of the shoe slightly beveled toward the outside to help spread the heels that much more. The shoe must be at least half an inch wider at the heel than the hoof is when the shoe is fitted, and generally one finds that by the time the shoes are to be replaced the hoofs have already spread nearly as wide as the shoes. Pads and packing with tar and oakum may be used if desired and may be necessary in case the animal is footsore. Whenever pads are worn there must be packing placed under them. I prefer a mixture of wool fat, neat's foot oil, and tar to be used with the oakum, rather than tar alone. It will mix better if slightly warmed. On a warm summer day, if the components are allowed to sit in the sun a couple of hours, they will become warm enough for easy mixing.

Corns may be caused by a combination of dry feet and stone bruises or pinching by the shoes. A true corn is actually a ruptured blood vessel, and while I have heard of corns being cured, I have never seen a true corn cured. I have heard my father offer a thousand dollars to anyone who could produce a recipe for curing corns, or could prove that he had really cured a corn. The offer was never taken up, so I assume there is no cure; however, that was perhaps twenty years ago, so there may be a cure developed by this time, but if so, I have never heard of it. Nevertheless, it is possible to keep the horse going sound, even if he has corns that are quite severe. The procedure is primarily to soften up the hoofs and keep them that way, by tubbing out, packing, etc. In some cases, this may be sufficient, but in others one may have to wear bar shoes and packing. The corn itself will need to be cut out and the sole around it pared to relieve any pressure. The bar shoes must give some frog pressure, but they need not have the web beveled toward the outside, as with contracted heels. In severe cases, the corns may be burned out with iodine crystals and turpentine, but the rest of the treatment will remain the same.

Quarter cracks are also largely due to hoofs being too dry. In this case, bar shoes may or may not be necessary. If the crack is back towards the quarters of the hoofs, bar shoes used with pads and packing are certainly advisable. The hoof must be softened up as before, and the shell for perhaps a half inch on each side of the crack will be pared low enough that it will not rest on the shoe. A line just at the top of the crack should be rasped in the hoof fairly deep to prevent further cracking. This line may be burned in with a hot iron, which is often necessary. Sometimes, two or more nails may be driven through the hoof horizontally and clinched on either side of the crack to help prevent further cracking. One will need an expert farrier for this job, as it is very easy to go too deep. Unless one has such an expert shoeing his horses, he had better not attempt it.

Stone bruises are perhaps best treated by the use of bar shoes, pads, and packing until the animal is no longer footsore.

Navicular trouble is not supposed to be at all common, but I have come across it several times lately, and it may be worth while to take the time to tell a little about it. The navicular bone is a small triangular shaped bone situated at the bottom of the hoof just back of the coffin bone. It is so well protected that one seldom hears about it, and it is impossible to get at it to treat it if it becomes infected or hurt. A horse with navicular trouble often walks more like a shoulder-sore horse than a footsore one, and often, even horsemen will call the animal lame in the shoulders on first examination; however, on closer examination, it can be seen that the animal will use its shoulders freely when necessary, as when stepping over obstacles, etc., but refuse to set the foot down hard. At times, it will appear very lame and sometimes it will travel nearly sound. To get the horse to travel reasonably sound, its hoofs must be kept absolutely healthy and soft, and it must be shod to cushion the blow, especially toward the point of the frog. Bar shoes, sometimes called butterfly bars, are not indicated unless needed for some other purpose and if used there must be little or no frog pressure. High heel caulks are usually necessary to help prevent contact of the frog with the ground. Some people advise a wide thin plate to be welded to the bottom of the shoe to further prevent any pressure on the frog, but I have found that rubber pads with high heels do the job about as well as anything. All excess portions of sole and frog are to be trimmed and packing must be very light, except at the heel. The high rubber heels help materially to cushion the blow to the foot as it strikes the ground, and most horses so afflicted will be found to go sound almost indefinitely if cared for and shod in this way.

Founder is generally caused by getting too much corn or green feed when not accustomed to it, but may also be caused by too much water when hot. It is actually a disease of the sensitive lamina or inner sole of the hoof, causing it to drop. If noticed immediately, it may be cured in most cases by a thorough physic and by packing the feet in ice and keeping them packed for at least forty-eight to seventy-two hours. This latter is best accomplished by cutting an old burlap sack in the form of a maltese cross and filling it with cracked ice and tying it around the pastern joint. The ice must be replenished as often as necessary. In an old case, about all one can do is to keep the hoof healthy, thin the sole as much as is permissible, and shoe with pads and packing, using either bar shoes or rubber heeled pads.

CORRECTIVE SHOEING

We now come to the use of shoes as a means of correcting or improving the action. The basic thing to remember in this case is that the horse will generally go to weight, and that the weight in front will generally improve and balance the trot, while weight in the rear will have a tendency to unbalance the trot or cause the horse to pace or rack, etc. Most important of all is that horses are individuals and are put up differently, and what works well on one may not be any good at all on another. This is perhaps the most common of all faults made by the uninitiated. That is, a beginner will often see some good horse shod thus and so and will be sure that that method of shoeing will help his horse, when in reality, it may be the worst thing for his horse. Each horse must be studied individually and, after carefully weighing possible consequences, an attempt may be made to improve its action, balance, stride, etc., by the trial-and-error method.

Everyone seems to want his horse to have more action. This is ordinarily accomplished in front by allowing the

Illustration XXIV

SOME COMMON TYPES OF SHOES

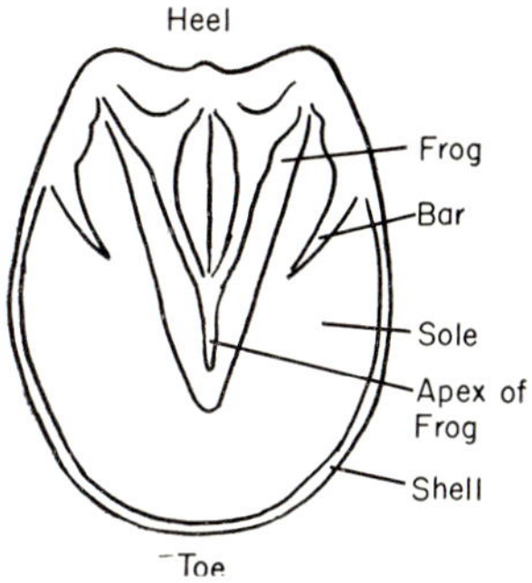

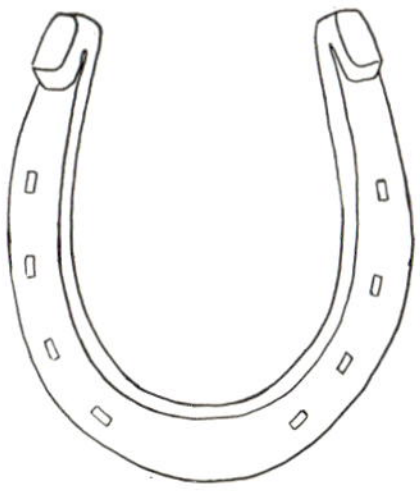

Heel Caulks Blocked. These are folded all the way over. They give more support than turned caulks and help some if the heels need to be raised.

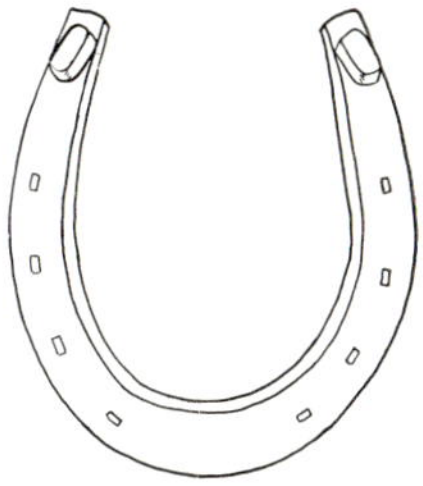

Jar Caulks. These are welded on almost but not quite parallel to the shoe. They help cushion the jar when the hoof comes in contact with the ground.

Blocked Caulk

Jar Caulk or Welded Caulk

Turned Caulk

When making shoes for horses wearing long hoofs, the nail holes must be punched farther in than is usually the case, so that the nails may be driven higher, in order to get them into firm solid wall, otherwise the shell will surely break off.

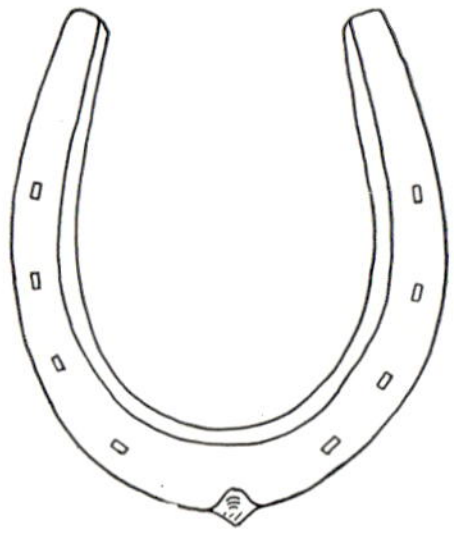

Shoe with a clip turned in with a hammer while the shoe is hot. Often two are used, one on each side where the toe meets the quarter. Clips if long enough will hold the shoe better than an extra nail, but may cramp the hoof unless done properly. Due to the way this clip is made, a small section of the hoof must be removed before applying the shoe. After the shoe is nailed on the clip is bent into contact with the hoof, using the driving hammer.

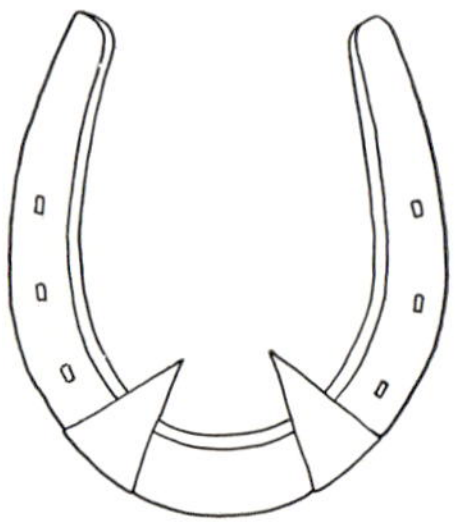

Shoe with welded clips. These clips are made of light weight steel, from an inch to two and a half inches long. They are welded to the outside of the shoe, thus are not as apt to pinch the hoof. They too are bent into contact with the hoof after the shoe is nailed on. These clips are particularly successful on thin shelled hoofs on which one has a hard time holding shoes.

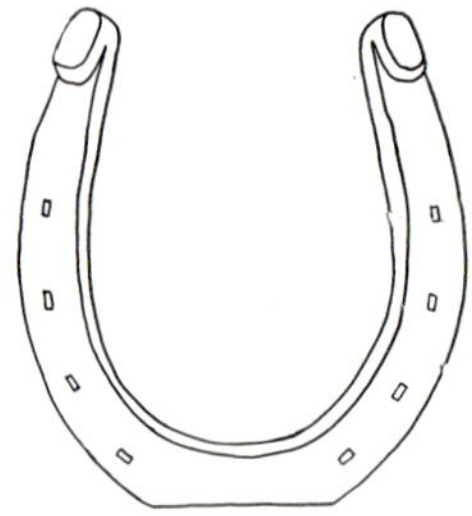

Hind Shoe with the toe squared, and blocked caulks (turned over). If toe is squared on the front shoe caulks are seldom used.

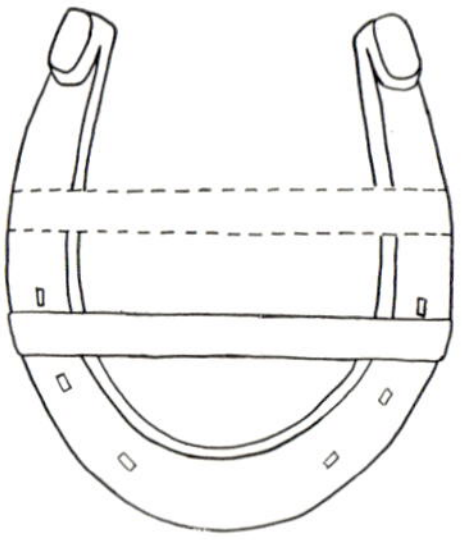

Single or double Memphis bars, with blocked caulks. Dotted lines indicate where second bar is usually placed. More often used on hind shoes than in front. Bars should be made of a piece of round steel bar, brazed on so that they may be easily replaced, finished to the same height as the caulks, about ½ to ¾ of an inch.

ILLUSTRATION XXIV (CONT.)

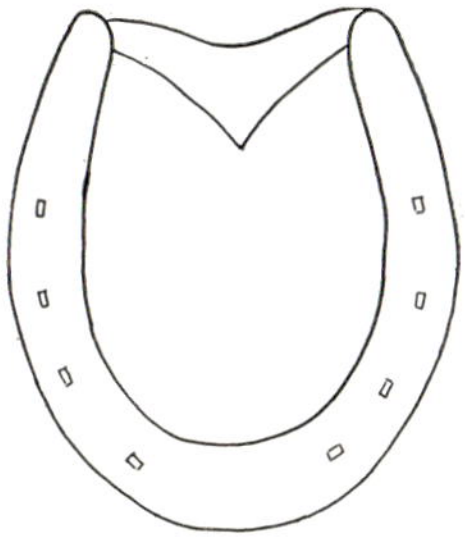

Butterfly Bar usually used in front where additional protection or increased frog pressure is needed.

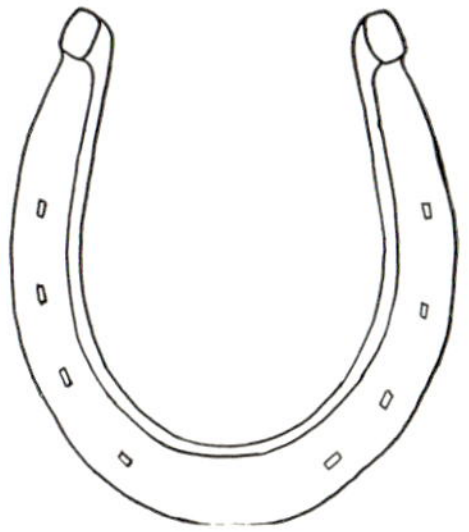

Heel Caulks turned. They help grip the dirt or pavement, and are also quite useful for mountain riding.

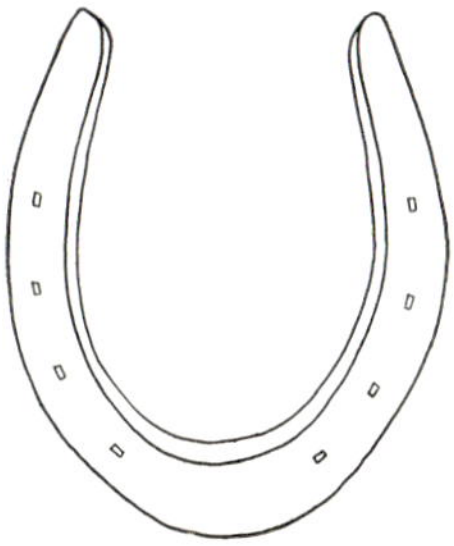

Toe Weight thicker and wider at the toe than at the heel. Usually a front shoe.

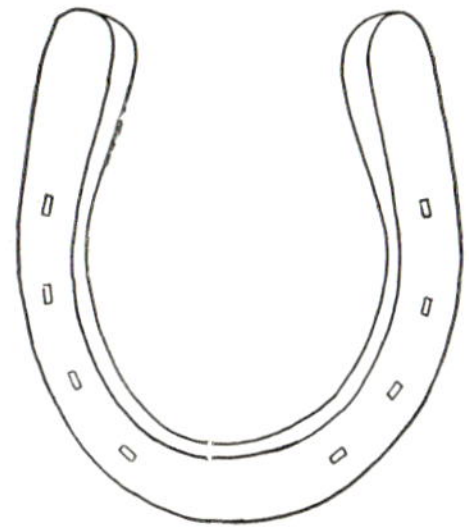

Heel Weight thicker and wider at the heel than at the toe. Usually a front shoe.

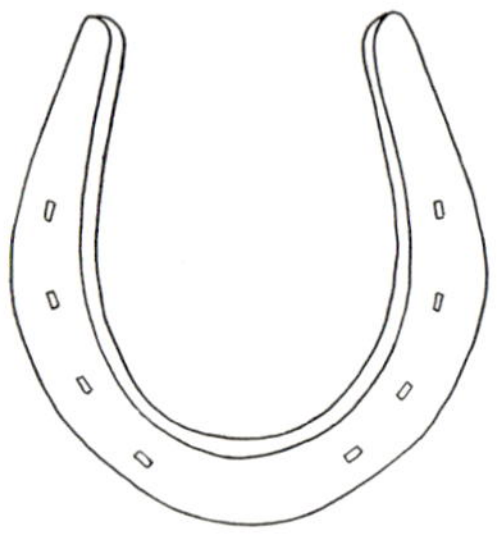

Side weighted shoe. May be either a front or a hind shoe. May be weighted on either side.

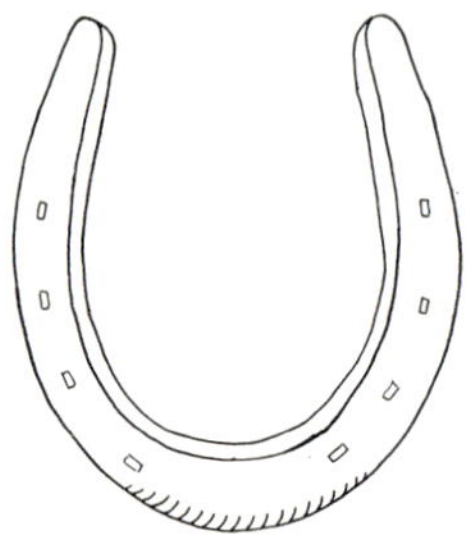

Roller motion shoe. Beveled for a quick break over. May be done at the center of the toe, or to either side.

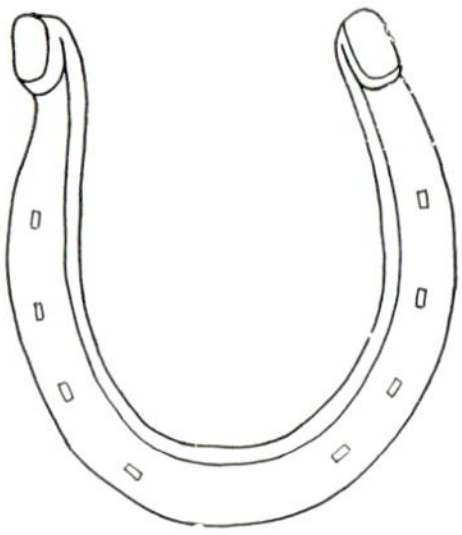

A type of hind shoe that often works well on a horse that is a little cow-hocked especially if it travels that way. It may or may not be used with heel caulks, if so they will generally be blocked, with the outside one a little higher than the one on the inside. Sometimes one will also want to roll the inside toe on this shoe.

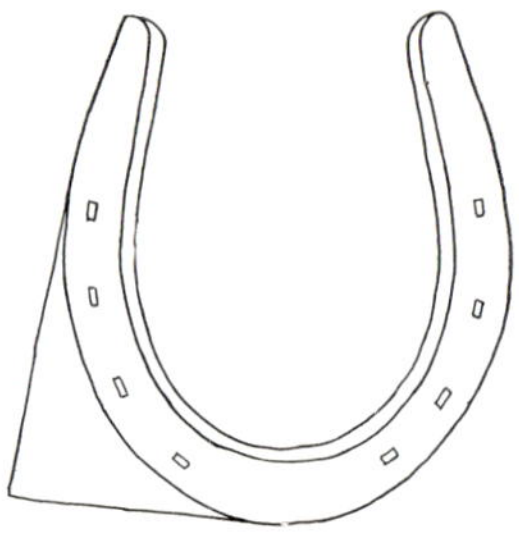

This shoe is often successful on a horse that breaks over on one side, instead of breaking center. The piece is welded on the side the animal is breaking over, and is welded on after the shoe has been made and fitted.

hoof to grow longer, especially the toe and adding more weight. By more weight, I don't mean a pound and a half or two pounds on each foot, as I have seen. Few gaited horses can carry more than fourteen to sixteen ounces in front, and a walk-trot horse seldom wants over twenty ounces. Many horses do far better with less weight. I have had horses go as high as horses ever go, wearing only twelve ounces. Many horses will travel better and higher with less weight than they are now carrying. Anytime the weight a horse must carry is increased, it causes an increase in the strain on both ankles and tendons, and if much weight is worn, one must decrease the amount of work he is giving the animal. He must also take special care of the ankles and legs if he does not want disastrous results. Everything said about more weight also applies to extra long toes on a horse. The more one gets away from the natural angle of the hoof, the more strain he places on both ankles and tendons. Whenever possible, the heels should be allowed to grow proportionately with the toes.

Little can be done about increasing the action of the horse behind, although long toes behind may be of slight help to some animals. Long toes and weighted shoes will generally be expected to increase the stride of the horse, as well as increase the height of the action, but one cannot put action on a horse that was never intended to have it. One can merely improve the action, but he cannot put it all there. A horse that is inclined to amble a little or is a little natural gaited will almost always be helped in its balance by having heavier shoes on in front and lighter ones behind—perhaps fourteen ounces in front and six to eight ounces behind. On the other hand, the gaited horse that is hard to make rack will probably be helped by wearing more weight behind. He may wear the same weight shoes behind as in front, or even a couple of ounces heavier. The amount of weight a horse needs will be governed both by its size and its way of going. If one wants his pleasure horse to amble a little, it will be helped by wearing shoes a trifle heavier behind than in front. If, however, the horse shows a tendency to pace, the hind shoes must immediately be lightened, lest it learn that gait and will do no other. Weight is often used in the hind shoes on stock horses to help teach them to get their hind feet under them and stop short on the haunches. In case the animal is particularly hard to teach, the front shoes are often removed altogether. The straight gaited colt is generally shod heavy behind and extremely light in front when first being started to rack. Toe weighted shoes behind are sometimes used for this purpose, but sometimes side weighted shoes will work better.

Toe weighted shoes in front are generally used to increase the animal's stride and are particularly successful on trappy-gaited horses. They may or may not increase the animal's action, and one can seldom be sure of the result in this respect, except by a trial and allowing the animal to wear the shoes about three days to get used to them, before any definite conclusions may be reached.

Heel weighted shoes are used on animals that do not bend their knees properly and travel stiff-kneed, or as we say, "shoot beans." If successful, they probably will increase the height of the action somewhat. On this type horse, it is often necessary to lower the heels somewhat in order to get the job done, on the other hand some horses will break better with high heels.

The side weighted shoe is used either behind or in front. Behind—it may be used for one of two reasons: to help start a colt racking or perhaps to help an older horse that doesn't like to rack, or it may be used on a horse that goes too close behind. Remember, the horse goes to weight. This type of shoe will often cure the horse that goes so close that it brushes the opposite hoof. This type of horse may be helped by trimming the outside wall of the hoof lower than the inside and perhaps using higher heel caulks on the inside. It may also be helped by wearing squared toes behind. Much depends upon the animal's conformation, as it is some fault of conformation that causes it to do this. In the above case, the weight is, of course, placed on the outside of the shoe. If the horse goes too wide behind, the weight will be placed on the inside of the shoe; or the shoe may be perfectly balanced all the way around, except that the outside heel caulk is higher and the inside of the hoof pared lower than the outside, or a squared toe may work. I have seen cases of horses that were a little cow hocked that went too close, but were helped immensely by making a deep roll on the inside corner of the toe of the hind shoe, which caused them to break on the inside and go wide enough to clear the other hoof.

In front, the side weighted shoe may be worn on either nigger-heeled horses (those which toe out) or pigeon-toed horses (those which toe in). The nigger-heeled horse breaks over at the point of its toe, causing it to swing in, and it often becomes a knee-knocker if it goes high enough, otherwise an ankle-knocker. If it uses its shoulders freely, it will probably go to weight, and a side weighted shoe made with a fairly heavy outside web and a very light inside web, with a deep roll inside, beginning at the point of the toe and extending around to the quarter, is indicated. This will often cause the nigger-heeled knee-knocker to go perfectly true, especially if the inside of the hoof is pared lower than the outside and if the animal uses its shoulders freely. Sometimes, trimming of the hoof is all that will be necessary. The pigeon-toed horse also breaks over at the toe, which causes it to throw its foot out or wing. This is not nearly as bad a fault as that of the nigger-heeled horse, as, at least, it stays sound. Nevertheless, no one likes to see it, and while most judges will not count it too much against the horse in the show ring, it certainly is no asset. In this case, the correct procedure is exactly like the nigger-heeled horse, except in reverse. Meaning, of course, that the weight is placed on the inside instead of the outside. Many horses that are not pigeon-toed also go to winging often as a result of too much weight. If this is the case and the animal can wear less weight, that, of course, is the remedy. Otherwise, one must be extremely careful in trying any drastic corrective procedure, as the animal may react to it too well and go to knocking its knees, which is far worse than winging, and if the animal learns this, it may be hard to correct.

The butterfly bar shoe is primarily used on horses with some little thing wrong with the hoofs, or to help hold pads, or for a horse that needs a little additional protection. It has been discussed earlier in this chapter, and there is no point in repeating it here. Of late years, we see quite a few horses wearing the so-called Memphis bar, either single or double, and in front or behind. It is welded across the shoe and seemingly may be placed at almost any point. I have seldom seen where they had much effect on the animal's action, except to cause additional ankle strain; but it has been quite a fad. It is a little like the story an old groom I once had used to tell about when he was a trotting horse man. He said one day, for a joke, one of the better known trainers brought his horse out to jog with a big piece of cow dung tied on the horse's head to the top of the bridle. When asked what that was for, he replied, "Oh, I found out that'll keep the horse from breaking." Well, that afternoon every groom on the track was out in a pasture field close by, hunting cow dung. While I can't vouch for the truth of that particular story, I do know that the general idea is true with horse people everywhere.

But to get back to the Memphis bar, there is one type of Memphis bar I have found to be very effective in cases where needed. It is a single Memphis bar placed on the hind shoe, just between the first and second nail holes, and made of about a quarter inch round iron or steel. It should be brazed on so that it may be replaced if it wears out before the shoe does. I always use heel caulks with this bar and have been very successful in curing horses that have a tendency to knuckle over behind. We quite often find this tendency in colts that are two and three years old, especially those with fairly long natural toes behind, and I attribute it largely to a weakness in the hind ankles. At any rate, I have found that by wearing the single Memphis bar placed as described above, the horse will nearly always stop knuckling over, and in time many will outgrow this tendency altogether. Naturally, what it actually does is to shorten the bearing surface and help the horse to break over. It, like anything else, is not a cure-all, and it surely will not help a colt to rack—quite the opposite, few colts can be gaited while wearing such a shoe. And, it means that if the colt needs such a shoe, we have to do one of two things—either wait a year longer before gaiting the colt or gait the colt before starting to wear such a shoe. If one thinks anything of his horse, the proper procedure is to wait a year before gaiting the colt and first develop his ankles.

I have been told by quite a number of people, including horsemen and trainers, that a single Memphis bar would help give the animal hock action and draw his hind legs under him. However, I had a chance to carry on a few experiments, taking motion pictures of horses both before and after being shod in this way, and have never yet found a horse that reacted in this way to Memphis bars. In fact, they seemed to act just the opposite. The animal would break faster but would generally have a tendency to drag its hocks behind it slightly. They do, however, make the horse travel more balanced in many cases, and they help a colt with a slight tendency to amble, to trot better. I have found that the heel caulks, in this case should be fairly low and blocked, or turned completely over rather than just turned down. Also, I always use a squared toe on this shoe, having the shoe first fit to the hoof and then the toe squared so that it sits back about a half inch under the toe of the hoof.

Half round shoes merely help the animal to break over easier, in any direction in which it naturally breaks. They are no good, except on the animal that naturally travels true. These shoes are often worn on colts when they are first asked to rack, which is the only time I ever use them. I like them very well for that purpose, however.

A rolled toe, or what is sometimes called a roller motion shoe, helps the horse to break over easier and quicker and at the point of the roll. They are useful on a great number of horses, especially those that do not break where one wishes them to, or for those that dwell too long on the ground. They are seldom any good on the trappy-gaited animal.

The squared toe merely shortens the bearing surface and helps the animal break over squarely and a little faster. They are successful on horses which have a tendency to forge while trotting. That is, over-reach and click the toe of the front shoe with the toe of the rear. Some animals seem to like to hear this clicking noise and do it from habit. Such horses are often cured by shoeing with a squared toe shoe behind, which is set back from a half to three-quarters of an inch. In this way there will be no clicking noise if the animal does forge. This helps the animal to break faster behind, making it less likely to forge, and the animal quits the habit if it is merely from liking to hear the noise. In most cases of this type, the front feet must also be worked on to cause the animal to break faster in front and get the front feet out of the way of the rear feet. This may sometimes be done by using a roller motion toe, and it may be necessary to lower the heel a little. If this doesn't help, one may try a heel weighted shoe. It will generally take a little experimentation to get just the correct thing. Many times, a toe weighted shoe is indicated instead of a heel weighted one.

Horses are shod slightly different for various purposes. Many animals travel better with small heel caulks on the hind shoes than with plates, and the horse that is to be used in the mountains will generally need them to help hold himself when coming downhill. These horses are generally shod with their toes dubbed off to help them be more surefooted, as a horse with long toes is apt to stumble in the mountains. The animal with a naturally long toe in front is often helped by the use of jar caulks. These are welded on parallel to the shoe instead of being turned and help a lot to take the jar off the ankles and tendons. The horse with weak tendons or strained tendons, which one is trying to get back in shape, will generally be somewhat relieved by the use of as short a toe as possible, as well as a blocked heel caulk to relieve the strain on the tendons. Oftentimes, rubber pads with high rubber heels work better than steel shoes on horses of this type.

While the above will give general hints on helping and improving the gaits of the horse, it must be understood that the individual horse may not react in the same way as most horses do. In a case of this kind, a man must watch the animal work and take notice of its conformation and how it uses its muscles and joints, then try to figure out what will work best on that particular animal.

Any corrective shoeing must be done with the thought in mind of the possible consequences on the animal's legs, as well as with the idea of improving the stride of the horse.

Chapter IX

VICES AND THEIR REMEDIES

Horses seem to develop quite a number of vices and bad habits in the stable and under the saddle. Many of these can be more easily prevented than cured. Some can be cured and others can either be helped or prevented. We shall try to list the most common ones and what methods have been generally successful in effecting a complete cure, or at least been a partial help. I shall begin with those bad habits the horse generally acquires in the stable.

Two closely related bad stable habits are *weaving* and *stall walking.* Some times the former develops from the latter. Animals confirmed in either of these habits must be considered unsound, as it is impossible to keep them in flesh. Both of these habits are found primarily in hot blooded horses and are, to a great extent, nervous habits. Many people believe that a hot blooded horse that has been worked hard all summer, if let down too quickly in the fall, will develop the habit of stall walking. Perhaps this is true and for that reason the show horse or trotter should have its work tapered off gradually in the fall, before letting it down completely. Confinement in a stall without proper exercise every day may also result in one of these vices. Therefore, if the horse is not to be used for a day or two, it should be turned out in a lot for exercise. Often young colts, when first brought up, develop the habit of stall walking for no known reason. If they are stud colts, castrating may prove effective and sometimes that is the only cure. Oftentimes, such a colt will quit if placed in a stall between two mares with bars between, so that they can see and communicate with each other. Mares will generally be more effective for this purpose than geldings. I believe that these habits are often the result of lonesomeness more than anything else, especially in young stallions. I once had a young mare, a three-year-old, that seemed confirmed in the habit of stall walking. We tried everything we could think of, such as hanging sacks partially filled with sawdust all around her stall, low enough so that she bumped them every time she moved, installing several alarm clocks in her stall to ring at intervals of every half hour, tying bells in her stall so that she would bump them and ring them herself. Each new trick seemed to work for about a day or so, until she got used to it, then she would start walking again. Finally, I bought a young stallion and placed him on the opposite side of the barn and moved this young mare over next to him. She quit walking at once and never did it again. We were never sure whether it was moving her to the opposite side of the barn or putting her next to a stallion that effected the cure, but she never did it again.

One thing that must not be done to the stall walker and that is to tie it up, as that will often cause the horse to start weaving, which is worse and perhaps harder to cure than walking. A confirmed weaver will not even stop if turned out in pasture. A stall too narrow to allow the animal to weave will effect a remedy, but will also prevent the horse from lying down and will effect no permanent cure. One needs to try anything he can think of and use both his ingenuity and imagination in trying to effect a remedy for either of these faults, hoping that he may eventually find the particular remedy that will work on that particular horse.

Crib biting or *wind sucking* is another stable vice closely related to the foregoing. Some people attribute it to the same reasons that they think cause stall walking or weaving, others say it is caused by a lack of something in the diet, and some think that one horse will learn it from another. It seems strange that if lack of something in the diet is the cause that only one horse in a large stable will learn it. I have known of several instances of a stable with one cribber in it for a number of years without the other horses ever learning it. The animal so afflicted sets its teeth on the tail board, ledge, or anything on which it can secure leverage and pulls down, making a peculiar noise as if sucking in wind. Many authorities say that the amount of wind actually sucked in is very small, but most cribbers are subject to periodic attacks of colic, which we term "wind colic." These horses are considered unsound and must be sold that way through a sales ring.

Any means which will prevent them from taking hold or prevent them from swelling up their throats in the act will be a temporary remedy. A strap, about an inch and a half wide, buckled quite tight around the neck just back of the poll, is perhaps the most common method used. Ordinary muzzles are generally not effective as the animal will crib on the muzzle. However, the bar muzzle made especially for this purpose is often quite effective. I have seen nails put in all over the stall at any place where the animal could take hold. These nails are allowed to protrude about two inches. It doesn't take long for the animal to get them bent down, after which he will continue as before. If one can put the horse in a stall in which there are no ledges, not even a feed box for him to take hold of, it may prevent him from performing the act. One may try any of these methods, and one or the other ought to work on most horses. A good veterinarian can perform a surgical operation on the throat, which will absolutely effect a cure if done right. However, one must secure a competent veterinarian who has had experience with such operations, as otherwise the operation is likely to be a failure, and one will have quite a lot of expense for nothing.

Kicking in the stall is another of these nervous vices. Sometimes, it seems as if the animal does it just to hear the noise, in which case, padding the sides of the stall so that there will be no sound produced may effect a cure. Chains attached to straps which are buckled around the ankles just below the fetlocks in such a way that they will bump the other leg each time it kicks will often stop the horse from kicking, and if this is worn a while it may effect a permanent cure. They may prove no good whatsoever on another horse.

Kicking at a person is an entirely different matter. This is generally done in viciousness, and immediate punishment is necessary. If the horse is young, it can generally be broken of this habit. Anyone entering the stall or having occasion to work around such a horse should always be armed with a good rawhide training whip and be prepared to use it at any time. If and when the animal kicks, it should receive a sharp crack with this whip around the hind legs. One should not continue whipping it, as that will probably only anger the horse, and it will learn nothing. But, each and every time it attempts to kick at a person, it must receive a sound hard crack with the whip at the minute it kicks. The proper timing of the punishment is the secret of breaking the habit. If the punishment is put off, it had better not be applied, as it will do more harm than good. The animal will not know the reason why it is being punished and will only lose confidence in the trainer. Whereas, if it is applied immediately to that part which is in error and if possible in such a way that the horse will attribute getting hurt to the act of kicking, it will generally soon desist. In no case should a man allow his temper to get the better of his judgment. As soon as one loses his temper, he also loses his power of reason and places himself on a level with the horse, in which case the horse has the advantage, as he is stronger than a man. A kicking horse is dangerous and should never be tolerated.

Striking is generally a vice of the stallion, as kicking is more likely to be a defense of a mare. A horse that strikes in viciousness is one of the most dangerous of all animals. There is no excuse for ever allowing a horse to develop this habit. If one has control of the young stud at all times, it will never learn this habit. If the young stallion strikes even playfully, it should immediately receive a good sharp crack of the whip around its front legs. It must be taught from the first that no such thing will be tolerated, even in play. I believe I love horses as much as anyone, have been associated with them all my life, have handled quite a large number of stallions, both young and old, due to the fact that a large part of my life has been spent on breeding farms. But, I have yet to find a single excuse for allowing any stallion, or any other horse, to develop the habit of striking. In the case of the older horse, I blame the early trainer rather than the animal, but still the habit must be broken. Anytime an old horse strikes viciously, it must receive not only a single crack of the whip, as is true in almost all other cases, but it must be soundly whipped around the front legs until it gives up completely. If this treatment is applied a few times, it will generally break any horse of this habit. This must be done as soon as the animal strikes in order to be effective, but this is the one time the trainer does not dare be chicken-hearted. A horse confirmed in this habit is perhaps as dangerous as any animal living, and when it comes to a choice of soundly whipping a horse or taking a chance of a man being injured for life, or even killed, there can be no second choice.

A stallion jumping a man comes under the same category as the one which strikes, and must be treated the same. There may be some super-sensitive persons with little experience who will not agree with me, but I doubt if there is in the country a man of wide experience with stallions who will not agree on this point. I know from experience, having at one time been knocked out by a stud striking me on the head and another time having my back badly wrenched and nearly broken by a stud jumping me. I have found that it is generally persons with little experience who think they know all the answers. I am reminded of a lady who got into a conversation with my wife. She knew all about colts and proceeded to explain the whole business to my wife. It developed that this lady had one mare that had had one colt and was with colt at the time; whereas, my wife has been on breeding farms for quite a number of years and is a registered nurse with a post graduate course in obstetrics. I find that it is often that type of person who is forever giving advice.

Biting or *nipping* is perhaps one of the most difficult of all bad habits to cure. Often colts get nippy from mere playfulness, and if they do it only in that spirit and little attention is paid to it, they will generally outgrow the habit. They should never be teased, and one should try to keep away from their mouths as much as possible. If the colt nips too frequently or if it begins to bite hard, it should be corrected by a crack across the neck. Nearly everyone will want to hit a nippy colt in the mouth or head. If one continues doing this, the colt will begin to look for it and will nip and then jerk its head away fast, and in so doing it will clamp its teeth down hard, making what would probably have been a playful nip a hard bite. For this reason, the horse or colt should never be struck on the head. If one uses a whip around a horse's head, the cracker may snap in the eye and blind it for life. I like to carry a wooden paddle around a colt that seems to be developing the habit of biting and use it on the colt's neck. It will make quite a noise and there will be no danger of injuring the colt. An older horse that has acquired this habit should wear a muzzle, as a cure is improbable.

Masturbating is a hard habit to break once acquired. A young horse that gets enough exercise, a certain amount of service during the breeding season, and is kept in a stall between two mares, will seldom acquire the habit. Sometimes the same treatment will effect a cure, otherwise a stallion ring placed just behind the head of the penis, tight enough to prevent an erection, will prevent the animal from practicing the habit. A stallion shield will also prove effective generally and is much easier to care for than a ring.

Rubbing tails is sometimes quite a problem. The horse may often do this because it has worms; in which case the remedy is apparent. Horses wearing tail sets often rub their tails if not prevented by means of tail boards. A dirty tail will often cause a horse to rub it, and for this reason if for no other, the tails should be washed quite often, every two weeks to a month, depending upon conditions. Salt rubbed in the tail immediately after it is washed will effect a remedy many times. Sometimes a parasite is the cause of tail rubbing. At one place where I worked, there was one stall in the stable that seemed to have been infected. At any rate, every horse I put in that stall would soon begin rubbing its tail. After washing the stall and tail boards down with boiling water, into which I had poured some creosote, I had no further trouble. Oftentimes absorbine rubbed into the tail will clear up a parasite condition. Another very good treatment I have found is one tablespoon of Tuttle's Elixir in a pop bottle of warm water applied to the tail bone about three different times. I also have found that an anti-tail-rubbing compound, made by Chas. F. Taylor, Bowling Green, Kentucky, is as effective for this as anything I have ever tried.

Halter pulling is another very bad habit and just how an animal acquires the habit, I am not sure. I believe if they are broke right as colts they will not learn the habit. The standard remedy is to fasten a rope in a slip knot around the animal's belly, passing it up through the halter ring, then tying the horse with this rope to a solid post, and attempting to force the animal back into this rope. This will break young horses and some older ones. However, an old horse, confirmed in this habit, probably has had this contraption on it and will refuse to back into it. I have seen horses that refused to back into such a rigging, even when scared with newspapers or other means. With such horses, perhaps the only thing to do is to always tie them with a strong rope around the neck and pass it through the halter ring, and if and when the horse does pull back, get behind it and whip it until it goes forward again. If one does this each time the horse pulls back, it will generally be effective for several months, but seemingly it will try again sooner or later even after such a lesson and can never be completely relied upon.

Eating the bedding is a fairly common habit. It may be from some deficiency in the diet, or the horse may be just gluttonous. I would first advise changing feeds for a couple of weeks at a time, including all known combinations and the addition of commercial minerals. If that doesn't help, about the only thing one can do is to bed with either peat moss or shavings. Peat moss is far better, as shavings are extremely drying to the hoofs.

Tearing the stable clothing is a habit developed by many colts, and if they are not prevented, many will carry the habit over into later life. Common preventions are: Wearing a muzzle all the time, except at feeding time, or wearing a special bib attached to the halter. This bib must be large to be effective and must be reinforced with light strap iron around the edges or the colt will finally chew the bib. A pole will generally prove as effective as anything. It has a snap placed on each end. One snap is attached to the halter and the other to a surcingle at about the middle of the side of the colt. This will prevent the colt from reaching the blanket, yet it can eat or lie down. It must be made the correct length, of course, for the particular colt.

The mean to trim, wash sheath, shoe, etc., horse: The aged horse that has learned to be mean at times like this can seldom be cured, and about the only thing to do is restrain it with a twitch. The twitch should be placed only on the nose and taken off as soon as possible, and the nose rubbed to restore circulation. Once in a long while one will find a horse that cannot be restrained with a nose twitch; in which case, he may apply it to the ear, which is the most effective. An ear twitch should only be used as a last resort, as it will almost always cause a horse to become head shy. Tying up a leg or throwing may be necessary in extreme cases. I prefer to try to get along without the use of a twitch on colts. The twitch doesn't teach them a thing, but merely restrains them for the time being, and generally they become harder to twitch as time goes on. For this reason, I far prefer to spend more time and teach them to hold still without the twitch. If necessary, this may be done by partially restraining them with cotton ropes or even by punishing with a whip. In this way, most colts may be broke to stand for the clippers and shoeing. It takes a little more time to do this, but it will save time later on, as it means that one man can do a job that would otherwise take two. Sometimes a stallion lead placed through the halter ring and over the nose to the other ring and snatched every time the colt misbehaves will effect a cure. This punishment is more severe than a whip and must be used with discretion.

The head-shy horse is one of the hardest to cure. In some cases, one may accomplish the desired result by merely being extremely gentle with the head and ears and attempt to gain the confidence of the animal in the trainer. I believe one reason why this vice is often thought incurable is that on the whole we do not have enough patience. In attempting this kind of a cure, the colt's head and ears are gently handled and rubbed several times a day, while an assistant holds the head if necessary. Sometimes a horse will be head-shy because of a sore ear or something of that nature, and an examination should always be made before pronouncing the horse incurably head-shy. Several years ago I got a Kalarama Rex mare that was extremely head-shy when being bridled, but only around the left ear. Complete examination failed to discover the cause; however, I discovered that if the bridle was put on from the right instead of the left side, and the right ear was first inserted into the bridle, she was perfectly gentle with the left ear also. Just why she should have been this way, I can't say, but that small change in the manner of putting on the bridle effected a permanent cure, just as long as we continued doing it that way; and she would never stand for having the bridle put on from the left. This is just another instance where a small change in the manner of doing something will oftentimes work when nothing else will. I find that many vices may be cured if we can just use our heads enough to figure things out.

This about completes the common vices which horses acquire in one way or another in the stable, but they will develop many bad habits and defenses under the saddle.

UNDER THE SADDLE

Shying is generally a vice of a nervous horse. It arises from one of several causes, either actual fear, an attempt to dislodge the rider, or sometimes mere playfulness. In most cases, we will assume that the animal shies because it is frightened by something unusual. We must remember that a horse is near-sighted and that even a familiar object at a distance or from an unusual angle will frighten almost any horse, and especially horses of a nervous temperament. Any unusual movement, such as a piece of paper blowing across the road, will frighten most horses. The remedy in many cases and whenever possible is to take the animal up to the object which is the cause of the fright and allow the mount to touch it with his nose and examine it from all angles, at the same time, caressing the horse and talking soothingly to it. One will often be surprised at the good he can do generally with a nervous horse by using a soothing voice. The main thing is to instill in the animal confidence in the rider.

Often, timid riders cause the animal to shy. The rider sees something which he thinks may cause the mount to shy and becomes frightened himself, and this in some way or other causes the horse to realize his rider is frightened and decides that there must be something to be afraid of. The horse isn't just sure what it is afraid of but partakes of the rider's fear, for there is no mistake about it—if the rider becomes frightened or loses confidence in himself, he cannot fail to communicate that fright or loss of confidence to his mount. I have had any number of experiences of being asked to ride an animal that was supposed to shy easily, or perhaps buck, and there was nothing I could do that would make the animal act up for me. I have had other trainers, as well as other good riders, tell me of similar experiences; so, in some instances, the cure lies with the rider rather than the horse. The rider must learn complete confidence in himself and his mount, and he must impart that confidence to his mount, because if the animal does not respect the ability of the rider, it may shy just to try to unseat the rider. If this is thought to be the case, it should be brought up on the bit with the spurs. At the present time, I have an Arabian in my charge which is always ridden by a competent rider, yet he is always on the lookout for something to jump away from. It appears to me that it does this maliciously, deliberately trying to find a moment when the rider is off guard and unseat him. I have not had the time or the opportunity to ride this horse for any length of time myself, and therefore, can't say whether it could be cured or not. I believe that I could partially break it of the habit; but the owner, I think, rather enjoys it. A horse like this should be kept up on the bit at all times and receive a reprimand with the spur, for this sort of behavior. It must learn to have a healthy respect for the rider.

Kicking under the saddle is generally done out of sheer exuberance of spirit, and if the animal merely indulges in this once or twice when first brought out, little notice need be paid to it. One should give such a horse more work and bring it into full collection soon after being brought out. That is, convert this excess energy into action and brilliance. The animal that kicks from meanness or at other horses, however, should immediately be punished with the spur and perhaps the whip also. Collecting it and moving it ahead faster at a trot will prevent it, as the animal will find it hard to do much kicking if it is trotting lively. This sort of thing must not be tolerated.

Bucking in a broke horse is generally done in an outburst of energy. The well broke animal will seldom, if ever, attempt it; but if the horse is so inclined, a strong rider can generally convert this energy into more useful channels. The novice who owns or rides a horse that does this will do well to work it on the bitting harness about ten minutes before riding it. This will take the edge off the horse and may prevent an accident. Raising the head as high as possible is a pretty good prevention, as a horse cannot do much bucking with its head up high. If the spurs are to be used on this kind of a horse, they should be used one at a time, as both spurs may cause it to buck more, but one spur will not.

Running away: In a very few instances a horse will become crazed and run wild. In a case of this kind, there is little anyone can do, except try to guide it to prevent it from running into anything, as it will not respond to any usual stimuli. Such cases are extremely rare, so rare in fact that most people who ride a lot will not run into such a case in a lifetime. In most instances, where one is riding a broke horse that attempts to run away, it is merely caused by fright or excess spirits. It should not be allowed to run and should be brought under control by producing a flexion with a give-and-take. Except in severe cases, the horse should not be brought to an abrupt halt. Most cases of runaways are caused by ignorant riders trying to race their horses and allowing them to get out of control. There is no excuse for this, and such riders should be arrested the same as automobile speeders are.

Pulling at the bits is closely allied to the foregoing and may lead to runaways. A horse that does this needs a lot of work on the bitting harness in order to teach it to give to the bits and make it easy to produce a flexion. The clever rider will have little difficulty with such an animal. It takes two to pull—the horse cannot pull the rider unless the rider does a little pulling also. The rider must use a give and take on such a horse, rather than a continuous pull. A severe bit with long shanks and a high port may be desirable on an animal of this kind.

Boring: When the animal pulls its head down, making it impossible to produce a correct flexion, it is called boring. This type of horse also needs a lot of work on the bitting rig and perhaps needs to wear a very small snaffle or a fishback snaffle bit, which may be severe enough to cause the animal to lift its head to the pressure of the snaffle bit. In working this sort of horse on the bitting harness, the secret bit must be very small but must not be adjusted tight, just tight enough so that it will hurt the horse's mouth whenever it attempts to lower its head, but loose enough that it can get off the snaffle entirely. After working a horse like this on the bitting harness for at least a month, it may then be saddled and the bitting harness placed over the saddle. The horse should be worked this way for several weeks so that the animal does not learn that it can bore under the saddle even if it can't in the bitting rig. Some horses develop the habit of jerking their heads down, just now and then. They must be treated as borers, although some of these horses can be broken of this habit by having a firm hold on the curb reins and by letting the horse hit the curb hard when it ducks its head.

Balking is generally a vice of a cold blooded horse, but not always. The cure lies in complete subjection at all times. In individual cases, the treatment is to try to destroy the rigidity of the muscles. This may be accomplished by turning one way, then quickly turning the other way; or even by backing a step, then immediately taking advantage of the relaxed muscles. One must remember that a horse has a one-track mind and oftentimes, if it refuses to move one way, it may be induced to move another, after which it will probably go in any direction it is asked. Sometimes if one will dismount and tuck the horse's ear under the bridle, it will start shaking its head and forget all about balking. After it starts off, one can fix the bridle later on. Sometimes a stroke of the whip or a touch of the spur at the right moment may prove effective and be just what the doctor ordered. More than that, however, will generally be worse than useless, angering the animal and making it more determined than ever. A sound whipping never yet cured any real balker, and one is just wasting his time and energy to try. A horse that balks in harness may often be started by rigging up a wet storage battery to a magneto from an old Ford car and running the wires up the lines and down to the crupper. Just at the command, "Get Up," if the animal is given a shock, it will generally move right now.

The herd-bound horse or the stable-bound horse are in about the same classification as the balker. In the first case, the animal is all right except that it will not leave a group of horses that it has been accustomed to being worked with. In the latter the animal does not want to leave the barn. In either instance, the animal must be brought under complete subjection of the rider at all times. I remember the case of a stable-bound horse that I had nearly twenty years ago at a riding academy and boarding stable. When I bought this horse, he seemed all right and continued so for about a week. One day after he had had a day or two of rest, he threw a girl rider in refusing to leave the stable. I mounted him and had quite an argument with him myself before he would leave. I finally discovered that he was all right if he was ridden every day, but if he was allowed to rest one day, he would refuse to leave the barn and would put up quite a bucking match if one tried to force him to leave. After I discovered how to keep him working, I would send one of the stable boys out on him the first thing every morning for about half an hour, and in this way he made a splendid school horse.

Rearing is also a defense closely related to balking and being stable-bound. The cure is the same as in the former cases; That is, getting the horse completely under the control of the rider at all times. When the animal rises, if spurs are poked into its ribs well back and hard, it will generally cause the animal to come down immediately, but it may rear again. In no case, should the rider ever dismount from a rearing horse, unless it actually falls over backwards. If the rider does this, it will teach the horse that it can get rid of the rider whenever it pleases, and it will resort to this practice more and more. One need not fear the horse coming over backwards on him if he does not pull on the curb reins while the horse is in the air. The horse so seldom rears high enough to come over backwards that it is the exception that proves the rule, and if it does, there is always plenty of time to get out of the way. Any experienced rider can easily feel the minute a horse becomes over-balanced and begins to fall backward, and he will then drop or jump off, running or rolling out of the way. It is certain that few horses ever actually attempt to throw themselves over backward, except in western stories, but many rearers can be cured by being deliberately pulled over backward when they are rearing. I had a little black mare that had developed the habit of rearing anytime she didn't get her own way. I completely cured her by one treatment of that kind. I remember another colt that I later discovered was broken by a timid rider. This colt would rear badly if one tried to ride it over a block away from the stable. I later found out that the former boy would then dismount and lead it back to the stable. I had one session with this colt in which I proved that I was not going to dismount and that it must go forward whenever I asked it to, after which I had no further trouble with it.

Getting behind the bit: This, too, is a defense against doing what the rider wants it to. The horse continually tosses its head and pulls on the bit when one tries to flex it, or it perhaps backs up at that moment, or does anything at all to keep from going up in the bit. It is sometimes a fairly difficult job to break the animal of this vice. About the best method I have found is to work this horse in the bitting harness, but instead of using side straps, use a pair of springs. The common coil door springs work very well. They should be adjusted so that there is always a slight tension on the bit, but very little when the animal gives to the bit and quite a lot if it pulls. One may have an assistant on the ground to force it up in the bit with a whip. After working the horse on the bitting harness a couple of weeks with a snaffle bit for the side straps and a little secret bit for the check rein, I then replace the snaffle bit with a stiff bit, preferably a Liverpool bit and fasten the side straps to the top hole for a week or so and then move them lower. A port bit should not be used, as it may cause the horse to cut its mouth. One should not use a curb chain on this sort of rigging. After about a month's work on the bitting harness, the horse should be worked under saddle again and forced into the bit by means of the spurs. It should always be ridden well in form for several months' time after this treatment.

Tongue over the bit: This defense is often the outgrowth of the former habit of getting behind the bit and is really a serious fault. The animal which does this will be continually cutting its mouth, and the rider will have little control over it. The sure remedy is to tie the tongue down, and this is done with race horses which have this habit. At best, this is unsightly, and as it cuts off the circulation, such a tie may not be left on for long periods of time. It is, therefore, impractical for Saddle Horses. A young horse just starting this habit may generally be broken by using a bit with a high port and adjusting it one hole tighter in the mouth than is usual and by tightening the nose band. Oftentimes even older horses may be prevented from getting their tongues over the bit by this procedure.

Stumbling is an extremely serious fault. In many cases, it may be remedied by calling the attention of the fault to the farrier, who may be able to suggest a remedy for that particular animal. Sometimes, shortening the toes will help such an animal. Stumbling may be caused by just plain laziness; in which case, keeping the animal well up on the bit at all times and keeping it awake with the spurs will often help. If the animal does it only when tired and leg weary, the rider will find that if he will dismount and lead it for a few minutes, it will rest both the horse and the rider. If the horse stumbles continually, however, from a structural defect, it is dangerous and may cause someone to get hurt badly. One will do well to dispose of such an animal, no matter what loss he may have to take. No horse is worth the price of injuring a person severely, and such a horse cannot be cured.

Chapter X

SELECTING AND BUYING A HORSE

We hope in this chapter to render a much needed help to the man expecting to buy a horse, as well as to bring a little better relationship between the dealer and the purchaser. There are two principal ways in which the prospective purchaser may satisfy his needs—either by private purchase or at an auction sale. In either case, there are certain things one may wish to ascertain before completing the contract.

First, the buyer must know exactly what he is looking for. This may seem a strange thing to say, but after one has been in this business for a good many years, he finds that a number of people who are looking for horses are not quite sure what they want. Many of these want an all-around horse; that is, one they can use on the trail and maybe jump a little, and then put in the show ring after wearing a tail-set about a week and expect to beat a stake horse. One may as well be satisfied before he starts looking, that there is no such animal. It is true that there are a few horses which can be used for pleasure riding and still do some showing at smaller shows. In cases of this kind, however, the horses are generally kept up and wear their tail-sets continuously; also, the rider is a very accomplished horseman who does not use his horse for trail riding, but who always enjoys riding his horse as much in form as a show horse. He does not over-ride the horse and keeps it shod up for show purposes. Such an owner is an excellent rider and gets his enjoyment out of riding as a trainer does, for the purpose of keeping the horse up and constantly trying to improve it. If the prospective buyer is such a rider, then he may have a combination pleasure and show horse; but even so, he should not expect to compete in the larger shows' stake classes. If he does, he must not feel hurt if the horse he has loved and lavished his attention and affection upon, should be beaten by a horse trained and ridden by a professional.

The professional always has a distinct advantage. He very probably has an animal that cost more and was worth more in the first place, then by long experience he has learned most of the tricks of the trade, of making the horse and getting the most out of it and showing it to the best advantage. In nearly all cases the professional is actually a better rider, even if he had no more ability at first. He generally rides from a dozen to a score of horses daily for six days a week, while the average amateur probably rides from a half hour to an hour a day for two or three days a week. The old saying that "Practice makes perfect" was never more true than with horseback riding. Furthermore, the professional must be good in order to continue making his living by riding; while to the owner, riding is merely a pleasant form of relaxation and exercise.

To the prospective purchaser, we say, know whether you want a pleasure horse, a jumper, a trail horse, or a show horse! If one feels that he is capable of training and showing his own horse and wants to do that, he must look long and carefully for that type and be prepared to pay the price, as such horses are rare enough to command high prices. He must also have the necessary facilities for keeping the horse in show form. The showing of horses in large stake classes has become big business and in most instances is not the place for an amateur, but there are thousands of smaller shows throughout the country where the owner may show his own horse with a fair chance of success.

Before discussing the subject of examining the prospect before buying, let us look into the methods of purchase; that is, private sale and auction. When buying privately one may buy from a dealer, a friend, or a friend of a friend.

In my experience, the hardest person from whom to buy a horse is the man who owns only a few horses and may or may not be a friend or an acquaintance. The average small owner loves his horses and values them far above their actual worth. For some strange reason he nearly always feels that the old-time gypsy horse dealing days are still with us, and that he must be just a little bit crooked or sly in order to be considered "horsey." This same man may be an outstanding business man in some other line of business, or a man of highest professional integrity and honesty. In his own business he may never think of overcharging or covering up the slightest detail of imperfection; yet, when selling a horse to a friend or acquaintance he will think that he is pulling a fast one if he can charge double what the horse is worth or cover up some fault, blemish, or unsoundness. I could relate literally hundreds of instances where this was the case, but will cite only a few to give the reader an idea of what I mean.

I know a business man in the Midwest who has owned horses all his life. He had a little bay mare worth about $125.00 that could have been bought for that from any dealer, yet he asked a friend of his $750.00 for her. I heard him tell his daughter that she must be careful when showing this mare to their friend, "as you have to be slick to deal in horses." This same man's business dealings are A No. 1, and he and his family are civic leaders and above reproach. I know another professional man, high in his particular profession, who sold a string-halted mare to a friend of his, and sold her as sound. Another business man sold a friend of his a gelding for $500.00 that was supposed to be quiet enough for his friend's wife. The horse was quite spooky and worth about $90.00. He knew his friend wouldn't bring a court action for so small a sum. A dealer wouldn't dare do the same thing. I know of cribbers and weavers being sold to friends as sound horses, and in one case even a horse with navicular trouble. Therefore, I can not honestly recommend buying a horse from a friend, relative, or business acquaintance, unless one knows the animal thoroughly and can purchase it for what it is worth.

There is also the idea that one can look over the backwoods of any of the breeding states: Ohio, Pennsylvania, Kentucky, Tennessee, Indiana, Illinois, Iowa, or Missouri and secure a horse far below its actual worth. This line of reasoning may have been all right fifty years ago, but today most of the better horses have been bought up by the larger breeding farms. Furthermore, the farmers themselves have become "city broke" and often times ask more for a horse than a dealer would. Besides one must travel many miles over some awful roads to get to some of those places, and in this way spend far more than the cost of the animal itself. There generally are some dealers located somewhere close to all these farmers who have anything worthwhile, and the dealers will pay fair cash prices for these prospects. Notwithstanding all this, if one wishes to take a vacation and enjoys such a trip in preference to spending his vacation in any other way he may have a good time and gain some valuable experience in this way. It is always possible that he may pick up a "gem in the rough," but from a purely economic standpoint it just does not work out.

Finally, we have the horse dealer. If one makes sure that he is reliable, this is no doubt the safest place the average buyer can purchase his mount. The old-time gypsy horse trading days are over and done with, and most dealers today conduct their business with as much care, intelligence, and honesty as the better stores. Oh! I well realize that there still are a few small dealers who have not progressed with the times, but the same can be said of a few small storekeepers, doctors, lawyers, and so forth. Therefore, first, make certain that the dealer to whom you intend going is reliable, then explain exactly what you want and take his advice the same as you would that of your doctor or the clerk in the store. He is really anxious to serve you and have you satisfied. His business is selling horses, and he knows them. Furthermore, he knows that sooner or later you are going to want a better horse, or more horses, or that you have friends who will one day be wanting horses, and if you are satisfied you will eventually help him sell a dozen or more other horses.

You will probably have to pay slightly more for an animal from a dealer than in the auction ring, but it is worth it many times over. Your safety, not to mention that of your wife or child, cannot be measured in dollars and cents; and at an auction sale you have absolutely nothing to go on, while the dealer will not sell an unreliable horse privately. Rather than take chances with his reputation, he sends all horses he does not want to stand behind to the auction block, takes whatever he can get, and "let the buyer beware."

Furthermore, the dealer does not price horses outrageously high. He knows horses and what they are worth and has taught himself not to fall in love with any of them, but to view them strictly as merchandise. He must sell horses and keep on selling them in sufficient quantities to go on making a living, so he will try to sell you what you want at a reasonable price.

Don't ask for a guarantee of soundness. Few dealers will give this, as one may buy a horse, take it home, and have something happen to it in a day or so, even unbeknown to the buyer, and blame the dealer, who may easily lose a court case. Rather, ask for and get a veterinary's certificate of soundness. Any dealer is glad to get this at his own expense, or the purchaser may call in his own veterinarian at his own expense. In either case, no veterinarian is going to risk his professional reputation by making out a false certificate, and this certificate protects both you and the dealer. No dealer can possibly guarantee what may happen to the horse after it leaves his stable. If one wishes to have his horse insured this is the time to do it. The insurance veterinarian will list any faults, unsoundnesses, or defects before insuring the animal.

When approaching the dealer, do not act smart or bring a knowing friend who will treat the dealer as if he were a "gypsy" and try to pick faults in the horse that it does not have. Consider how you would feel under similar circumstances. If the buyer goes to the dealer with a know-it-all air or takes a friend so disposed, who disbelieves everything the dealer says, it may get his dander up, and just to prove that the buyer or his friend is not so smart, he may put one over. Remember, the dealer is only human too, and he has had experience with hundreds of horses for every one the average buyer has. I know of dealers who sell five to seven hundred head of horses a year, which is about a dozen times as many as the average owner has anything to do with in a lifetime. If, however, one goes to a good dealer in a businesslike way, the same as if he were going to buy a suit of clothes, and explains just what he wants and about what he can pay, the dealer will try his best to satisfy him or will tell him that he does not have anything at that time that will fill the bill. He very likely will refer the buyer elsewhere. Anyone is always welcome to visit a horse dealer's stable or farm, whether he is ready to buy or not, and this is a good way to get acquainted with a number of horses, but one should not try pricing several horses he has no intention of buying. This kind of person is soon spotted, and the price quoted to such a visitor may be anything from half to ten times what the animal is worth or for which it will be sold.

There is also the auction block as a means of securing a horse. There are getting to be a number of these all over the country. In most instances this is probably the cheapest place to buy a horse; not only from the standpoint of actual cost, but also because of the fact that one can see a large number at one place and at one time and therefore make his selection easier and cheaper. The auction block, however, is probably the trickiest place to buy a horse and is the place for the expert rather than the novice. Even the expert gets stung many times. The annual auctions are used for the most part by dealers to get rid of stock that they refuse to stand behind in private sales, for culling out animals that are not worth keeping any longer; and by breeders for culling over their breeding stock and colts that they do not think will pay the cost of raising.

Few good horses go to the auction block, except at dispersal sales, those sent by a few breeders who use this means of disposing of all their young stock each year, or in unusual circumstances. For the most part the motto seems to be, "let the buyer beware." Some sales rings have a veterinarian examine all horses for soundness before being sold and announce the findings at the time the animal is brought up; others depend upon the owners' statements, which may or may not be misleading. In some cases where the veterinarian findings are announced, they may be softened up to a point where the novice does not catch the meaning; such as, "He is a little anxious for water," or "He likes the wood" for a cribber. A nickel's worth of feather may mean that the horse is all but stone blind. In no case will blemishes be called unless they actually cause unsoundness, nor will faults of disposition be called, and sometimes these are the worst faults of all. In any case, the buyer has no recourse once the sale is completed and he has paid his money. Therefore, while the expert who is going to buy a dozen or more horses may profitably buy at an auction sale, and if he gets stung on one or two of them has bought the others cheap enough to make up for it, the novice who intends purchasing one horse for himself or his family to ride had better be extraordinarily careful and use all his knowledge as well as that of any horse minded friend he may have.

He should, if possible, get to the sale ring a day before the auction starts and look over any horses he thinks he may be interested in. He should then ask as many questions as he can get answered, and decide how much he will pay for a certain animal. At the time of the sale he should stick close to his original valuation of that animal. One must not allow himself to be swayed too much because the bidding is brisk and perhaps get himself bidding against one or two by-bidders who are merely trying to bid him up. It happens at every sale. If it looks as if this is happening, the only thing to do is drop out and wait until another horse that one is interested in comes up. I know of one particular case where a young man was so anxious to get a certain horse that he bid himself up from $1,800 to $2,950, with no one bidding against him. On the other hand, if one decides to pay just so much for a horse he is better off not to stall along trying to get the horse five or ten dollars cheaper. Oftentimes a jump bid will shut the other bidders out, and one will actually get the animal cheaper than by going up slowly.

Many bidders will decide to pay so much for a horse but will stall along on their bids and finally allow the horse to be knocked down to another bidder for a smaller amount. This happens quite a few times at almost every sale, and at most sales many horses are resold at a good profit just in this way. The man who originally wants the horse fails to bid at the sale and after he does not get it he wants it all the more and will offer a substantial profit to the successful bidder. I know of one case where a stallion was sold for $2,500, and the successful bidder was immediately offered $4,000 for the animal. I, myself, have been offered double the price I paid for a horse by some bidder who failed to get in and bid at the right time, when he could probably have secured the animal by an extra ten or twenty-five dollar bid at the right time. To sum it up; the prospective purchaser at the auction ring should find out all he can, use all his and his friends' judgment, and know when to bid and when to quit bidding.

Now, as to selecting the horses and how to evaluate soundness, blemishes, etc., I will try to set down certain basic rules and try to omit as much hocum as possible. In every work on this subject that I have ever read, the author tries to explain that the horse must travel straight, his legs must set just so, etc., until the reader begins to feel that he must buy a perfect horse or none at all. As a matter of fact, there is no such thing as a perfect horse any more than there is a perfect man, and the man who starts out to buy a perfect horse is either going to get cheated or never buy a horse. The art of buying or dealing in horses comes from evaluating the different faults or blemishes and realizing how much or how little damage each one does and which can be corrected. On one hand, if one is buying a horse for himself and he is a very good rider, he will not discount it any if the horse is a trifle skittish; but on the other hand, if he is buying the horse for a young child or a lady who has ridden very little, then perfect manners are more important than looks or even soundness. Therefore, the use to which the animal is to be put must always be kept uppermost in the mind of the prospective purchaser.

Any horse one buys should be at least usably sound. In order to determine this, the animal should be trotted over firm ground or a hard road. Any limping or soreness, unless purposely covered up, will then be revealed. I certainly would not advise anyone, unless he was sure he knew what he was doing, to buy any lame horse. They can go lame fast enough after one owns them. The expert may notice the cause of the lameness and know how to correct it, but the novice should stay clear of anything that shows the least sign of lameness, as it may get worse. At the same time, the purchaser should notice how the animal travels; whether in a straight line or with any noticeable swinging in or out with either front or back feet, the amount of action, and whether it appears to travel loosely or if it is all stiffened up. Extreme action is not at all necessary, except for a show horse; but the horse should travel freely, as the looser it moves, in most instances, the easier ride it will give. If the animal comes out of the stall a little stiff or sore in front and soon warms out of it, it is a good guess that it is lame in the shoulders. Such an animal should be observed standing in the stall and if it paws or continually holds one front foot ahead of the

ILLUSTRATION XXV

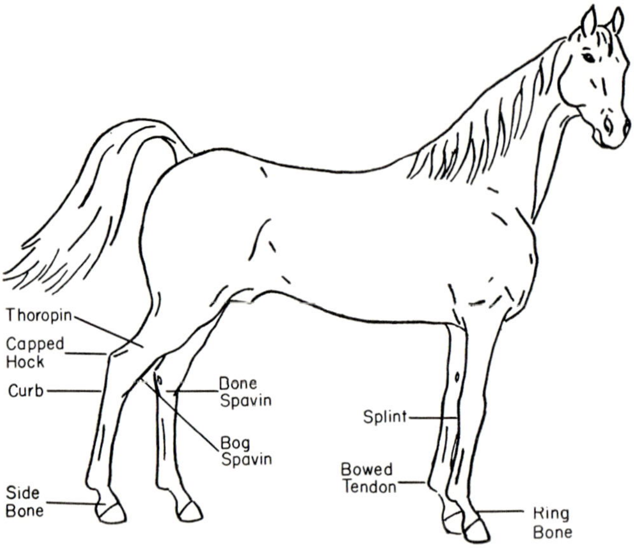

POINTS AT WHICH UNSOUNDNESSES OCCUR

other, it is a further indication of shoulder soreness. Both front feet forward may be an indication that the animal is sore in both shoulders or that it has been foundered. An animal that is sore in the shoulders may completely rest out of it; however, it may take anywhere from three months to a year and it may never get over it. An animal that has an old case of founder can never be completely sound, but may be shod so that it is nearly so, for usability.

The footsore horse may be so from a bruise, which will in time right itself; from contracted heels, which can easily be detected by close examination and for which it can probably be shod so that in time it will become perfectly sound; from corns for which it can be shod so that it will be serviceably sound; or from navicular trouble for which there is no cure, but even in this case it may be shod so that it can get around fairly or even quite well. If the animal swings its feet in, it is an indication that the animal may become a knee or ankle knocker, unless it can be shod out of it. If the horse moves extremely free in the shoulders it is very likely that it will go to weight and can be shod out of it. If, on the other hand, the horse travels stiffly in the shoulders it is very doubtful if it can be shod so that it will travel straight, and anytime it becomes tired it will, no doubt, begin hitting its knees or ankles, depending upon how high it goes. This, in turn, may cause the animal to become lame. It should, therefore, be put in the category of an unsound horse, or nearly so. Such a horse will generally stand toeing out or, as we say, nigger-heeled. A horse like this should be closely examined and be considered a bad bargain, unless one is very sure what he is doing. One should remember this, that if the horse does stand nigger-heeled and swings in with its front feet, it is merely a fault of conformation and not an unsoundness, unless it has already caused the horse to become unsound; and, in no instance, will any fault of conformation or blemish be called to one's attention. This is for each and every man to find out for himself.

The animal that stands pigeon-toed and wings as it travels or throws its feet out sideways instead of traveling true, is just the opposite of the foregoing and by being shod the opposite way, the fault may or may not be corrected. As can readily be seen, this is not likely to have the severe consequences as in the case of the nigger-heeled horse, and therefore, little attention need be given to it, unless it is very bad or if one contemplates showing the horse. In a show ring this will, of course, be counted against a horse, but not to a great degree, and if the horse is superior in all other respects to a horse that travels straight, it will still win.

In the rear the horse may also travel in or out; in either case it is quite a problem to shoe such a horse so that it will travel straight, although it sometimes may be helped considerably. Swinging out too much slightly weakens the animal's usefulness or its showing ability; while swinging in, if bad enough, may cause the animal to hit itself and become lame. A very little out of line, either way, need hardly be noticed. Any soreness in the hip or stiffle joint will generally show up as the animal is trotted forward. Oftentimes a horse will rest out of such soreness by being turned out to graze for some length of time. Soreness in the hock joint can generally be detected easier by backing the animal by short turns or by raising the hind foot backwards. Such soreness is generally quite serious.

The front legs should set on the animal straight and come out of the body well apart, rather than too close. It makes both for better appearance and more usefulness, and a horse with a chest that is too narrow is often quite hard to resell in case one tires of him. The knees must bend neither in nor out and, as viewed from the side, must set straight, with no tendency of dishing back and very little if any tendency of bending forward. A horse over in the knees nearly always shows signs of excessive strain.

The hind legs as viewed from behind should set in a straight line; however, most of us would prefer the hocks to point slightly in rather than out. It is what we call cow hocked, and while it is objectionable, it is not as much so as the animal with hocks spread too far apart. When viewed from the side the foot should set slightly forward, rather than directly under the hock. A very little variation need not cause one any concern, but too much is undesirable. The whole appearance of the animal must be taken into consideration, rather than any one particular part. If one is a pretty fair horseman and the whole appearance from front, side, and back is pleasing, then the animal is, no doubt, correctly proportioned; on the other hand, if it does not seem symmetrical at any particular point, that part should be examined carefully.

Splints are enlargements of the splint bones and may occur on any leg, but are more generally seen on the inside of the forelegs. They are merely considered blemishes and in most cases do not bother the animal's usefulness at all, unless they are set well around the cannon bone where they may cause pressure on the tendons. If the prospective buyer does not mind the looks of these bumps, he may think little of them, but if one must have a clean limbed horse, he should take note. Filled tendons are a sign of weakness or lameness and probably will cause a lot of trouble keeping the animal going sound. Filled ankles or fetlocks, if soft or wind puffed, need generally cause little concern. They may usually be taken down with bandages or as the animal hardens he may quit puffing there. If these filled fetlock joints are hard, it may indicate that the animal has had quite a lot of strain or abuse and will in many cases be impossible to remedy. Such a horse may or may not remain sound. Ring bones, or side bones, are bony growths just above the hoof on the pastern joint. Ring bones on the front of the foot are especially bad and generally will cause the horse to go lame. Side bones may or may not cause lameness. They are not considered quite as bad as those in front, but are, nevertheless, quite serious.

The hoof should be well shaped and firm. Thrush is an evil smelling disease found on either side of the frog, that V-shaped horny growth on the bottom of the hoof. A case of thrush, even if bad enough to cause lameness, can generally be cleared up without too much trouble. Contracted heels may also be remedied in most instances. While one is looking at the feet it is a good idea to notice how the horse is shod, for if it is excessively weighted, it is likely to lose much of its action if lighter shoes are to be worn, and it may be hard to keep the animal sound wearing heavy shoes. If, however, the animal is to be used for the same purpose as it has been used for, in most cases it is not wise to change the shoe drastically, especially if it has been worked by a dealer or professional trainer. Exceedingly long toes are in the same category as heavy shoes and act much the same, i.e., increasing action but causing a lot of strain on the tendons. Special shoes, long toes, etc., are probably on the horse for a good reason, and while this may not deter the prospective buyer from purchasing a certain horse, nevertheless he should take note of these things and take them into consideration before making the purchase.

There are several other forms of unsoundnesses a horse gets on its hind legs. Thoroughpins are hard projections just above the hocks in the soft part of the legs. They can generally be pushed through from one side to the other. I have never heard of them being taken off, but they seldom cause a horse to become lame; however, they may. A bone spavin or a jack, as we commonly call it, will generally cause lameness. Jacks are bad business and cannot be cured. They may sometimes be killed, and the horse may then be given moderate use. Jacks are bony growths on the lower inside of the hock joints. The jack spavin is generally the result of an accident or strain. The blood spavin or bog, as we usually call it, is also generally the result of an accident or strain. As its name implies, it is not a bony growth but an enlargement and a separation of the blood vessels in that area, causing a gathering of the blood which becomes semi-hard and makes moving of the hock joint painful. It is located on the front of the hock joint. It may sometimes be cured but may reappear at the first excuse. In any event, both bog and jack spavins are quite serious. Most breeders dislike brood mares which have had spavins, unless they are sure that it was the result of an accident, as it is believed that a weakness in that direction may be inherited. There may be something to that theory. I once had a colt out of a spavined mare that sprung a pair of bogs while still a suckling. As far as we could ascertain, that colt had no undue strain of any sort. One hears quite a lot about blind jacks, which in my opinion covers a multitude of ignorance. In most cases, it simply means that it is impossible to correctly locate the true cause of the lameness. Of course, jacks vary in size and there are times when they may be so small as to be hard to see or feel, but still cause lameness.

A curb is a bony growth on the rear of the hock joint, generally found on horses whose hocks are not well let down. Curbs are generally the result of excessive strain and may cause severe lameness or periodic lameness. They may often be taken off but may reappear again at the slightest strain of the hock joint. Any lameness of the hock joint must be considered serious. String halt is the act of jerking the hind foot or both hind feet up sharply, well under the horse, as it is first led from the stable. The animal may warm out of it by use, but it will again be present after the animal has been standing a short while. It is said that it may be cured by a surgical operation, but in most instances it does not render the animal unserviceable and need not cause one too much concern, if he is looking for an ordinary using horse. It is called an unsoundness and must be considered as such. It is easiest detected when the horse is first led from the stall, after it has been standing awhile and before it has had a chance to warm out of it.

These are the most common blemishes and unsoundnesses of the legs to look for, with the exception of scratches, scars, and wire cuts. Corrective shoeing procedures will be found in the chapter on shoeing and other corrective measures in common use will be found in the chapter on stable management.

The eyes and wind must also be examined before purchasing a horse. A colt may have a white speck in its eye which does not cause blindness and which may disappear in time, or may get worse. Such a colt will not be worth as much as a perfectly sound one; on the other hand, it will probably be as good as a sound horse for utility purposes. In a case like this, if one remembers that he is gambling on whether or not it will recover and, if not, that the colt in question will be slightly harder to resell, there is no reason for not buying it. One must always suspect that a horse which has moon blindness or periodic ophthalmia will eventually go completely blind. Complete blindness in one or both eyes, while not rendering a horse worthless, considerably decreases its value. Moon blindness is often hard for the novice to detect, as it occurs periodically about once a month, lasting from a few to several days and may be in one or both eyes. In between times, the animal will generally have a thin bluish film over the eyeball, which can be seen on dull days or in the stable, but seldom in bright daylight. No reputable man will sell a moon blind horse as sound, but if one does buy such a horse, his only recourse is through the courts of law, in which case, the burden of proof that the animal had shown unmistakable signs of it before the purchase, is on the buyer.

A roaring horse has, no doubt, had overwork or strain at one time or another. If valuable enough, it may be completely cured by a surgical operation, but it is an expensive operation, the cost of which must be taken into consideration before the purchase is completed. A heavey horse, on the other hand, can never be cured. Heaves can be detected in severe cases without even taking the horse out of the stable, as it will have trouble breathing, seeming to draw in two breaths before expelling one. The flanks show labored breathing and the animal will probably cough slightly, a dry hacking cough. All these signs are increased when the horse is used. It is generally the result of dusty hay or feed and is thought by many to be inherited. If the heaves are not too bad, such a horse may be used moderately if it is fed small portions of hay that is dampened down well before feeding. The grain ration will have to be increased and also dampened.

Cribbing is considered an unsoundness for which there is no cure, except a surgical operation. However, except for the fact that one can expect periodic attacks of wind colic, a horse may be considered usably sound even if it is a cribber. Care and treatment will be found in the chapter on stable management. A weaver, or a stall walker, if confirmed in this vice, probably can never be cured, nor considered sound, as such a horse is almost impossible to keep in flesh. If one's riding will be neither hard nor prolonged and he doesn't mind riding a skinny horse, then such a horse may prove satisfactory. While not considered unsound, a parrot mouth on a horse is, nevertheless, a serious defect in conformation. It is generally easy to detect if bad enough to do a great deal of harm. The upper lip overhangs the lower, and upon closer examination it will be found that the front teeth do not meet, but the upper ones overlap the lower by an inch or more. It can easily be seen that such a horse will have a hard time eating, and, in fact, may have to be fed chopped grain and hay for life. In many cases of this kind, the horse can hardly get sustenance even in an exceptionally good pasture, and the prospects for resale are nil.

The foregoing will be looked for in any horse, for any purpose. Other features that one will look for when expecting to buy a horse will be mostly according to the type of horse one wants and the purpose for which he expects to use it. In all types of horses to be used under the saddle, one will naturally look for a comparably short back, meaning the length of the coupling, or distance between the hip bone and the floating rib. One will also want good withers on a horse that is to be used under the saddle.

A five-gaited show horse must have extreme action at the trot and rack. The three-gaited show horse does not need or want speed at the trot, but must have extreme action at all four corners. The show horse must have a very flat croup, a long fine neck set well on a pair of sloping shoulders, a lean, bony, beautiful head set well on the neck, with a pair of smart ears, big eyes, and a clean fine throatlatch. It must be exceptionally well broke to all of its gaits, as well as backing and standing in a correct pose and have a good mouth, which takes a firm yet gentle and light hold on the bits. Just a word of caution, few novices are competent in correctly judging a show horse, and as the cost may range from five to twenty-five thousand dollars, it will be wise to consult a professional horseman before buying a show prospect. One should remember that a horse may look beautiful and that it may have what seems to be a lot of action and speed when by itself but may not look so well when in the company of several other good horses. Even a professional must keep up with the best horses showing and know pretty much what they look like and how much they are able to do, in order to be able to judge a prospect's chances of winning.

A three-or five-gaited pleasure horse should have most of the foregoing attributes, except probably it may lack extreme action or speed, which is needed to qualify the horse for show purposes. An animal of this type should be secured at between $250 and $1,000, depending upon its age and particular excellence or lack of it, in different respects. When approaching the $1,000 class, thc animal should be good enough to go to some of the smaller shows, with some chance of winning in its respective classes. There is almost no limit for a top gaited horse that can go out and win anywhere. There have been reported prices up to $50,000.00 and $20,000.00 for this type of horse is not too uncommon.

If one is simply looking for a pleasure or trail horse, he will not be quite as concerned about looks as he will soundness and the animal being well broke, which, in a trail horse, will probably also mean well reined, especially if one lives in the western part of the country. In the western trail horse, or the stock horse particularly, one will want an exceptionally well reined animal and will look primarily for strength in the quarters. This will be especially true if one expects to use the horse for roping. A right decent trail horse can generally be secured for from $200.00 to $500.00, and a well trained roping horse will be worth considerably more, up to several thousand, depending upon its particular excellence and the locality, as well as the training, conformation, soundness and general usefulness. A roping horse should be low headed and low tailed.

At present, parade horses are selling quite high, up to as much as $25,000. They must have size, style, and a flashy color. In jumpers, one will look especially for very strong quarters and consistency in taking the jumps. Jumpers will range in price from $200 for the cheaper grades, up to as high as $5,000 for top show jumpers of excellent conformation and breeding. They should be of Thoroughbred type.

Color is mostly a matter of personal preference, with chestnuts and dark grays being the easiest to resell generally. Stallions, if especially good, and particularly if they have established reputations either as show horses or producers, are worth much more than mares or geldings; but otherwise they are often worth far less. The exception to this is in the case of yearling registered colts in the midwest, where they will generally bring a little more than geldings. Throughout the midwest or the breeding states, registered mares of good type will generally be worth far more than geldings or most stallions; on the other hand, in the coast states as well as the states where there is little breeding done and with animals of slightly inferior quality, such as livery horses and trail animals, geldings are always preferable and worth more money.

On page 274 is found a diagram showing points at which various types of unsoundness occur. Pictures of the unsoundnesses are not clear enough in most cases to do the reader any good, and drawings are always so enlarged and exaggerated that they in turn are of little practical value.

In buying registered horses of any breed one must practice caution: first, to be sure that the papers are authentic, which, no doubt, will generally be the case; and second, to be sure that one is buying and paying for the horse and not the papers. It is very easy to become so enthusiastic about certain breeding that one forgets it is the animal and not the papers that he will be riding or showing. When anyone has a registered horse for sale that is not quite up to par, he will usually dwell on the breeding of the animal, rather than on the horse itself. That is only good salesmanship, but one should not be taken in by it. The really sure way, is to never look at the papers or discuss them until one has first examined the horse. Just because a horse's brothers or sisters have been famous is no reason that he will ever be. Even when buying breeding stock one will do well to obey this rule, except that here the primary consideration should be the quality of the offspring already produced. Of course, when buying breeding stock, registration is more important than otherwise.

Just a little personal incident to explain what I mean and how easy it is for even a smart man to be unduly influenced by papers. At one particular position I held, my employer had a friend who was going over the country buying some of the best breeding stock he could find. He had by that time become a pretty good judge of a horse's value, but, at times, he would ask my opinion of a certain animal. He heard of a certain Rex Peavine brood mare for sale and went to see her. He was asked $1,300 for this mare, although she was fairly old. Before buying her he asked me to look at her and see what I thought. I like Rex Peavine breeding in a good brood mare as well as anyone, but when I went to look at this mare she was definitely not up to standard. She had two or three colts which were nothing to write home about. Later when I went back to see this gentleman and told him I had looked at the mare, he asked me what I thought of her. I replied, "How much would you give for her if you didn't know how she was bred, but only that she was registered?" He answered, "Oh! about $150. I said, "Well it is your money, and if you realize that you are paying $150 for the mare and $1,150 for the papers, go ahead and buy her." He said, "That's right, that is just what I would be doing; wouldn't I?" Of course, he didn't buy this mare, but many people have paid $500 for a gelding with papers that could do him no good, when they wouldn't have given $250 for the same animal if it were not registered. Now, don't mistake me, I believe in registration. I believe particularly in honest registration, as that is the only way in which we are ever going to continue building up any breed; but I don't believe in buying papers instead of horses.

To sum up, one should know just what he wants and not expect to find an all-purpose horse, nor a perfect one. In most instances, a reputable dealer is, no doubt, the best and safest place a novice can make his purchase.

CHAPTER XI

BUILDING A STABLE

Due to the many inquiries and requests for suggestions for building a stable, I have been led to believe that a few notes or suggestions along this line should be included in a book of this kind. I sincerely hope that they may prove of some benefit. I do not intend to supply complete details or plans, as each and every horse owner and lover has a slightly different problem confronting him with regard to his stabling arrangements, and the amount of time, size, and expense that he will wish or need to expend. Rather, I shall try to give certain general facts that may prove worth while and discuss various arrangements which may be made, and as far as possible, some of the good and bad effects of each type stable.

I, like most other men in my business, have at one time or another worked from coast to coast and have been able to visit, as well as work in, various kinds and types of stables. Some are good, some not so good, many handy work barns and others not so handy, some beautiful and some that were anything but beautiful; some were round, some square, tee-shaped, rectangular, oblong. Nearly all of them have certain advantages, as well as some disadvantages. A man may spend anywhere from a few hundred dollars to several thousand dollars to build a stable, and after he has finished it he generally finds that he has forgotten something or left out something. Oftentimes, because of the fact that few owners actually work with their mounts, the builder leaves out many small things which would make for handiness and be time savers and, also, money savers. Few architects have the experience, and therefore do not think of these things, and must be depended upon primarily for size of supports to hold the required load, etc.

Before actually going into the different types of stables, let us discuss certain things necessary or desirable for every stable. The first consideration will be the stalls. They should be the box stall type. All good stables are so built, and they are the only type worth discussing. They really should be from twelve to fourteen feet square, or if not square then at least twelve feet across the smallest dimension. Smaller than twelve feet absolutely does not give a horse enough room to turn and rest properly and roll. Furthermore, if one intends to use the stable for any length of time, stalls less than twelve feet are not cheaper in the long run. In a small stall the animal will mess up his bedding and get it all chopped up in almost no time, and the saving in straw, plus the saving in cost of time trying to clean and shake out small stalls, will soon overcome the extra cost of building the larger stall. A man can clean out a fourteen-foot stall in about half the time and with a waste of about half the bedding than with a ten-foot one. Then, if one ever intends putting in tail boards, they will be at least a foot wide (fifteen to eighteen inches is better) and that much more space is taken up. An animal will get himself cast far easier and much oftener in a small stall than in a large one, and he will be much harder to get up, due to the small space for the man or men to work. If I can succeed in nothing more than convincing the prospective builder of the advisability of building the stalls large enough, I feel that I have accomplished a great deal.

The partitions should always be of two-inch material and be boarded up solid to about four feet six inches. Anything less than two-inch material will soon be kicked down, and the cost of rebuilding and patching up will very soon far exceed the cost of putting in two-inch material in the first place, and if the stall is built against the wall, it must still be boarded up on the inside with two-inch material to a height of about four feet. Above four-feet six-inches, partitions partially opened are better than if closed entirely in. This may be either bars of iron or wood or heavy metal screen about one and one-half inch to two inch mesh. Never wire. The bars may be placed about four inches apart. One will find that his horses will do much better if the stalls are built so that they can look out and at the other animals in the stable, but are not able to get to them to bite and fight. Stallions especially get along far better this way than all boxed up, as they, particularly, get very lonesome and really need company. The ceiling should be at least eight feet high. The fewer projections of any kind in the stall the less danger there is of a horse getting skinned up or even badly hurt. Hay racks made of iron rods and shaped round to fit in the corners are far better than wooden ones built in, or wooden mangers. Metal feed boxes shaped to fit in the corner and rounded on the outside and bottom are safer than square wooden ones. They should, if possible, have a drain plug in them so that they may be washed and cleaned easily; otherwise they should fit on a bracket so that they are removable for cleaning occasionally.

Tail boards should be at least a foot wide, and fifteen to eighteen inches is preferable. They should be placed about four feet high and if possible made of two-inch hard wood, and very well braced, both up and down, as some horses will sit on tail boards, and others will come up under them and tear them off, if possible. Mr. Emil House of Payson, Illinois, has perhaps the best arrangement for tail boards I have ever had the privilege to see. Instead of several braces, the whole thing is solidly braced and boarded up, making a right triangle out of the complete tail board. No horse can possibly come up under it, as the slope is enough to push him away, and I believe it is strong enough for a horse to walk on without the slightest damage. Tail boards for the doors may be hung directly on the door if it is the type that swings out, or they may be hinged and swung upward out of the way; in which case, some type of mechanical catch should be used to hold it in place, both while up and when down. Otherwise, the horse will surely knock it down on someone's head when it is supposed to be up, and when down he will soon develop the habit of playing with it with his nose, continually raising and dropping it. Probably the best plan is to arrange for it to slide back over the other fixed tail board in a brace and hooked into place. A two-inch pipe may be used successfully for this purpose.

If convenient, it is very nice and adds much to the animal's comfort to have fresh water accessible at all times. A bucket may be hung in the stall for this purpose or a tub may be hooked or strapped in to be filled at intervals, but it must be removable in order to be cleaned. It is a time and labor saver to have water piped into each stall, in which case a faucet may be placed above the tub or receptacle, or regular drinking fountains may be purchased into which the water when turned on flows into the bottom of the trough, and by turning another valve the water may be drained out of the same hole for cleaning; or automatic drinking fountains may be purchased from which the animal soon learns to water himself by placing his muzzle on a lever at the bottom, which releases the water. In this case, the lever must be placed low enough so that there will be little chance that the animal will overflow the tank with too much water, and the tanks must have a drain plug for draining and cleaning. Electric lights in each stall make for greater convenience and are almost a necessity in a dark barn or in a foaling stall. The switch should be just outside the door, or if in the stall proper it must be enclosed so that there is no way in which the animal can touch it, and all wires must be encased in metal tubing. The dimensions of a foaling stall, if needed, should be at least fourteen by eighteen feet, or no less than 250 square feet of floor space, and no smaller than fourteen feet across the smallest side.

Windows and awnings. Every stall next to the wall that does not have any other outside opening should have a window for light and air. It should be protected against breakage by the horse by bars or heavy iron screen. Individual permanent wooden awnings may also be built outside each window and are well worth while. They protect the stall from the direct rays of the sun and slightly darken the stalls, thus help to keep down flies and protect the stall in summer from sudden heavy rains, and therefore, are worth all they cost.

Doors may swing out, but sliding doors are always preferable and are absolutely necessary in stables so designed that an animal will be ridden or worked inside, or in a stable with a narrow aisle.

Good clay, no doubt, makes the best flooring where it is possible to secure it. It is easy on the animal's feet and legs, and if kept clean it will last for years, except in the case of an animal that paws quite a lot or when one allows his animals to get bad kidneys. In the first instance, about all one can do is place the animal on a board floor, and in the second instance, the horses' kidneys should be taken care of. Other kinds of dirt will not last as well as good clay but are still preferable to other types of flooring, especially if there is a certain amount of clay mixed in. Board flooring is permissible if the animal will be bedded very heavy, and it makes it easier to clean the stalls; however, the boards will soon rot out unless properly drained. This is probably best accomplished by laying the boards about an inch apart and by drilling several holes about an inch in diameter at the spot where the animal urinates, and by setting the whole thing up on a foundation under which there may be a cement floor with a good slope of several feet, or one may use a mixture of sand and cinders to allow for good drainage. In no case, should the stall floor itself be built on a slope, and if a cement floor is placed several inches under the stall floor, it should have a good outlet and some way of flushing it out occasionally.

Board floors are also permissible and are very handy in cases where each stall has its own lot for the animal to run in, and where the animal is allowed free use of the lot all or most of the time. In this case, there must still be suitable drainage; however, it need not be bedded so heavy, as the horse will spend much of his time in the lot. The lot may be anywhere from double the size of the stall up to as large as is desired. If one will shut the horse outside in the first place until he starts his manure pile and never clean this pile up entirely, most horses will continue to use the outside lot for this purpose, and it is a big saving in bedding and time. The wet straw may be thrown out into this lot to help keep down dust and to dry for re-use.

The stable should also include a tack room for saddles, bridles, harnesses, medicines, records, etc.; and a feed room, even if the main quantities of grain and hay are to be kept upstairs, the feed room will have shoots for dropping the required amounts, and will be used for mixing, etc.; a work room for cleaning tack, doing minor repairs, etc.; and a wash rack for washing tails, legs, sheaths, buggies, etc. This wash rack may be combined with the work room. One may also wish to have a buggy room or shed for show buggies, jog carts, and breaking carts, and an office or lounge, or the two combined.

The tack room may be almost any size and may be elaborate if one so wishes. In some cases, it may be purely a tack room, while in others it may be quite large and include office or lounging furniture, and even a fireplace. Wooden brackets may be made for both saddles and bridles, or metal ones may be bought. It will, in most cases, be finished off, and the recesses in the walls may be used for medicines, spare equipment, and whip closet, by merely putting the finishing on in the form of doors. A larger closet may be built in for storing blankets, tail sets, cotton, or any of the bulkier things. This may as well be left to each one's ingenuity and his own ideas on the subject.

The feed room will depend very much upon the type of stable. If hay, bedding, and grain are to be kept there, it will have to be quite large. On the other hand, if hay and bedding are kept elsewhere and only grain is kept there, one will not need so much space. Generally one will wish to keep his grain upstairs in large bins, especially in a stable of fairly large size. In this case, there will be chutes coming down from the different large grain bins upstairs into smaller containers, where it will be easily accessible. There should also be a place to store salt and a metal bin for bran, perhaps one for minerals and either a metal bin or feed wagon for mixing feeds. There should be plenty of space for the feed wagon or cart.

The work room and wash rack may or may not be combined. In the work room there should be places to hang dirty tack and harness until it is cleaned and ready to be hung away. This room should have a sink and running water, preferably both hot and cold. It is well to have the sides lined with closets and drawers, as there is always an accumulation of old blankets, pieces of harness, etc., that one shouldn't throw away, as they may well come in handy for some repair job. The drawers may be used for buckles, snaps, rings, keepers, rivets, and a riveting machine. Many other saddle making tools can profitably be included and also needles and heavy thread. This is a good place for one's medicine cabinet. One should make about four times as many cabinets as he thinks he will ever need, as it is surprising the number of things one will accumulate over a period of years. Of course, lights are a necessity. The wash rack must have a non-skid floor and a good drain and water outlet, a hose and a pair of cross ties for the animal. If it is to be used for washing buggies it must, of course, have a door large enough to make it possible to conveniently get the buggies in and out.

The buggy room may be built in the stable, or could be a separate shed outside somewhere, in which case it is just as well to have the blacksmith shop adjoining. The blacksmith shop should have a wooden floor. A small forge, anvil, vice, and a few blacksmith tools do not cost much and will many times come in handy to the owner, as well as to the horseshoer. There are times when a horse will lose a shoe when it is impossible to get a horseshoer right away, in which event, anyone can tack a shoe on well enough to hold the foot until the horseshoer arrives. A few spikes in the studdings along the wall will serve to keep the better shoes in cases of emergency.

Whether one wishes to include an office or lounge, or combine the two, is purely a matter for each individual to decide, and I only bring them up in order that they will not be overlooked. I, personally, prefer to combine the tack room and lounge and have a small office completely separate.

The only practical way to keep down flies in a stable is to have it completely screened in. Electric fly killers throughout the stable will aid considerably, and having the upper part of the doors specially wired for killing flies will prove nearly one hundred per cent effective. Heated stables are neither practical or desirable, as it is almost impossible to prevent the animals from taking cold if they have been kept in heated stalls. Of course, your tack room, work room, lounge, etc., may be kept heated; and in parts of the country where the weather gets severe it helps to preserve tack to keep a small fire in the tack room all the time.

In large stables where the hay and bedding will be kept upstairs a hay fork on a track is very desirable to facilitate handling the quantities that will be used. Stables of this kind should also be equipped with grain elevators for raising the grain into the bins. Grain bins, of course, must be lined with metal.

Before discussing the various types of stables I wish to make one other observation. If one's stable is the only place he will have to keep his horses, he should build it with a view to the future, which, in most cases, means a far larger stable than he thinks he will ever need, or it should be of some design that may easily be enlarged. In about nine cases out of ten, the man who can afford it starts out with one or two horses, never expecting to own more, and ends up with a dozen or more. It is something to bear in mind when one starts to put out money to build a new stable.

The types and designs of stables are almost as many and varied as the number of them in the country, however, they can be divided into several general groups. Perhaps the most common of these is the stable with an aisle down the center and stalls on each side. In a small stable, eight feet is as wide as the aisle need be, however, two to four feet wider will allow for greater convenience. The floor should be non-skid material, clay, cement, or brick. The ceiling does not need to be higher than the stall ceilings, as no horses will be ridden in a barn of this size, or there need be no ceiling at all, and the grain, hay, and bedding may be placed on either side above the stalls. Holes with removable covers above each hay rack is a great convenience in feeding and less droppings will be scattered around the barn. Sliding doors above each stall, large enough to easily drop large flakes of bedding through, also make for greater convenience and cleanliness and add very little to the cost. In the event a fireproof stable is being built, the ceiling should extend entirely across the stable and should be made of about eight inches of cement to confine possible heat, as well as fire upstairs; in which case, the sliding door and removable cover over the hay rack must be made of metal.

In a larger barn of the same type, one will often want to ride horses inside, therefore, the aisle should be at least eighteen feet wide, and if one expects to use a jog cart he will need about twenty-five feet for turning. The ceiling, if any, should be at least 15 feet high, and the floor should be either of good clay or tanbark, or a mixture of sand and sawdust. In parts of the country where limestone is plentiful and cheap, the very smallest size crushed limestone (not powdered) makes a very good flooring if covered about eight inches deep. Hay or bedding is easily raked off, and dust may be washed down through with a hose. In this size stable, the stall doors should slide to prevent any possible injury to the horse or rider when working the horse inside. The outside doors should be large enough to permit a truck loaded with hay to enter, if hay and bedding are to be kept on either side above the stalls. If a ceiling is used over the center, a hay fork on a track coming outside one end of the barn is almost a necessity in order to handle economically the amount that will be used. A grain elevator used in filling the grain bins will be worth its cost in a stable of this size, as quite a lot of grain will be used. In this type of stable the tack room, work room, etc., may be on either side of the aisle as one enters, or it may be all built to connect across one end of the stable.

Another type of stable, closely related to the foregoing, is the one built in a T shape. Practically everything said about the former could be repeated here with the exception that generally only the body or the cross of the T will be used to work horses in, and in some instances the cross of the T contains no stalls at the top, but rather, the whole cross is built in a big block formation and is used for a riding hall. This makes a very good arrangement in any country where there is a great deal of inclement weather, but it is quite expensive and is only adaptable to large stables. Large mirrors may be placed along the wall at such an angle that it will allow the rider to watch his own horse work.

What I shall call the oblong type of stable is perhaps the nicest type of all for the parts of the country that have a good deal of inclement weather. They are, however, quite expensive and to be completely effective are really only adaptable to large stables of twenty or more stalls, which will give one about 160 feet of straight-away. However, even a stable of ten stalls, if built this way, will allow a fair sized work ring. They are built with a double row

ILLUSTRATION XXVI

The hallway of the new well appointed stables at Oak Knoll Farm, Milford, Michigan.

ILLUSTRATION XXVII

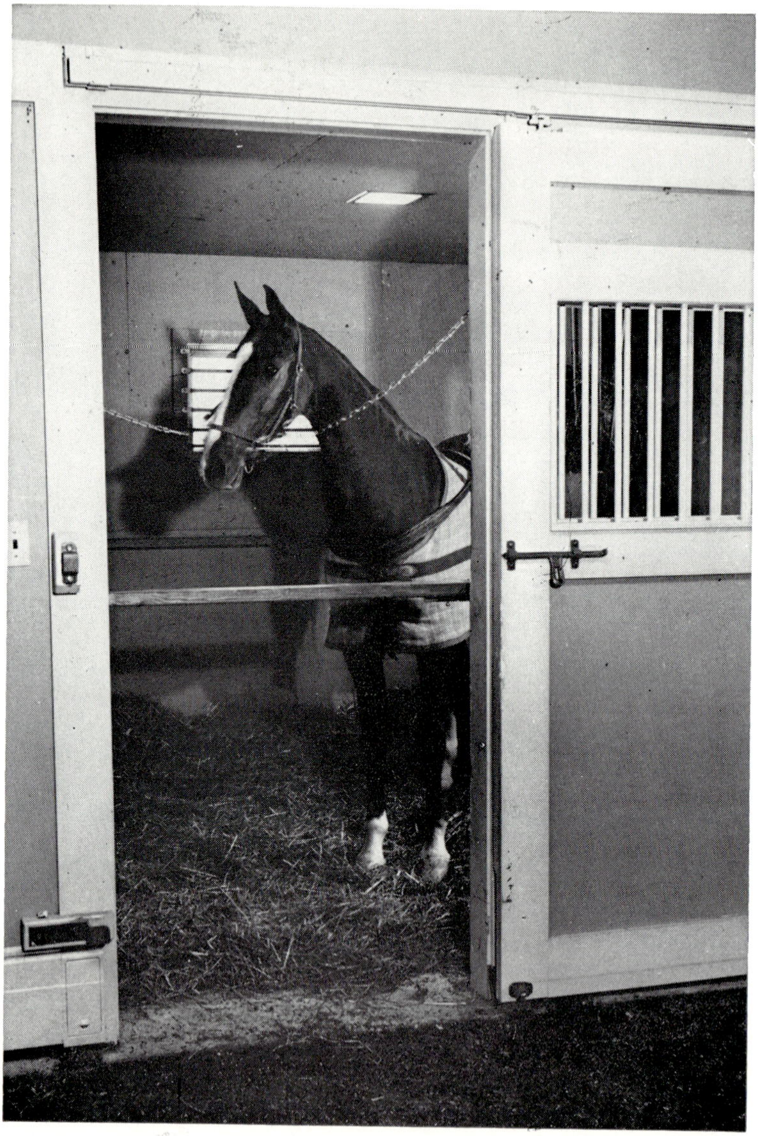

Another view of the inside of Oak Knoll's new stables showing the spacious stalls, sliding doors, cross ties in each stall and bars between the stalls for light, air and better communication.

of stalls, back to back down the center of the barn, with the isle or work ring around the stalls and all enclosed under one roof. In this arrangement there is no chance for drafts of any kind, and windows along the sides will regulate the temperature and afford plenty of light.

The very smallest barn of this type may be built with about eight twelve-foot stalls, a work room and a feed room each the size of a stall, and a ten-foot isle, with the tack room and office at the front. This would give a work ring sixty feet long and thirty-two feet wide. Of course, a much better arrangement is more stalls about fourteen feet square and a track about twenty feet wide, which would give a width of sixty-eight feet and a length of forty feet, plus fourteen times half the number of stalls. The ceilings should, of course, be high, as one will intend to work horses in the barn, and the upstairs should be large enough to store sufficient quantities of hay, bedding, and grain, with the grain bins so located that the chutes come directly down into the feed room. Of course, a grain elevator and a hay fork on a track should be included. The hay and bedding will be placed toward the outside, as the trap doors for hay and bedding will be directly down the center. The floor should be of good clay or tanbark, or a mixture of sand and sawdust, or limestone. A walk around the stalls of soft asphalt or non-skid cement will provide a clean place to walk and an easy place to push the feed cart, without interfering with the work ring, if it is wide enough. Bruce Seabright of Bridgeport, Ohio, has such a stable, and it is very effective. An accommodation for a large number of horses may be made in a stable of this type by adding rows of stalls along each wall, in which case, sky lights must be placed above the aisles. In a public stable of sixty or more horses, an extra riding hall may be built in addition to the stable.

The square barn is built with rows of stalls along each side of the stable, and generally is large enough for either a single or double row of stalls down the center, or two single rows of stalls down the center with an aisle in between. Personally, I see little advantage in this latter type and would prefer to have a double row of stalls down the center and devote the extra space to making the outside aisles larger.

The round barn is in most instances too costly for what good it is. There are few of them in the country. Dr. A. L. Sheffler of Joliett, Illinois, has an extremely good one, which is quite large, with a row of stalls around the outside, then a work ring and another row of stalls, with a center aisle all the way through the barn. It was built a long time ago, when labor and materials were much cheaper than is now the case. It is built of oak two-by-fours laid one on top of another, making the walls and partitions four inches thick, and is, of course, extremely solid. However, such a barn today would be economically impractical. The stalls cannot be square and are always shorter across the inside dimension.

In the Southwest many stables are built in the form of courts, or horseshoes, which amounts to practically two rows of stalls, with the feed room, tack room, office, and so forth across one end and the other end open. The enclosed lot is generally landscaped. This is the type of stable at Kellogg's Arabian horse ranch at Pomona, California. In this type stable, the roof must always extend out about eight feet in a porch-like effect so that one may stay out of inclement weather. This type of building may also be used with a double row of stalls on either side, in order to house more animals.

Any of the aforementioned types of stables may be finished as elaborately as the owner desires. All stages from rough lumber to select hardwood can be seen and everything from nothing to whitewash to the best of varnish is used. These things remain entirely up to the individual to do as he sees fit. There is one thing one should remember if he intends to finish his barn elaborately. The finer the stable is finished the more time, trouble, and expense will be used to keep it in shape, and a nicely furnished stable must be kept in A-1 shape to look like it should. Hay is always more or less dusty, making cobwebs form over night, hence a stable of this kind must be dusted every day. This, the usual owner overlooks and seldom does he want to provide enough help to keep up a fine stable as he wants it kept and as it should be kept. It takes a man about as long to keep up his part of a finely finished stable as it does to take good care of three horses. Hence, the man who owns a stable that needs only a rough dusting about once a week can get along well with a good groom for every six horses, while the man with a nicely finished stable will need just as good a groom for every four horses, or else he will have to have one man whose sole duty is to keep up the stable and tack. This is one reason many horsemen dislike to go to work in a fine stable, as they well realize it entails so much extra work for which the usual owner gives them no credit.

There is one other type of stable, which consists mainly of a row of stalls. They are seen at race tracks, summer homes, resorts, etc., but they are not so practical for all year around, as they do not provide sufficient shelter nor do they have a dead air space above to provide for insulation from both heat and cold. They are inexpensive, and, especially if a separate lot is attached to each stall into which the animal may roam at will, they are very easy to take care of. Hence, they are admirably suited to summer homes, camps, etc.

We sincerely hope that the foregoing may be an aid to the prospective builder in helping him select the type of building that may suit his particular need and in preventing him from making costly oversights.

Chapter XII

OTHER METHODS OF TRAINING FOR ACTION

Of all the controversial methods of training a gaited horse, so-called "High Schooling" probably causes the greatest amount of comment. I say "so-called High Schooling" advisedly, as it is not true high schooling, but nearer trick training in an attempt to teach the Spanish Trot particularly in front, then converting that to a saddle horse trot, and therein lies the problem. Firstly, a true high schooled horse is first trained from the rear and the front naturally follows through (the Spanish Trot as such has no place in the true classical "Haute Ecole" or high school, being thought of as an artificial gait or trick). Secondly, in a Spanish Trot the horse raises its knees, and should also raise its hocks to full height, then pauses a fraction of a second before lowering its feet, but the gaited horse should not pause at the height of its stride; rather the whole stride of the gaited horse should be a smooth even-flowing movement like the rippling of water flowing down a mountain stream. Few, if any, trainers are skilled enough to get this smooth-flowing gait from an animal that has once been "High Schooled."

There is a great controversy among judges as to just how much to discount a "high schooled" horse and I doubt if any judge likes to see evidence of it. Personally, I don't, and if possible will tie down any horse that shows effects of having been "high schooled." On the other hand, I well remember one show I judged. In the fine harness class was one little mare that was outstanding, a dream girl if there ever was one. Yet, at times, she hesitated just a trifle at the height of her stride showing unmistakable evidence of having been "high schooled" at some time during her training. I still tied her first, and would do it again, even though the show committee approached me after the show, wanting to know my reasons for tieing that particular mare, when she showed unmistakable evidence that she had been "high schooled." I explained that, in spite of that, I thought she was still the best fine harness mare in the class, by a large margin. With that the committee was satisfied, but I am sure many spectators were not.

I have been asked many times how this "high schooling" is done, and perhaps there are a few horses with which one can get more action in this way than in any other. In my opinion, it is one of those methods that should only be undertaken by an expert, and even then perhaps on only one horse out of a thousand.

The method used for gaited horses is really quite simple. One must first pad the legs, particularly the cannon bones, and protect the quarters with quarter boots to prevent the horse from banging its legs and injuring itself in the early stages. Only a plain snaffle bridle is used and one will need a short stiff stick. I have a light piece of bamboo I use for many purposes and it is ideal for this. The horse is led to a small enclosure where the trainer can easily maintain control and the animal is placed against the wall or fence. As the trainer allows the horse to move out a step, he cracks it rather sharply on the knee; one more step, one more crack. Several full strides and the animal is stopped and caressed, then the whole thing is repeated. The object is to get the horse to strike out at the stick. Sometimes it will strike at the trainer instead but even if it does this, it must not be punished. At this stage it is up to the trainer to keep out of the way and to encourage striking. The horse should be worked this way for only very short periods of five to ten minutes at a time, never longer than that. If after a few days the animal still has not shown any inclination to strike, sometimes a little more harsh treatment is necessary and may work. A small horseshoe nail is driven through the end of the stick and this is used to prick the horse at each stride. If these extreme measures are taken, the horse's legs must be washed well with soap and water on being returned to the barn, then alcohol or other good astringent and antiseptic is applied to prevent any danger of infection. It should go without saying that nothing but a clean new bright nail will ever be used for this purpose.

There are, no doubt, some horses so phlegmatic that they will never learn to strike, and if one has a horse of this type he might just as well not waste his time trying to "high school" such an animal; however, just because a horse is gentle and kind doesn't mean that it won't learn to strike. It may be the first one to learn.

Once the trainer has his charge striking at the stick without his having to crack the animal's knees, the battle is won, but not the work. The work has just begun. The trainer then begins working the bit, lifting and slightly jerking with each stride; on the side the horse will strike out. Here one must use care that the horse strikes out equally high with both feet. In order to do this, the trainer may have to work part of the time on one side and part of the time on the other side of the horse, spending the most time on the side that doesn't raise as high.

For a time, both stick and bit are used; gradually the stick will only be used for pointing rather than for hitting the horse, then eventually the use of the stick will be discontinued entirely and all reliance for a signal to strike be placed on the bits. Once this is accomplished, the next step is a few steps at a time at a trot, and the trainer may again have to make use of the stick until the animal gets the idea of striking out with each stride on the signal from the bits. Always and forever he must only be allowed to strike out on signal, never of his own accord.

Once the trainer has his charge well enough along that it will strike out at each stride, both at a walk and at a trot, and only on the signal from the bit, he may then begin mounted work. Here he'll have to start all over again, except that he'll ride and control the bit while an assistant will use the stick to encourage the horse to strike out. Work will be done only at a walk again until the rider has all the control with the bits and the use of his legs and heels. He must by now begin using both legs and heels augmenting the lifting by the bits. When work is begun at the trot, the assistance of the helper may again be called for, or the rider may be able to do this job himself by the use of two fairly long riding whips as aids. At no time during this type of work shall the horse ever be worked long enough to tire. Few horses can take this type of work for ten full minutes, many will progress faster with far shorter periods of work. Finally, all reliance is placed in the trainer's hands and legs, and the animal now does a Spanish Trot, at least in front. This work may also have heightened the animal's stride behind, but maybe not.

From then on the trainer attempts to keep this increased action and gradually converts it into a saddle horse trot or the nearest semblance of one he can reach. He tries to smooth out the trot and get rid of the hesitation in its height that has become apparent to a marked degree. How long will that take? Who knows. One year? Ten years? Forever perhaps. I don't think I have ever seen a horse that had been "high schooled" that didn't show the effects of it, at least at times, and I've never talked with a judge who liked to see it. Should you "high school" your horse or have it "high schooled"? I've been asked that question so many different times. If I say yes, the probabilities are that I'll be "cussed out" for life, and if I say "no" I am just an old "fuddy-duddy" who doesn't know what he is talking about. You pay your money and take your choice.

Developers

There is at least one other quite well known method of helping to obtain increased action on gaited horses. The use of developers has become quite general. It seems as if it should work and probably does sometimes, but in my experience, it has always seemed to do the owner more good than it does the horse. Especially in a large public stable where several horses are being worked for a number of different owners, many of them often wonder if their particular pet is receiving his just share of attention, and perhaps all of them would like to see improvement faster than is sometimes possible. If these owners are allowed to see their horses worked in developers now and then, most of them are better satisfied. These owners begin to see how much action may be possible from their horses, not that many of them will ever go that high. On the other hand, some horses, particularly those that don't use their shoulders as freely as they might, are really helped by the judicious use of developers, which helps to loosen these muscles and call them into play.

Developers are used in so many ways that it is impossible to describe all of them, but the principles remain the same, and if a few methods are explained, I feel the trainer can then go on from there and devise other methods that may suit his purpose. Perhaps the most generally used rig, especially in a large stable is made up by the blacksmith out of a couple of old rasps. This rasp is split down about three inches, these ends are then spread out and turned back to about a 40 degree angle and the rest of the rasp is left solid and cut off about four inches long. This latter part goes under the horse's hoof and the two split ends come up in front from the toe. A small rawhide loop is then fastened to all three ends through which a small strap, such as a curb strap, passes to secure the developer to the horse's hoof. A ring is also attached to the heavy loop at the rear of the hoof to which a rope may be attached. This type of developer may then be moved from one horse to another, and used on any number of them. The person with only one horse on which he intends to use developers can work out something a little neater and better. For instance, on a horse wearing a butterfly bar shoe, a hole may be punched in the center of the bar by the horseshoer, into which a ring may be placed for attaching the rope, or some horses may wear pads that are heavy and strong enough for this purpose. The main thing is that when the ropes are attached, they will pull from the feet directly and not from the pasterns as when a "W," described earlier, is used.

ILLUSTRATION XXVIII

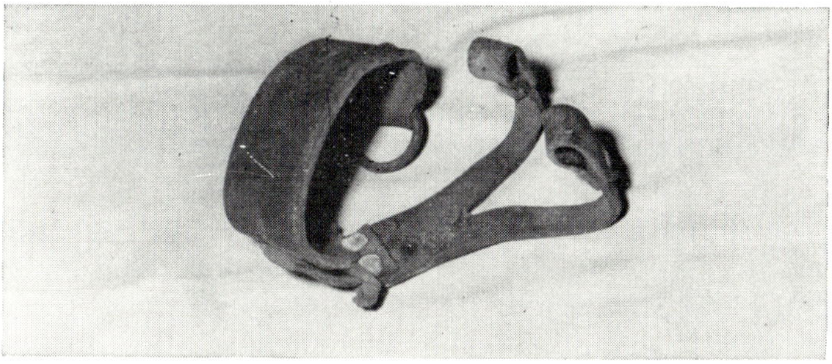

Developer—one of a pair.

When working the horse in developers, one should really have a helper to drive the animal while the trainer works the ropes. I've seen trainers try to use one rope fixed up as with a "W," but it always seems to me that the job can be done better with the use of two ropes, one to each foot. Developers are essentially ropes run through rings in the surcingle of a bitting harness, directly to the horse's feet. As the animal is driven at a trot, the trainer jerks quickly on the proper rope to help the horse lift its feet faster and higher than it normally would. He must be very careful that he does this at the precise instant and in perfect cadence so that he will not trip the horse and throw it. As can easily be seen, this work can best be done where the ground is fairly soft, and is much easier in a small ring, or even a small circle, as both the trainer and his assistant must run alongside of the horse while it is trotting. The smaller the circle, the easier it will be for the men to travel in relation to the horse. The animal will learn faster and better if only trotted this way for short stretches at a time, a couple hundred feet. Stopping at the end of this also gives the trainer a chance to catch his breath. About five minutes a day on the developers is ample for any horse, generally done just before its regular workout. Usually the fetlocks will have to be padded, as it seems that no matter how the developers are applied, they will rub sores on most horses.

These developers can later be put on the horse when it is being worked in the cart, and can be worked quite successfully in that way. They may often be used while the horse is worked under the saddle; however, in this case, one will generally want to fix up a little different arrangement, perhaps fairly heavy springs or heavy rubber bands attached directly to the girth. This keeps the rider from needing the services of a helper or from trying to work the ropes himself, which is quite a chore for the mounted man. Of course, springs or rubber bands may also be used on the harness horse but that never seems to me to give quite as good results as when ropes are used. In any case this type of work should never continue for longer than five minutes a day.

There are, of course, obections to the use of developers, as with anything else. As I mentioned before, one of these is the problem of trying to keep from rubbing sores on the horse's fetlocks, another is the fact that it is almost impossible to get the ropes, springs, or rubber bands to pull straight up. If they pull out they may easily teach a horse to wing, and if they pull in they may teach it to become a knee knocker. Ropes or springs attached to the girth or to the shafts of a horse in harness will cause the saddle to pull one way then the other and may easily cause a sore back. The continued use of developers may or may not help a horse to break loose in the shoulders, but they impede, rather than help any reach the horse may have and, therefore, hamper the development of a true saddle horse trot and in many cases cause it to become "trappy."

Therefore, like any other training method, it must be used judiciously.

No, my friends, there is no royal road or easy way of obtaining action from a saddle horse. I've seen stock horses with no particular breeding go out barefooted with more action than some saddle horses after all the training one could give them. Primarily, high action is a matter of natural ability and natural way of going with a particular horse. This may, of course, be changed to some extent, heightened and improved, by a combination of training and shoeing, but nothing can put it all there. After one has done all he can in the way of shoeing and training, the horse is then "fired up," or animated sometimes merely by yelling at it, sometimes by scaring it with a whip, almost anything to get it anxious to move on. This energy is then converted into the greatest amount of action possible for that particular animal. Some horses respond much easier than others, and, with some, the greatest amount of action is obtained by producing flexions and asking the animal to move slower, converting all the excess energy into action. These, of course, generally make the best walk-trot and fine harness horses. Other horses need speed to get the most action of which they are capable; the more speed the more action these horses have. These make five gaited horses.

Chapter XIII

QUESTIONS AND ANSWERS

Soon after publishing my other book, "The American Saddle Horse," I received quite a number of questions about the various phases of the care and training of Saddle Horses; and at a number of meetings which I was called upon to address, I also received questions at the conclusion of the talk. Many of these questions seemed to me to be of general interest, which prompted me to include this chapter in this book. Some of these questions are those I have been asked while editing a column called "Equestrian Queries" in the Horseman's Review; while others are some which I remember only in a general way, but have been asked of me at one time or another. Many of them have been asked several times in slightly different forms.

QUESTION: My horse does not go as high as it did several months ago, when I first bought him. Do you recommend using a bitting harness on him?

ANSWER: I have been asked this question a number of times in slightly different forms. I cannot tell you what your particular horse needs without seeing it work, and probably then only by working it myself for some time. I can, however, give you several general hints. In the first place, we must understand what makes a horse have action. Summed up, it is his natural ability, coupled with shoeing and the degree of flexion possible to obtain. Added to this the horse is keyed up, then that energy is converted into action. A horse may be going perfectly right for one rider, but if another rider gets on it and does not keep it so well primped or up on the bit and flexed, it may not do nearly so well. Some horses need to be keyed up quite a bit, while others having a lot of natural fire will need it but little. Hence, when buying a horse, especially if it is to be shown, after the deal is made one should always find out all he can about how it is prepared for shows and how it is ridden and shod. Any trainer or dealer will be glad to give you all that information that he can, and it is vitally important that the horse be shod and ridden, as nearly as possible, the same as it was before changing hands. If after getting well acquainted with the new mount, one decides that he may be able to improve it by changing shoes, he should first take all measurements; i.e., length of toes, angle of hoofs, weight of shoes both front and behind, before making even the slightest change. By so doing, one can always get it back the same as it was before, if the new method does not work out as expected. One should remember that if he bought the horse from a trainer or dealer he very likely had a very good reason for putting on the type of shoe the horse was wearing at the time of the sale, and that he had, no doubt, tried several different combinations until he thought it was doing as much good as it was possible for that horse. Any special shoes the horse was wearing were put on for a very good reason. People don't put fancy high priced shoes on a horse if a common shoe will do just as well.

Many people will buy a good horse that is going just as good as the horse can go, then right away try to change and improve it, generally knowing far less about what they are trying to do than the man from whom they purchased the animal. Usually, unless they are truly expert, their experiments result in failure, and oftentimes they get the horse so mixed up that it is impossible to get it right again. The best advice I can give to one asking the above question is to try to have the horse shod as near like it was when it was purchased as possible, then write to or talk with the man from whom the animal was purchased and ask his advice on how to ride and care foi it, and then do your best to abide by those directions.

QUESTION: What is the difference between an unsoundness and a blemish?

ANSWER: An unsoundness is anything which impairs a horse's way of going or his usefulness, such as bad eyes, broken wind, lameness for any reason. A blemish is merely a disfigurement which, while detracting from the animal's appearance, does not interfere with its general usefulness. In this class primarily are scars. A splint is merely a blemish unless it is the actual cause of lameness, in which case it becomes an unsoundness.

QUESTION: Should a horse be set back in a show for being restless on the line up?

ANSWER: It depends entirely upon the reason for the restlessness. If it is only because of the excitement, it will be discounted very little if at all, but if the judge considers the restlessness to be caused by improper training or not enough training, it will be set down some. If it appears that the animal has been doped in any way, the judge will surely tie it down. The degree of restlessness must be taken into consideration in all cases.

QUESTION: Are spurs permissible in a show ring?

ANSWER: Yes, a great many of the best showmen wear spurs at times, whenever necessary.

QUESTION: In an open class should the age or sex of the rider influence the judging?

ANSWER: In an open class neither age nor sex of the rider, nor for that matter should style of riding, influence the judging in any way. Only the horse counts.

QUESTION: My horse knuckles quite a lot behind. Can you suggest a remedy?

ANSWER: This is quite a common fault, especially with colts that have been ridden or worked a little too young or with horses that are inclined to be a little weak in the rear fetlock joints. I have found that the use of a single Memphis bar shoe behind will often remedy this condition. I use very low blocked heel caulks and a square-toed shoe and have the bar made of round steel and brazed on just behind the first nail hole, that is, between the first and second nail holes. More specific directions on shoeing will be found in this book in the chapter on shoeing and under the heading "Corrective Shoeing."

QUESTION: Is a horse that has been shown in open classes eligible to compete in a pleasure horse class?

ANSWER: I am aware of no ruling barring horses from showing in pleasure horse classes just because they have formerly been shown in open classes. Many shows specify that pleasure horses must not have been shown in open classes in the same quality show for a certain period before entering that show, or that they must have been used as bona fide pleasure horses for a certain period before entering the show. A few shows merely state that horses showing in open classes in that show may not compete in pleasure horse classes. In making entries one must be governed by the rules of that particular show in which he is entering. He should, therefore, read these rules carefully before making his entries.

QUESTION: Is it possible for a professional rider to revert to an amateur status? If so, what are the specifications?

ANSWER: Yes, a professional rider can revert to his amateur rating if he goes into a wholly different kind of business and derives no part of his income from buying, selling, or training horses. If he then refers these facts to the National Horse Shows Association, he may be given an amateur rating, after a period of probation. I believe this period is one year in most cases.

QUESTION: How should horses be treated for worms? What is the best tonic for rundown horses? Is copperas safe to give horses? If so, how much is a dose, and how should it be given?

ANSWER: I am a trainer, not a veterinarian, and shall only attempt to answer the parts of this question which properly come under the head of a trainer's duties. Worms (with the exception of bots) are effectively destroyed by a number of patented drugs which can safely be given and may be purchased at the nearest drug store. One should follow directions to the letter, as many of these preparations can cause serious consequences if not given correctly. The nicotine worm powders to be given in the feed are generally less drastic and easier given, if the horse can be persuaded to eat them. I sometimes use them as a sort of tonic, feeding minimum doses at intervals. Common chewing tobacco may be used also, about half a pack daily for about a week. If the horse is badly rundown, it should be treated by a veterinarian, and its teeth should be examined. At least, one should buy the drugs directly from the veterinarian and follow his directions. A veterinarian should be consulted before giving copperas. As a tonic, green grass fed daily cannot be beat in the summer time. A flake of legume hay, either alfalfa or lespedeza, daily is also a good tonic. Fowler's solution of arsenic is good, but one should follow the directions of a veterinarian before giving this. Along this line, I firmly believe in keeping a horse in condition all the time, rather than depending upon periodic dosing. Bran should be fed along with the grain daily. Salt is a necessity and loose salt should be easily accessible at all times. In parts of the country where the soil is deficient in minerals, some commercial form should be made available so that the animal can take it at will.

Question: Is 14.2 the division line between a horse and a pony?

Answer: Yes, unless a particular horse show committee makes a definite specification to the contrary for that particular show.

Question: What is a rack?

Answer: A rack is a four beat gait, each foot hitting the ground separately. It is the intermediate gait between the trot and pace. It is practically the same gait we used to call a single foot, but speeded up and with much action. A horse should rack freely about twelve miles an hour.

Question: Should a fast racking and trotting horse be placed over a horse going not so fast but in better form?

Answer: This is the old question of form versus speed. The show ring is not a race track, and the rules generally call for a rack at least twelve miles an hour in correct Saddle Horse form; therefore, the Saddle Horse should go in correct form. He should also have a reasonable amount of speed. In judging a five-gaited class too many people do not remember that there are other things to be taken into consideration, and that the horses are being judged on the whole performance and not just one particular gait. If the horse going fast lacks perfect form but is obviously the better horse otherwise, he will be tied first. On the other hand, if the best horse in the ring lacks only extreme speed, then, of course, it will be tied first.

Question: Is 15.2 the standard size horse?

Answer: There is no standard size. Rather, let us say that 15.2 is about the average size Saddlebred horse.

Question: Are most gaited classes judged primarily on the basis of a fast rack?

ANSWER: Most gaited classes definitely are not judged solely or mostly on the basis of a fast rack. All conscientious judges take all five gaits into consideration in a five-gaited class, as well as conformation, form and true Saddle Horse way of going. However, if a slight emphasis is placed on any one gait, it is the rack correctly performed, as that is the gait which distinguishes the five-gaited American Saddle Horse from all other breeds. The rack must be correctly performed, not merely fast. I recall a case of this kind that happened several years ago. I was judging a class in which there was one big bay mare that had worlds of speed at the rack but very poor form and not too much form at the trot. There was another chestnut mare in the ring that kept in form and had plenty of speed at both rack and trot, but did not have the extreme speed of the bay mare. I, of course, tied the chestnut mare first. I had quite a lot of comment about it for awhile, as the bay mare had been beating the chestnut mare. Later I had a conversation with the gentleman who had tied the bay mare up in two shows. He said, "I have been wanting to tie up the chestnut mare for some time, but she never was doing quite enough. I told the rider of the bay mare that she was going to get beat the first time the chestnut came to herself if he didn't get his mare in form first."

QUESTION: In an equitation class, where all riders are riding the forward seat, should perfect form be primarily considered?

ANSWER: I do not think so. In judging an equitation class, whether the forward style of riding or any other seat is used, suppleness of the rider and especially suppleness of the arms and wrists is the most important factor to be taken into consideration. An instance of this kind took place not so long ago. I was judging an equitation class along with a military man (a Captain, I think) in which all riders were riding the forward seat. One rider had perfect form but was riding mechanically and with very stiff wrists, while another rider carried her legs slightly forward of the correct position but was perfectly supple and relaxed. The Captain, at first, wanted to tie up the first girl, but after I called his attention to her wrists, he was perfectly willing to tie her down fourth, while the other girl placed second.

In this connection, I would like to make one other point clear as to riding in horsemanship classes, and that is the importance of little things. As an example, I was judging a girls' horsemanship class of about fourteen girls from a camp where complete horsemanship was taught. I had four ribbons to tie and had selected six girls, without yet placing them in their respective positions. When called upon to change horses, only one girl out of the lot even looked at her girth and tightened it before mounting. She was immediately placed first in my mind. Another girl allowed a strange horse to walk away as she was mounting because she did not have hold of her reins. This same girl almost pulled her saddle off because the girth was so loose. She was disqualified in my mind right then. Another girl was on a strange horse, and when asked to canter she allowed the horse to slop into it, and, as was expected, it took the wrong lead. Now, if she had asked for the lead correctly and the horse got off wrong and had she noticed it immediately, I would not have counted it against her. As it was, I eliminated her right then. Oftentimes it is little things done right or wrong that make the difference between a first or a third, or being eliminated entirely.

QUESTION: What is meant by a collected gait?

ANSWER: Many people have the wrong impression of this. Too many seem to think that all they need to do to obtain collection is to slow down their mount, when the exact opposite is generally true. A collected gait is, of course, any gait at which the horse is traveling in collection. To obtain this, the horse must be forced up on the bit with the heels, then a flexion is produced at the poll; the animal is then physically collected and under the rider's will. The collection should be both physical and mental to be complete. This mental collection will generally follow physical collection if the flexion is obtained by coaxing and give and take, rather than by brute force. When in perfect collection, the animal is between the rider's legs and hands, with its legs well under it, and is perfectly ready and willing to do anything it has been taught to do. Collection implies movement or propulsion under control.

QUESTION: What is meant by two-track work, or work on two tracks?

ANSWER: I am afraid that many riders who consider themselves horsemen do not understand what two-track work is. It is used primarily in dressage work and merely consists of the horse doing the movements with the hind feet following in a different path or track than the front feet, thus making two tracks. It is not actually a side step, as the animal does not move completely sideways, rather the forward movement is still the principal movement, but the rear quarters are forced to one side, making two distinct lines as it moves. The object of two-track work is to teach the animal to have its hind quarters controlled by the rider's legs; and in a show ring, to determine how well the horse obeys the rider's legs.

QUESTION: How can I prevent colts from rearing up and sometimes throwing themselves over backward when I am breaking them to lead?

ANSWER: I wish I knew. Many colts do this, some more than others; and I have seen colts hurt badly as a result. Sometimes they may be prevented from doing this by breaking them to lead with a rope around their hips and up through the halter, rather than by pulling on the halter shank. Some may be prevented by having a man in the rear to help force the colt forward; and at times it seems as if no known method will prevent them from throwing themselves. If the colt is inclined to rear, one can often prevent it from rearing, or at least from falling hard, by giving it plenty of slack just before it begins to rear.

Many colts also do this when first being broken to drive. One can sometimes prevent them in this case by having both the girth and the check rein quite loose, sometimes wearing blinders, and sometimes by wearing an open bridle. For the most part, one has to be as easy as possible with colts and hope for the best.

QUESTION: Why should a horse not be allowed to take a canter from the trot?

ANSWER: Because, allowing it to take a canter from a trot will teach it to break its gaits. We must understand that a gallop is the natural gait a horse takes when wishing to go faster than a trot. If the horse, when being ridden, is allowed or asked to take a canter from a trot, it will break into a gallop every time it is called upon for a fast trot, and soon learns to mix its other gaits. If, however, all gaits are taken from a walk, the horse will keep its gaits pure.

QUESTION: What is meant by the expression, "behind the bit"?

ANSWER: A horse is behind the bit when it is attempting any kind of a defense, rather than obeying the will of the rider. Getting behind the bit may take a number of forms. The horse may continually toss his head rather than go up into the bit and set his head. He may back up whenever he is asked to tuck his head. He may keep jerking his head down, or he may merely refuse to take enough hold to give the rider any control over him. In any case, when the animal is behind the bit, the rider loses all control, and he must force the horse up into the bit before he can regain control.

QUESTION: Can you give me a few hints to help me win equitation classes?

ANSWER: That is a big order. Equitation classes are perhaps the hardest of all to judge and to show in. Besides being a good rider, one must also be a good showman. Dress in good taste, but if possible just a little different from most of the riders. A boy may wear a flower in his lapel, or a girl a feather in her hat, etc. Make yourself just a little outstanding. These little tricks will not help put you across if you cannot ride, but they will help in a class of evenly matched riders by making the judge aware of you. The rider that is easily picked out of the crowd always has a little advantage over those who dress and look pretty much the same, especially in a large class.

QUESTION: How do I stop my horse from rubbing its tail?

ANSWER: That's a good question; I wish I knew. I have heard many answers to this question, none of them all-inclusive. There are many things to try, and eventually one can nearly always find the solution. First and foremost is to wash it often and keep it clean, and second is to check for worms. Only very seldom will a horse that does not have worms, and does have a clean tail, rub it. However, it happens. Some horses have a scaly itch which may be either relieved or often cured by one preparation or another. In this case the services of a veterinarian are necessary; as these itches are actually skin infections, or sometimes the result of a fungus growth, what may help one case may be actually harmful for another. Therefore, the veterinarian should prescribe for them. I have been able, in some cases, to clear these up and stop the animal from rubbing its tail, with Absorbine, sometimes with a ten per cent mixture of sulphur salve, and sometimes merely by rubbing common table salt into the scalp of the tail after a thorough washing. Of course, many horses will try rubbing the tail while wearing a set. Whether the tail itches, as it perhaps does after being cut, during the healing process, or whether the animal is merely trying to rub off the set is a question. Therefore, tail boards are nearly always a necessity for horses wearing sets. While most tail boards are about one foot wide and about forty inches high, it will be found that some horses will need boards fourteen to sixteen inches wide, and some will do better if they are only about thirty-six inches high. This type of tail board may also be a considerable help for the horse that rubs its tail for no apparent reason, even though it is not wearing a set.

QUESTION: What is a hoof leveler?

ANSWER: A hoof leveler or level is merely a device to measure the angle and the length of the animal's hoof. It is a dummy shoe made with a prong at the toe which is graduated in inches, as well as a marker graduated in degrees. This is placed on the horse's hoof after it has been pared and rasped. The prong is pushed against the front of the hoof, and the pointer then shows the angle at which the

ILLUSTRATION XXIX

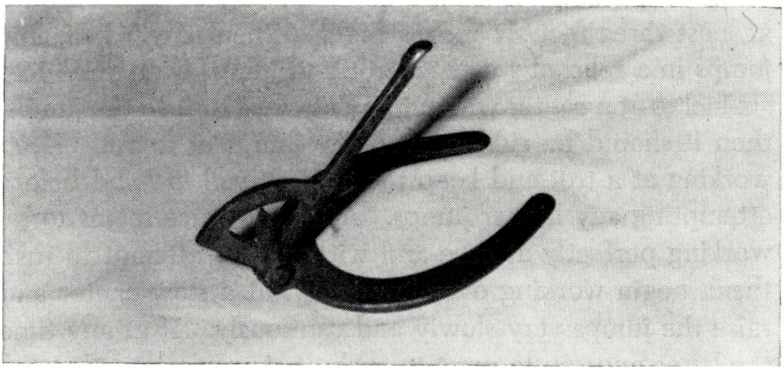

Hoof Level—Movable prong graduated in inches, cross bar graduated in degrees.

hoof has been trimmed; to lower the angle one lowers the heel and to raise the angle the toes must be lowered. The length of the hoof is measured at the same time by checking the graduated markings on the prong. The hoof is, of course, measured to the top of the coronet. The hoof leveler being perfectly flat will show up any unevenness of the hoof which must then be rasped level. We can readily see that if a definite angle and length of hoof is needed on a particular horse, that hoof should be checked before any trimming is done, as once toe or heel is taken off it cannot be replaced. Often gaited horses and some race horses, particularly some trotters, are very sensitive to minor changes in either hoof length or angle, in which cases the farrier needs to exercise caution not to take too much either heel or toe until he checks, as dropping the heel very little can cause a change of more than one degree in the angle on that hoof. The hoof leveler is surely one of the greatest aids a farrier has when he must do precise shoeing.

QUESTION: My horse always wants to rush the jumps. How can I prevent this?

ANSWER: A horse of this type needs a thorough re-education. In my opinion, the best way to correct this very serious fault is to put the animal back on the lunge line and jump it over low jumps at a trot. Even after the jumps are raised, that horse should be kept at a trot until they are at least three feet six inches high. When it will take low jumps in a relaxed way at a trot and jumps over three feet six inches at a canter without any attempt to rush the jumps, then it should be ridden over low jumps at a trot. Keep working at a trot and keep the animal well in hand before attempting any higher jumps. After the horse seems to be working perfectly at ease and without any attempt to rush them, begin working over low jumps at a slow canter and raise the jumps very slowly and cautiously. If at any time the horse appears to want to rush, it simply means that the work has progressed too rapidly and one must move back to lower jumps or a slower gait. I wonder if this isn't often the fault of the rider rather than the horse. If the rider gets nervous and excited he is bound to communicate this feeling to his mount, or if the rider falls back or is thrown back on the animal's kidneys, at the same time he jerks the horse's mouth just after they clear the jump, it will naturally have an adverse effect on the horse's way of jumping. Either it'll refuse altogether or it'll try to rush through and get it over with as fast as possible.

QUESTION: Can you explain to me just exactly what the different gaits are? I often go to horse shows and can't always tell just what gait the horses are doing.

ANSWER: Elsewhere in this book you'll find pictures of horses doing different gaits; however, perhaps the following explanation will be of some help also. First are the three natural gaits. All horses should do a good flat footed walk, we all recognize that I am sure. It is a four beat gait (i.e.) each hoof striking the ground separately; however, the gaited show horse which is both spirited and nervous during a show oftentimes closely approaches a two beat walk with the diagonal legs moving almost in unison. The show horse carries its head up and set, that is almost vertical, and takes short mincing steps rather than long slow strides. Any judge will allow this as long as the horse doesn't actually prance. This horse looks more animated and is really putting on a show for the crowd.

The next natural gait for the horse to do when it moves faster than a walk is the trot. It is a two beat gait, that is, the diagonal legs move in unison. The diagonal feet should raise and hit the ground at exactly the same instant. The slightest deviation from this is called "saddling" and is counted against any horse. The three gaited horse should trot in perfect form, well up on the bit, with head set high and as nearly perpendicular as possible. This trot should be done rather slowly, a park trot with extreme action both in front and behind, with the front legs well folded at the height of the stride, and the hind legs carried well under the horse. The trot of the five gaited horse should be fast. It gains it's action from speed. It reaches out both with the front feet and the hind. The very fact that it does move so fast means that it is impossible to ask for the same degree of collection as is required of a three gaited horse, however, even with this extreme speed the show horse must not travel all strung out, completely losing form. It should carrry its head high, fairly well tucked in and be responsive to the will of the rider. In other words, collection is still required but not to quite the degree that is required of the three gaited horse. The five gaited horse should also be able to do a good park trot if asked to do so.

Normally, when the horse wishes to move faster than an easy trot it breaks into a gallop or a lope. This then is the third natural gait. The gallop is a three beat gait which we all recognize. It is a series of leaps or jumps. It is a true three beat gait, with one front foot leading out, followed by the diagonal pair, that is the other front leg and the hind leg diagonally across from it, then the other hind leg. In the gallop or lope there is always a silent beat, it sounds something like tat tat tat—tat tat tat. The lope is merely a slower form of the gallop, and the canter is exactly the same gait performed in a greater degree of collection. We say the stock horse "lopes" and the gaited horse or jumper "canters" but the placing of the feet are exactly the same.

The pace is never a saddle gait, it is used racing with sulkies, but never should be used under the saddle. Some gaited horses if tired out or improperly trained or ridden, will resort to this gait in order to relieve themselves, but any judge will seriously score against such horses and rightly so, for in this gait there is no way for the rider to relieve himself as he can by posting to the trot. The rider is shifted from side to side and, especially on a long ride, it tires the rider more than any other gait a horse can do and often rubs him raw. There are a very few horses that seem to be able to pace only with the legs not shifting the body noticeably. Some people like to ride this type of pacer for pleasure. The pace is also a two beat gait, just the opposite from the trot, that is instead of the diagonal legs moving in perfect unison, the lateral legs move together.

Horses sometimes naturally do an intermediate gait between the trot and the pace. It is upon this intermediate method of moving legs that the artificial or man-made gaits are based. The ability to do an intermediate gait has been bred and cultivated for many years and has by now been brought to the peak of perfection by a combination of breeding and training. The difference in these various intermediate gaits is in degree rather than in kind, which makes a diagram of the way a horse moves in these gaits almost an impossibility. The stepping pace is the next one the judge calls for in the show ring. Actually he calls for a slow gait, which in one hundred per cent of the cases in the show ring these days means a stepping pace. It is an off pace with the lateral legs moving together, but not exactly together, as in a true pace; rather the hind foot on one side strikes the ground a very short interval before the forefoot on the same side. Thus, it is actually a four beat gait but the beats are not evenly spaced. It sounds on hard ground something like 1-2—3-4. It is a very showy gait with high front action and with the head well up and set beautifully. On some horses it is quite easy to ride; other horses shift the rider back and forth almost as much as a true pace.

The rack is the true saddle horse gait. It is exactly midway between the trot and the pace, a true four beat gait with each foot striking the ground separately at exactly spaced intervals. One can easily hear it as well as see it. It sounds 1-2-3-4 perfectly in cadence. It is a very fast, showy gait, a trifle less in form than a fast trot, with the front legs developing both reach and height, but the hind legs do not lift far off the ground as they do at the trot. It is without a doubt the easiest of all gaits for the rider, merely giving him a quivering sensation, no jar, no bumping, no shifting from side to side, but as easy as it is for the rider, it is the hardest of any gait on the horse. Each hoof strikes the ground separately and must therefore carry the entire load at each step. Particularly is this gait hard on the front tendons, as the action is high which means the front foot comes down hard carrying the entire weight of both horse and rider; therefore, a horse should never be asked to hold a rack for too long at a time. Many of you have heard some old-timers speaking of a singlefooter and how fortunate one was to be able to secure one such animal for a personal mount. This of course is the same gait, slower, done naturally—not artificial, not showy nor nearly as hard on the horse as a rack, but just as easy to ride.

You'll probably never see a fox trot in the show ring. Legally it may be used as a slow gait of the five gaited horse, but I have not seen it so used in the last thirty years. It is an "off trot," a saddling trot, just as the stepping pace is an "off pace"; the diagonal legs move almost in unison but with just enough difference to keep the rider from getting the bouncing he gets (if he doesn't know how to ride) on a true trot. It is easy on the horse, not fast—perhaps about six miles an hour is about average—but is a mile-eating gait as the horse can keep at it all day long with less strain on its heart than any other gait except the walk. For this reason it always was and still is highly prized by people who must spend many hours and travel many miles horseback.

One other gait may legally be used as the slow gait of the five gaited horse, but is no longer ever used as such. It is the running walk or plantation walk. Today it is only used on plantation horses, which also do the flat footed walk and the canter. This gait has been changed perhaps more than any other in recent years and for the worse. Originally it was a fast saddling walk, at about six miles an hour with the horse's head carried not too high, and nodding in time to its foot movements. It was a very easy gait to ride for even long periods of time and was much favored by the plantation owners many years ago, from whence comes its name. Breeding of walking horses fifty to a hundred years ago were along similar lines as the saddle horse, and those that had a natural tendency to "walk" or saddle a little, particularly if they had not enough bloom to make a gaited horse, were developed into walkers. And great horses they were too; one could ride them after the mail, chase the cows home, examine vast plantations easily and comfortably on one, or if need be, hitch it to the buggy to go after the week's supply of groceries; yes and even put it in the plow as a third horse on many occasions. Twenty or more years ago they began a registry for this breed as well as a big promotional deal, and more and more shows began having classes for walking horses. This, too, was good, if they would have kept them walking, but each exhibitor tried to get more and more speed, more and more action, until they have lost their walk, and for the most part today they do everything from a hop skip and jump to a pace or a true rack with the head lowered. They have lost everything for which they were once famous, and have gained nothing in its place. It is one of the sorriest spectacles that has happened to horses in the last century.

QUESTION: I have an eight year old gelding which has hoofs that are very brittle and continually break off causing it to lose shoes and making it extremely difficult to reshoe. I keep him bedded on shavings. Can you give me a good hoof dressing that will remedy this condition?

ANSWER: In the first place, you need to get rid of the shavings you are using for bedding. Shavings are extremely drying to the hoofs. Try using either straw or peat moss. I am afraid you'll never be able to use shavings for bedding with a horse of this type, no matter what kind of a hoof dressing you use. All horses' hoofs need moisture, and especially one of this type. I believe packing this horse's hoofs with a good clay will do this horse more good than a hoof dressing. If, and only if you keep your horse in the stall all day long, then a good hoof dressing may also be used for some extra benefit, but it should be made up of greases that mix with water. I only know of two that will do that, neatsfoot oil and woolfat. I make my own hoof dressing out of these two greases, mixing them warm to such a consistency that they may easily be painted on the hoof. Woolfat has a tendency to get very stiff in cold weather, therefore one needs more neatsfoot oil in the winter than in the summer; even then one may need to warm the mixture slightly before applying in very cold weather. But do NOT use this or any other hoof dressing composed of any type of grease if you turn your horse out in a pasture or a lot any part of the day. Nighttime is all right. The sun will bake any kind of grease and cause the hoofs to get even more brittle than they originally were.

Until you have corrected this condition, try feeding two tablespoons full of gelatin each day in the feed. I think you'll find that this will help you get better hoofs; also until the hoofs have grown out, ask your farrier to drive the horse shoe nails higher and use but three to a side rather than four. I can't emphasize enough how important moisture is to the horse's hoofs. Of course, some horses' hoofs seem to dry out much easier than others. Several years ago I bought a pleasure horse for one of my sons. As he used her only intermittently, I gave her a stall with a lot attached to keep her where she could run in and out at will. Soon she went lame, for no apparent reason. The hoofs seemed a little dry, but not feverish, but as I could find no other trouble, I tubbed her out and packed her hoofs with clay. The next day she was sound. I then instructed my boy to allow the watering trough to run over about every other day, so that the mare would have to tramp through the mud to get a drink. That kept her sound for years, except when the boy would forget to run over the water at the trough. At any time he forgot for as much as a week, she would begin to show signs of being sore, and he would immediately make a mud hole by the watering trough and that fixed that.

Question: At what age should I start shoeing my colts?

Answer: Keep them trimmed level and at a natural angle from the time they are a month old. Don't shoe them until you have to. Probably this will be after you start working them. You may want to put shoes on for showing in halter classes, in which case use the lightest plates that will do the job, and try to stick as close as possible to a natural angle.

Question: I have a sixteen year old mare that has been bred three times this year and is now in heat again. She was also bred last year but didn't catch. Is she too old to breed?

Answer: I don't think your mare's age is bothering her too much. I have successfully bred mares up to ten years older than that. Of course, the older the mare is before she has her first colt, the harder it may be to get her with foal. In your case there are several factors to be taken into consideration. Is the stallion to which you are breeding getting most of his mares in foal? Be sure you are breeding to a sure foal getter. In some parts of the country, they breed this type of mare to a jack, believing that the jack will settle the mare better than a stallion, and that she will in later years settle easier when bred to a stallion. I doubt if these extreme measures are necessary. I know if I had this mare, I'd feed her wheat, or wheat germ oil for at least a month before attempting to breed her. Then when she came in heat, I would examine her before breeding her. Many mares, particularly of this age, show a heat period that is not a true heat. In other words, while they are mentally ready to accept the stallion, they are not physically ready to get in foal. These are false heat periods and can fool anyone. In examining the mare at this time, the hands and arms must be washed thoroughly, then a preparation known as K-Y is rubbed over the hand and arm. It is a sterile slippery substance especially made for this purpose. The hand and arm is inserted into the vagina until you can feel the cervix of the uterus. The cervix of the uterus is examined. If it is extremely tight there is little use in breeding at this time as there is almost no chance of the sperm entering the womb even if the egg has descended, which is probably not the case. On the other hand, if the cervix feels loose and flabby, there is very little chance of settling the mare at this time; but if the cervix is elastic and about two fingers can be inserted with little difficulty, the mare is then physically ready to receive the stallion. I believe I'd breed this mare twice in one heat period, skipping one day in between. If that didn't work I'd capsule her on her next heat period.

QUESTION: I have a three year old registered mare that won't show in heat. Can you tell me how to get her to show her heat periods?

ANSWER: Many young mares do not show heat periods very clearly. For riding purposes we all like this, but for breeding it isn't so good. Most breeders these days feed either wheat or wheat germ oil regularly to both brood mares and stallions during the breeding season. This alone may cause your mare to show her heat periods better. I understand that veterinarians now have a preparation which can be injected into the muscles which will cause a mare to show heat periods. As I have never had an occasion to use this I can't say just how it works. Old-timers had their own methods, which I have used successfully on many occasions, particularly with young mares. The mare in question is "opened up." To do this, one has breeding hobbles placed on the mare and an assistant should hold her. The hands and arms are then washed thoroughly, leaving a copius amount of soap suds on the arm and hand which is inserted into the vagina. The cervix of the uterus is found and very gently massaged, one finger may be inserted carefully into the cervix during this procedure. The mare is then placed in a stall next to a stallion, with bars or a screen between them, where they can both see and nuzzle one another. She will, almost without question, show the next heat period clearly enough to be easily recognized, within a week to ten days at most. If there is any chance that the mare is coming in heat or may possibly be bred at the time she is opened up, then soap suds must not be used. Soap itself is, of course, an antiseptic and any left in the vagina will kill all the sperm cells. Instead, a sterile but not antiseptic preparation known as K-Y should be used. Some old-timers "open up" a mare each time she is to be bred. I've never believed in, nor followed this procedure.

Question: I have a six year old mare which will foal in about four months. I have been riding her nearly every day. When shall I discontinue riding her?

Answer: That is a good question, and you'll probably get a different answer from every horseman you ask. On most breeding farms, brood mares are never ridden; on the other hand many private owners ride brood mares right along, some of them right up to the foaling date and with no apparent ill effects. Of course, good judgment must be exercised and a mare in foal, especially after about the fifth or sixth month, should never be ridden hard nor overheated. A brood mare does need exercise, every day right up to the foaling date; I believe everyone will agree on that. She will have an easier delivery and the foal will be healthier for this daily exercise. If the mare is in a pasture, or a lot big enough that she can and will take her own exercise daily, that is probably ideal.

REGISTRY ASSOCIATIONS

The American Albino Club, Inc., Butte, Nebraska; Ruth White, Secretary. The American Albino Quarterly publication, devoted to the Albino Horse lover.

American Saddle Horse Breeders Association, Inc., 929 South 4th St., Louisville, Kentucky; Col. C. J. Cronan, Jr., Secretary.

Arabian Horse Registry of America, Inc., 120 South La Salle St., Chicago, Ill.

The Morgan Horse Club, Inc., and American Morgan Horse Register, 90 Broad Street, New York, N. Y.; F. B. Hills, Secretary.

Palomino Horse Association, P. O. Box 446, Reseda, California; Willard R. Beanland, Secretary.

American Quarter Horse Association, P. O. Box 271, Amarillo, Texas; Harold K. Linger, Secretary.

American Trotting Horse Register Association, Inc., Goshen, New York; Charles E. Koons, Secretary.

Jockey Club (Thoroughbreds), 300 Park Avenue, New York, N. Y.; Marshall Cassidy, Secretary.

Tennessee Walking Horse Breeders Association, Lewisburg, Tenn.; Miss Syd Houston, Secretary.

INDEX

The letter "i" indicates an illustration